Making Teachers
BETTER
—*Not*—
BITTER

ASCD MEMBER BOOK

Many ASCD members received this book as a
member benefit upon its initial release.

Learn more at: **www.ascd.org/memberbooks**

Making Teachers
BETTER
—— Not ——
BITTER

Balancing Evaluation, Supervision, and
Reflection for Professional Growth

TONY FRONTIER | **PAUL** MIELKE

Alexandria, Virginia USA

1703 N. Beauregard St. • Alexandria, VA 22311-1714 USA
Phone: 800-933-2723 or 703-578-9600 • Fax: 703-575-5400
Website: www.ascd.org • E-mail: member@ascd.org
Author guidelines: www.ascd.org/write

Deborah S. Delisle, *Executive Director;* Robert D. Clouse, *Managing Director, Digital Content & Publications;* Stefani Roth, *Publisher;* Genny Ostertag, *Director, Content Acquisitions;* Julie Houtz, *Director, Book Editing & Production;* Jamie Greene, *Editor;* Georgia Park & Khanh Pham, *Graphic Designers;* Mike Kalyan, *Manager, Production Services;* Kelly Marshall, *Senior Production Specialist;* Keith Demmons, *Production Specialist*

PAPERBACK ISBN: 978-1-4166-2207-9   ASCD product #116002
PDF E-BOOK ISBN: 978-1-4166-2209-3; see Books in Print for other formats.
Quantity discounts: 10–49, 10%; 50+, 15%; 1,000+, special discounts (e-mail programteam@ascd.org or call 800-933-2723, ext. 5773, or 703-575-5773). For desk copies, go to www.ascd.org/deskcopy.

ASCD Member Book No. FY16-9 (Aug. 2016 P). ASCD Member Books mail to Premium (P), Select (S), and Institutional Plus (I+) members on this schedule: Jan, PSI+; Feb, P; Apr, PSI+; May, P; Jul, PSI+; Aug, P; Sep, PSI+; Nov, PSI+; Dec, P. For current details on membership, see www.ascd.org/membership.

Library of Congress Cataloging-in-Publication Data
Names: Frontier, Tony, author. | Mielke, Paul W., author.
Title: Making teachers better, not bitter : balancing evaluation, supervision, and reflection for professional growth / Tony Frontier & Paul Mielke.
Description: Alexandria, Virginia USA : ASCD, [2016] | Includes bibliographical references and index.
Identifiers: LCCN 2016021746 (print) | LCCN 2016032009 (ebook) | ISBN 9781416622079 (pbk.) | ISBN 9781416622093 (PDF)
Subjects: LCSH: Teachers--In-service training. | Teachers--Rating of. | Teachers--Job satisfaction.
Classification: LCC LB1731 .F76 2016 (print) | LCC LB1731 (ebook) | DDC 370.71/1--dc23
LC record available at https://lccn.loc.gov/2016021746

23 22 21 20 19 18 17 16   1 2 3 4 5 6 7 8 9 10 11 12

Making Teachers
BETTER, NOT BITTER

Balancing Evaluation, Supervision, and Reflection for Professional Growth

1. The Need for Balance 1

2. Evaluation as a Component of a Balanced System 41

3. Supervision as a Component of a Balanced System...................70

4. Reflection as a Component of a Balanced System 118

5. Guidelines for Navigating Change That Results in
   Balancing Evaluation, Supervision, and Reflection 160

Appendix A: Protocols to Support Systems of Valid, Reliable Evaluation.............. 165

Appendix B: Protocols to Support Systems of
Empowering, Focused Supervision.. 191

Appendix C: Protocols to Support Individuals'
Meaningful, Purposeful Reflection... 211

Appendix D: Collaborative Protocols to Support Individuals'
Meaningful, Purposeful Reflection... 229

Appendix E: Matrix of Protocols for Balancing Evaluation,
Supervision, and Reflection 243

References 245

Index... 252

About the Authors 261

1

The Need for Balance

"This process isn't making me better. It is making me bitter."

— Cindy Alexander, Middle School Teacher

"We've spent all our time trying to figure out how to make this process more manageable when we should be asking how to make it more meaningful."

— High School Principal

A familiar scenario unfolds in schools each year. It is the final day of state testing. Students meticulously fill in bubbles on answer sheets. They respond to a few open-ended questions. They are not exactly sure how the test will be scored, but they know it is important and that they will be judged based on the results. Later that day, the responses are collected and sent away to be evaluated.

After a few weeks, students forget that they have even taken the tests. Then, near the end of the school year, each student receives a document—a report that judges the student's competence in several domains. Students look at the scores, but don't know exactly how they were calculated or what they mean. Without this understanding, they (or their parents) reach a broad generalization: *I am good at math*, or *I am OK at science*, or *the test must not have been fair*.

Teachers and administrators understand the realities of student accountability, but they question the benefits of such large-scale standardized student assessments. After all, accountability tests take time away from student learning, the results provide little information that students can use to improve, and the process forces students to passively accept a judgment from an outside source on the basis of a sliver of their performance from the entire school year.

Unfortunately, we believe that in our current push for more rigorous systems of *teacher* accountability, we are in danger of duplicating the flaws of systems of high-stakes *student* accountability. Three days of high-stakes testing does not improve student learning, and three days of high-stakes evaluation does not improve teacher performance. Like high-stakes student assessment, teacher evaluation is seen by many as an occasional event that is disconnected from day-to-day teaching and learning, consumes too much time, produces results that do not help teachers improve their performance, and places those who are supposed to benefit from the system in a passive role as mere recipients of an external judgment. Given the amount of time, effort, and energy invested in systems of evaluation, it is critical that those systems provide benefits that empower and build—rather than merely measure—teacher capacity to support student learning.

This book is not about whether teacher evaluation is *good or bad.* This book is about ensuring that all stakeholders are clear about what teacher evaluation *is and is not.* It is about transcending the misconception that teaching is easy—and that anyone who struggles to address a single student's needs simply lacks the reward or consequence to do so. It is about understanding why evaluation will never improve teacher performance and what to do about it. It is about eliminating the dangerous notion that teachers become expert at their craft after a few years of practice. It is about developing processes of supervision that are less reliant on supervisors. It is about helping stakeholders understand that using comprehensive frameworks of effective teaching to guide personal reflection and changed practice—rather than solely to evaluate—carries the greatest potential to help teachers improve and feel valued. And finally, it is about changing a system that has grown woefully out of balance—with its emphasis on visits, forms, and deadlines—into a system that is productive and supportive of teachers and the students they serve.

The Other Sides of the Pyramid

Our perception of what something is often has more to do with our perspective than reality. This concept is important when considering how comprehensive frameworks for instruction are currently used in schools.

Consider this anecdote. Three nomads converge at a small marketplace, far from where they usually trade, to exchange some goods. Despite the long, harsh journey, the trip is worth it; each nomad has brought goods that cannot be acquired in the others' native region. One has come from the North, one from the West, and the third from the South. As night falls, they meet near the marketplace, start a fire, and talk about their journeys.

Eventually, the conversation turns to the great pyramid that stands, in the distance, between each of their native regions. The nomad from the North says how much he admires the pyramid's beautiful red walls. The nomad from the West laughs and asks if he meant to say yellow. The nomad from the South says they are both wrong; the walls are clearly green.

The nomad from the West claims that according to legend, most of the riches inside the pyramid were placed along the western wall, as a tribute to the good people of the West. The others argue that it was their side of the pyramid that was the most significant. Voices are raised; fingers are pointed.

The nomad from the South claims that not only did his side of the pyramid have the greatest significance, but the wall facing south was the most important because without it, the other sides of the pyramid could not stand. A shouting match ensues.

The argument escalates; no one concedes. Despite desperately needing the goods that each has brought, they are all so angry that they decide they do not want to do business with people whose judgment is so deficient. They break camp in the darkness.

As they head back down their respective trails, the sun rises and the pyramid comes into view. Each nomad looks at his side of the pyramid, satisfied that he was right and the others were wrong. They never do business together again.

Each nomad was correct in articulating his perception of the color of one wall of the pyramid. Unfortunately, each was wrong in defending his perception of what the other walls *were not.* The truth is the pyramid was built with three types of stone, and the walls were different colors. Each nomad was right about a portion of the pyramid but failed to acknowledge that the other walls could be different.

Furthermore, each was correct in articulating the significance of *his* wall to the people in his region. But this "all or nothing" reasoning failed to acknowledge why the other walls might be significant to others. Unfortunately, each nomad was wrong in his analysis of what part of the structure was *most* important. Although each wall was equally important, the portion that was most important was not a wall at all but the single foundation that supported each wall.

Without a solid foundation, a structure cannot be built. Without balance among the walls, the structure cannot stand.

The pyramid anecdote is analogous to much of the debate we've seen unfold around teacher evaluation. Teachers, administrators, and boards argue about the details of comprehensive frameworks for instruction and the evaluation systems that are often attached to them, yet the purpose of the system is rarely articulated. Furthermore, the debate about why teacher evaluation is so import-ant seems to miss the notion that a solid foundation of trust and credibility is essential if the system is going to stand.

There is one important difference between the pyramid analogy and teacher evaluation. The nomads knew the structure was a pyramid; they were quibbling about the color and the value of *their* wall. We seem to be sitting at the base of the wall that has clearly been labeled as "evaluation," yet we are oblivious to the fact that other walls even exist. What are these other walls that must be present to bring balance to the evaluative component of comprehensive frameworks for instruction?

This era of high-stakes accountability for teachers has spurred an unprece-dented emphasis on teacher evaluation. In general, this focus has been on tech-nical, transactional components of the evaluative process, such as the number of administrative visits, which forms need to be completed, and how various scores result in a single rating. We've sat so long at the base of the pyramid—staring at the imposing wall of evaluation—that we've forgotten why we convened at the pyramid in the first place. What started as a conversation about quality and accountability has devolved into negotiations about visits, tracking forms, and online management systems.

Furthermore, we seem to have forgotten that the other walls exist. By itself, *evaluation* is not a pyramid. It is a two-dimensional triangle balancing on a thin edge that cannot stand. An empowering system of *supervision* and processes that support meaningful *reflection* are equally important walls. We need to clarify the purpose, distinctions, and interrelationships among *evaluation, supervision,* and *reflection* if we are to use comprehensive frameworks in a manner that makes teachers better, rather than bitter.

The Potential of Comprehensive Frameworks for Effective Practice

Much of the discussion of new systems of evaluation has focused on the underlying frameworks that states, districts, or schools have adopted. What follows is a brief overview of some of the more popular teaching frameworks. Each is research-based and uses a standards-based approach to evaluation, with specific criteria described along a continuum of quality. The rubrics can be used for judgment and evaluation, as well as formatively to establish a common language for individual goal setting and professional collaboration. None of the frameworks uses a checklist approach whereby every element needs to be present in every lesson; instead, they honor the systemic and complex nature of teaching and learning.

The Danielson Framework for Teaching

Based on her research for Educational Testing Service on evaluating preservice teachers, Charlotte Danielson (1996, 2007) developed a framework that sought to capture the complexity of teaching in a manner that was practical yet didn't reduce teaching to a set of simple steps. The Danielson Framework divides teaching into four domains: Planning and Preparation, Classroom Environment, Instruction, and Professional Responsibilities. Within these domains are a total of 22 components of effective practice. These components are further divided into a total of 76 elements. The Danielson Framework uses a four-point rating scale to evaluate teacher performance: Distinguished, Proficient, Basic, and Unsatisfactory.

The Marzano Observational Protocol

Based on his comprehensive framework for effective teaching as described in *The Art and Science of Teaching* (2007), Robert Marzano developed the Marzano Observational Protocol for supervision (Marzano, Frontier, & Livingston, 2011) and evaluation (Marzano & Toth, 2013). The framework has four domains: Classroom Strategies and Behaviors, Planning and Preparing, Reflecting on Teaching, and Collegiality and Professionalism. Across these domains are 60 elements that are further divided into specific instructional strategies aligned to various instructional outcomes. The Marzano Observational Protocol uses a five-point rating scale to evaluate teacher performance: Innovating, Applying, Developing, Beginning, and Not Using.

The Strong Teacher Evaluation System

James H. Stronge developed the Stronge Teacher Evaluation System, and after years of field testing, he has simplified his framework to make it more practical to implement. The performance standards outlined in it are Professional Knowledge, Data-Driven Planning, Instructional Delivery, Assessment of Learning, Learning Environment, Communication and Advocacy, Professionalism, and Student Progress. Each performance standard has subcategories. The eight performance standards contain 54 sample quality indicators. Because of the complexity of teaching, Stronge advocates the use of multiple data sources (such as observations, student surveys, and teacher-created artifacts) to create a portfolio that documents teacher performance. The Stronge system offers the option to use a three-, four-, or five-point rating scale (Stronge, 2013). The four-point rating scale to evaluate teacher performance is as follows: Exemplary, Effective, Developing/Needs Improvement, and Unsatisfactory.

Evaluation in Schools Today: The Need for a High-Quality Teacher in Every Classroom

Effective teaching matters (Hattie, 2009; Lezotte & Snyder, 2011; Marzano, 2007), and expertise in the complex craft of teaching requires a career's worth of focused effort and is difficult to obtain (Marzano et al., 2011). Unfortunately, educational policy in the United States has focused on external, higher-stakes accountability for teachers and students as a means to improve our collective capacity to meet students' learning needs. This approach is destined to be counterproductive unless it can be significantly reframed. As noted author and researcher on change Michael Fullan (2011) states,

> [If higher-stakes accountability is] based on the assumption that massive external pressure will generate intrinsic motivation, it is patently false. Instead . . . what is required is to build the new skills, and generate deeper motivation. Change the underlying attitude toward respecting and building the profession and you get a totally different dynamic around the same standards and assessment tools. (sec. 3, para. 3)

We believe the recent emphasis on evaluation has further distorted a culture in which acknowledging the need to improve is already perceived to be an admission of incompetence. Too often the mere mention of a comprehensive teaching framework is assumed to be about ranking and judging teachers.

Consider the following perspectives and associated concerns about evaluation that capture just some of what we've heard expressed by various stakeholders:

- A teacher argues that the new emphasis on evaluation is evidence that legislators, administrators, and school boards don't trust teachers and this is another attempt to catch them "being bad."
- A state lawmaker believes that educators have failed to ensure quality in their field; therefore, legislation and oversight from governmental agencies are required to ensure teachers "get their act together."
- A parent who is pleased with his child's current level of education is worried that principals and teachers will need to spend all of their time filling out forms and justifying ratings—time they could have spent working with students.
- A veteran teacher argues that it doesn't matter what evaluation system is used, nor does it matter what incentives are given to teachers; it is just a "dog and pony show" anyway.
- A local board member doesn't like the district's current evaluation framework and is eager to begin the board's work of adopting the framework that a neighboring district is using successfully.

- A principal is eager to implement a new evaluation system because it will allow her to finally get rid of the "bad teachers," and the great teachers can finally be rewarded and recognized for their work.

There are two paths we can take to address these critical perspectives. Path 1 asks that we determine which perspective is correct and then dig ourselves into political or ideological trenches and argue our point. When the argument is done, we will feel vindicated. If we engage the argument by talking to others who already agree with us, we can be assured that not only were we correct, the people we associate with were correct, too. Path 2 asks us to acknowledge that each perspective has a kernel of truth in the eyes of various stakeholders. We can then work to develop an understanding of these different perspectives to inform our school's or district's implementation of a new, more effective system of evaluation.

Path 1 is useful if the goal is to feel right. If that is your chosen path, you need not read any more of this book! Path 2 is essential if the goal is to build capacity in schools to better meet each child's learning needs. Before we start down the second path, we need to acknowledge why the first path will merely result in maintaining the status quo of frustration and confusion that permeates so much of the current discourse about teacher evaluation.

The Paradoxical Effect of Evaluation

Performance evaluation takes time, causes significant stress among supervisors and employees, and tends not to be very effective. Although these statements may ring true for many teachers and principals today, the points were raised in a seminal article in the *Harvard Business Review* in 1972 by Douglas McGregor, a noted researcher and author on human behavior in organizations. Specifically, McGregor argued that performance appraisal systems often result in the manager feeling intensely uncomfortable in the role of "playing god," and the employee dislikes being inspected like a product coming off an assembly line. Then the person being evaluated is subjected to the judgmental feedback of someone who has seen only a small portion of the person's work.

Concerns similar to McGregor's are supported by contemporary experts in the field of human resources and management. Samuel Culbert (2010) of UCLA argues that many systems of evaluation are not only ineffective but also counter-productive. Rather than improving performance, they can actually undermine it. Some of Culbert's concerns about evaluation systems include the following:

- *They prevent individuals from acknowledging the need for improvement.* In a system of high-stakes review, no employee wants to acknowledge any area of need. Many fear that acknowledging the need for improvement might be held against them.
- *They undermine collaboration and teamwork.* If resources for rewards are limited, there is little incentive to support a colleague's efforts to improve. Her gain could become your loss.
- *They create disincentives for individuals to be critical of the organization's efforts.* For fear of retribution, the people who know the system best may resist sharing important observations about day-to-day inefficiencies or offering constructive criticism to management. This situation isolates managers from receiving open and honest feedback that may be difficult to hear but could ultimately benefit the organization.
- *They require significant time, effort, and energy—often for justifying behaviors or practices rather than for using strategies that ensure growth.* The processes and paper trails that are generated for evaluative reviews often have more to do with avoiding lawsuits or justifying and denying pay raises than they have to do with honest, clear feedback about employee performance.

Although McGregor's and Culbert's perspectives may differ from your own experiences with systems of evaluation in education, we've heard many of these concerns throughout our careers as educators and across our work in educational research. Recent studies looking at systems of evaluation in K–12 schools imply additional challenges, including the following:

- Not enough specific feedback to improve teaching (Weisberg, Sexton, Mulhern, & Keeling, 2009).
- A failure to discern meaningful differences in performance, so that nearly everyone gets the highest ratings (Toch & Rothman, 2008).
- Unrealistic expectations related to time for principals and administrators to keep up with the required paperwork and protocols (Ramirez, Clouse, & Davis, 2014).

Moving forward with a balanced system of evaluation, supervision, and reflection requires stakeholders to better understand why neither refining existing evaluation systems nor implementing new ones is likely to result in better teaching or more student learning.

The Systems We Have

What percentage of teachers in your school or district have demonstrated such a high level of expertise that you think they should be nominated for a statewide or national teaching award? We've asked this question across dozens of states to thousands of participants, and the responses are remarkably similar: the vast majority say fewer than 10 percent of their teachers have demonstrated this level of performance. We've also asked a more challenging question: *What percentage of teachers in your school or district are so incompetent they need to leave the profession?* We get the same results as we do with the first question. The vast majority say fewer than 10 percent of their teachers demonstrate this level of performance.

Then we ask a few questions rooted in how the system responds to those different levels of performance. *What percentage of teachers have typically received the highest overall rating on their evaluations?* Now the numbers turn dramatically. About 80 to 90 percent of participants say that 90 percent of their teachers receive the highest rating. And finally, we ask this: *Think about those 10 percent of teachers who are really struggling in the profession. When you intervene with those teachers to put them on a course of corrective action, how many of you call the intervention to address those concerns an "improvement plan" or a "plan of improvement"?* About 80 to 90 percent of participants raise their hands.

These responses raise some concerns. First, the majority of teachers are evaluated as though they are as skilled in their craft as the most accomplished professionals. This results in a false sense of accomplishment for the vast majority of teachers and fails to acknowledge the depth of expertise obtained by a small group of educators in each school. Second, when "improvement plan" becomes synonymous with a "job action" for the weakest teachers, we've turned improvement into a liability. Some states have even adopted frameworks in which the lowest levels of performance are "incompetent" and "in need of improvement." If only those who are struggling are in need of improvement, wouldn't it be in all teachers' best interest to deny any such need?

Too often, evaluation results in a few people being told they are incompetent and thus in need of improvement, while everyone else is told they have achieved excellence. This predicament—casting the need for improvement as a liability and accepting competence as excellence—is typical in an evaluation system whose purpose is either to acknowledge competence or to weed out *in*competence.

A Different Approach

The "good enough" or "in need of improvement" approach is completely counter to research on systems that develop and support high performers in their respective fields (Ericsson, Charness, Feltovich, & Hoffman, 2006). Systems that support the highest levels of performance acknowledge that there is always room for growth. The need for improvement is not seen as a liability; it is embraced as an opportunity to develop higher levels of skill. These supportive systems do not merely measure competence; they create pathways toward growth that ultimately yield expertise.

In these systems, high performers constantly seek new ways to improve. For the high performer, finding an opportunity for improvement and learning a new skill is a badge of honor. The world's best athletes work with coaches every day. The best musicians are always finding pieces to add to their repertoire. The best surgeons relish the opportunity to work on the most difficult cases or learn the most challenging techniques.

Additionally, fields that critically discern levels of quality across a broad range of skills create clear and rigorous pathways toward excellence. In martial arts, for example, the path toward a black belt is clearly defined; there is not simply a white belt and a black belt. Each belt has clear criteria that represent the attainment of more complex levels of skill. The dedication, discipline, and effort required to rise to the challenge of obtaining the next belt result in a marvelous sense of accomplishment once that goal has been obtained—which fuels the dedication, discipline, and effort to rise to the next level. The delineation among levels is so widely accepted that individuals who have reached the next level are revered by those who aspire to achieve it.

How We Got Here: Ensuring Competence or Supporting Expertise?

Systems of evaluation in the field of education are rooted in a history of inspection and efficiency. Late 19th century models of supervision largely consisted of clergy or bureaucrats traveling from town to town to inspect schools and ensure funds were being used as expected (Tracy, 1995). Early 20th century models of schools and evaluation of schooling were based on the principles of scientific management—the belief that the effectiveness of schools and teaching could be measured and monitored no differently than production at a factory (Cubberley, 1929; Taylor, 1911). The goal of these early systems was largely to ensure competent teaching and efficient use of resources in classrooms. However, systems designed to measure performance must be designed differently than systems designed to support growth (Marzano, 2012). Most teacher evaluation systems in K–12 education remain rooted in the legacy of the former; but to improve performance, we must move toward the latter.

Ensuring Competence

Teacher evaluation systems have historically been designed to ensure competence. Competence is typically defined as meeting job demands and having the skills and attributes to perform a specific set of tasks (Burgoyne, 1988). An evaluation of competence allows us to answer this question: *Is this individual good enough to maintain a job in this organization?*

Competencies are the specific knowledge, skills, and attitudes required to be successful in a given field. Lists of core competencies and judgments of competence exist in any profession. The idea that only teachers are subject to evaluation, or high-stakes evaluation, is a fallacy. In law, medicine, engineering, education, or any other professional field, competence is typically judged in a system that includes the following attributes:

- Competencies are defined by practitioners and researchers in their respective fields.

- Competence is determined through a judgmental process of evaluation by a superior.
- Competence is a baseline level of performance associated with being good enough to maintain employment status.
- When level of competence determines job status or pay, the evaluative process used to render a judgment about competence is typically governed by legal and contractual obligations of the specific organization.

In education, competencies are typically associated with strategies and skills of planning, teaching, assessing, and collaborating. The extent to which a teacher has developed these *competencies* and uses them effectively determines a more holistic judgment of *competence*. A person may demonstrate skills associated with highly competent teaching (e.g., is highly engaging, plans meaningful lessons, uses assessment to inform instruction) but be a horrible employee because he or she lacks basic professional competencies (e.g., comes late to work, is disrespectful, continually misses important deadlines). When a teacher is judged as competent, it typically means he or she has demonstrated a baseline of skills as both a teacher and an employee.

Systems of evaluation in education have historically been designed to ensure competence. Or stated a bit differently, systems of evaluation in education have historically been used to root out incompetence. This is the reason why findings from the widely cited studies titled *The Widget Effect* (Weisberg et al., 2009) and *Rush to Judgment* (Toch & Rothman, 2008)—which found that most teachers get the highest rating possible and only a tiny percentage are given the lowest ratings—did not shock practitioners in the field. Unfortunately, too many practitioners have interpreted a rating that signified competence to mean that they had obtained excellence. Conversely, only those who were deemed incompetent were viewed as needing to improve.

Supporting Expertise

If competence describes the minimum level of quality required to maintain employment in an organization, expertise describes a ceiling of excellence that is obtained by an elite group of individuals in the entire field (Ericsson et al., 1993).

Experts develop a very broad, deep, and flexible skill set that requires focused dedication, practice, and time to acquire. Whether a lawyer, a concert violinist, a surgeon, or a teacher, an expert embraces the most difficult challenges in the field and finds a path to success. When we judge someone as an expert, we have made a judgment about that person's ability to demonstrate and integrate the highest levels of skill in various competencies by answering this question: *Does the individual demonstrate expertise by consistently using the right strategy, in the right way, at the right time, to obtain desired results—even with the most challenging cases, under the most challenging conditions?* Expertise is calibrated to a radically different standard than competence.

Expert performance includes a number of specific, distinguishing components as compared to mere competence (Chi, Glaser, & Farr, 1988). Expert performers (1) excel within their field; (2) perceive meaningful, interconnected patterns missed by others in their field; (3) are faster and more accurate than novices performing skills in their field; (4) have better short- and long-term memory than novices; (5) recognize problems in their domain at a deeper level than others in their field; (6) spend a larger portion of time analyzing and constructively addressing problems; and (7) self-monitor effectively during problem solving.

Dozens of examples illustrate how these components of expertise are valued by those who rise to the top of their field. In sports, LeBron James is widely considered the world's best basketball player. Coming off MVP seasons in 2009, 2010, 2012, and 2013, James was asked if he could get any better as he headed into the 2014 season. He responded by saying this:

> I know I still have room for improvement. I feel I can improve on my shooting, on my ball handling, on my low-post game. . . . I've only been in the low post for two years now, playing with my back to the basket. So that still needs a lot of improvement to catch up with the rest of my game. (Broussard, 2013)

James could rest on his laurels, but instead he has placed himself on an improvement plan to further increase his ability to use the right strategy in the right way to obtain the results he desires.

In the field of music, consider Pablo Casals, who is widely noted as the preeminent cellist of the first half of the 20th century. At age 93, he still practiced three hours a day. When asked why, legend has it that his reply was "I'm beginning to notice some improvement." When asked if he was still learning, he didn't even pause to answer: "Every day." He continued, "I still do the same things as when I was 13—the scales, the arpeggios, the thirds" (BBC, n.d.).

Although James and Casals are from different continents, from different generations, and engaging in dramatically different crafts, their pathways to expertise are remarkably similar. Rather than accepting their current practice as good enough, they break their craft into small, manageable pieces and identify specific areas for improvement. They strategically and deliberately attack these areas in search of the next level of quality. They are experts because they are perpetually focused on action that results in improvement.

Applying the concept of expertise to teaching is not new. Noted educational psychologist David Berliner (1988) believed that creating expertise begins with increasing awareness of the developmental stages of pedagogical expertise. Berliner described these stages as a continuum from *novice* to *expert* as follows:

- Novice: The teacher follows general rules, regardless of the nuance of the circumstance.
- Advanced beginner: Experience affects the teacher's behavior but with little sense of which skills or strategies are most important.
- Competent: The teacher makes a conscious choice about what to do; priorities are set and plans are followed. The teacher feels responsible for what is happening and has an emotional attachment to success and failure.
- Proficient: Intuition or know-how becomes important. The teacher has the ability to predict events more precisely and is analytical and deliberative in how to respond.
- Expert: The teacher understands what to do or where to be at the right time. There is automaticity in accomplishing goals. The teacher recognizes meaningful patterns in others' behaviors quickly and is flexible and focused in applying strategies and behaviors that support intended outcomes.

Although we've grown accustomed to looking at descriptors on a continuum of competence as being synonymous with ratings for evaluation, Berliner believed that defining various levels of expertise would help increase teachers' ability to self-reflect on their current performance, their ideal performance, and closing the wide gap that exists between each level on this continuum.

Unfortunately, these levels of competence have been taken away from teachers and placed in the hands of evaluators. They've been co-opted as ratings in a system of evaluation when their most powerful application is in a system of goal setting and reflection.

Evaluation, Supervision, and Reflection: Three Systems, Three Purposes

Any system can be better understood by clarifying the *purpose* and *premise* of its components. For example, the *purpose* of an orchestra is to perform orchestral music. The *premise* of an orchestra is that it includes various percussion, string, woodwind, and brass instruments. Different instruments produce not only different sounds but also different pitches. For string instruments, the *premise* of the design of a violin and a cello allow them to serve the *purpose* of producing similar sounds. However, the *premise* of the length of the strings on these two instruments is different, so that the violin's *purpose* is to play much higher notes than a cello. The expert violin player cannot play a pitch lower than that produced by a child playing a cello. You can tune and retune the violin a thousand times and you will still fail. The violin isn't *bad*. The violinist isn't *bad*. The fault lies in the inability to acknowledge the premise and purpose of the components of the instrument. Until this occurs, frustration and confusion are the predictable result.

Too often, we have not distinguished the *premise* and *purpose* of systems designed to measure teacher performance, support teacher growth, and develop teacher expertise. We've asked evaluation to play every part of the orchestral arrangement, yet we act surprised when the music is discordant; frustration and confusion have been the result. We believe several fallacies about the premises and purposes of evaluation have contributed to the misalignment.

The Need for Balance: Fallacies About How Evaluation Alone Supports Expertise

Systems that improve, rather than merely measure, teacher effectiveness must balance the urgency of valid, reliable evaluation with systems of supervision that empower teachers to focus their efforts on goals for growth. This must be done in a manner that honors teachers' capacity to engage in meaningful reflection as they chart their own path toward expertise (Mielke & Frontier, 2012). In such systems, teachers use comprehensive frameworks throughout the school year and collect data to reflect on their teaching in a way that informs deliberate practice as they progress toward expertise. We believe there are five fallacies about the potential of evaluation to improve teaching that need to be confronted if we are going to create systems that balance the role of evaluation with systems that support teacher growth.

Fallacy 1: Evaluation elicits expert teaching.

Our discussion of how the premise and purpose of different systems support intended outcomes—illustrated by the difference between a violin and a cello—applies to systems of evaluation. Although systems of evaluation can elicit valid ratings, they are not designed to elicit expert teaching.

Looking at research from a broad range of disciplines, systems that support expertise have five common components (Marzano et al., 2011). These components are (1) a shared language of practice, (2) opportunities for feedback and deliberate practice, (3) opportunities to observe and discuss expertise, (4) clear criteria and a plan for success, and (5) recognition of status as one makes incremental progress toward expert performance. As shown in Figure 1.1, teacher evaluation frameworks are aligned to the first component of systems that develop expertise—a shared knowledge base and language for effective teaching. However, the similarities end there.

Ironically, evaluators are more likely to improve their expertise in teaching through engagement in the evaluation process than are teachers. Almost daily, the evaluator is immersed in opportunities to understand the nuance of the framework's language as it relates to effective teaching, is given the opportunity to visit dozens of classrooms to observe and learn from others' practice, and discusses teaching with many teachers. Teachers, on the other hand, remain isolated and have only a few conversations with their evaluator each year.

The best evaluation framework in the world may yield highly accurate ratings from highly reliable raters, but it is unlikely to elicit expert teaching. A balanced approach to evaluation, supervision, and reflection honors the fact that the purpose of evaluation is to elicit valid, reliable ratings. Eliciting and supporting expertise requires an emphasis on the other walls of the pyramid: supervision and reflection.

FIGURE 1.1

Systems That Develop Expertise Compared with Teacher Evaluation Systems

Characteristics of Systems That Develop Expertise	Alignment to Teacher Evaluation?
1. A well-articulated knowledge base and shared language for teaching	Aligned; but the shared language is primarily used by the evaluator, and the evaluator is the primary user of the framework.
2. Opportunities for focused feedback and deliberate practice	Not aligned; feedback from the evaluator may be focused, but it is not frequent enough to support deliberate, reflective practice.
3. Opportunities to observe and discuss expertise	Not aligned; the evaluator builds expertise through classroom visits, but the teacher remains isolated.
4. Clear criteria and a plan for success	Not aligned; criteria are clear to the evaluator but not necessarily to the teacher. The plan for success may be too vague to implement as specific instructional strategies or may lack frequency of developmental feedback required for growth.
5. Recognition of status on pathway toward expertise	Not aligned; recognition of status may occur but is more likely to be about competence rather than expertise.

Note: Characteristics in Column 1 are based on Marzano et al., 2011.

Fallacy 2: Comprehensive teaching frameworks are to be used exclusively by administrators for purposes of evaluation.

Teachers who understand formative assessment teach their students how to use rubrics to guide their work. They know that the rubric can't simply "appear" after the work has been done. When used to improve learning, the language of the rubric becomes the ongoing language of the curriculum.

In the same way, administrators and teachers need to use comprehensive teaching frameworks for more than just evaluation. When used effectively, frameworks create a common language for practice to focus teachers' collaborative efforts in building their repertoire of instructional strategies to more effectively meet students' learning needs.

A balanced approach to evaluation, supervision, and reflection honors the fact that teachers should be the primary users of comprehensive teaching frameworks. At a minimum, they can use such frameworks to guide their daily practice—for example, to assist in lesson planning, prioritize strategies for whole-group instruction, or select alternative strategies for students who require more challenge or support.

We've seen tremendous professional growth among teachers who have used frameworks as the starting point for a comprehensive self-assessment process; they identify specific skills for improvement and obtain feedback through such activities as peer observation, video analysis, peer discussion, and student surveys. The opportunity to self-reflect and engage in professional discussions with peers helps teachers clarify how they should invest their efforts to grow in the profession.

Fallacy 3: Teachers fail to improve because they lack the incentives or consequences to do so.

Becoming an expert in a complex field such as teaching is difficult and elusive. We believe that developing expertise is the central goal of a high-quality system that balances evaluation, supervision, and reflection. Evaluation systems that rely on consequences and incentives for teacher growth assume that teachers already have frequent opportunities to dramatically improve their performance; they merely lack the will and incentives to do so.

As a profession, we need to transcend the idea that teaching is easy and that rewards and consequences will elicit good teaching and extinguish bad teaching. If systems of evaluation view "needs improvement" as a liability worthy of sanctions, then we should not be surprised when educators become defensive when asked to acknowledge their need to improve.

A balanced approach to evaluation, supervision, and reflection honors the fact that improving one's practice requires specific, structured opportunities for growth. Changing incentives for growth without creating new pathways for that growth to occur assumes teachers have already mastered the complex craft of teaching. Becoming an expert teacher does not occur because of carrots and sticks but because of a belief that there is always room to grow and structured opportunities to make growth happen. Here's what one teacher told us after engaging in a self-assessment process designed to elicit reflection and deliberate practice:

> You see movies like *Freedom Writers* and you get this idea that there are magical teachers who come in and do this amazing job, and all the

kids are enraptured with learning. Then you think, "Oh, I don't have the gift." You know what? I just need to keep working at it. . . . It's really about my own commitment to growing as a professional and continuing that process indefinitely.

A culture that acknowledges the need for everyone to improve and provides opportunities to engage in protocols and strategies that empower teachers to expand their instructional repertoire can create a clear, reliable pathway toward teacher growth.

Fallacy 4: Evaluators are the only source of meaningful feedback and can provide enough feedback to help teachers improve.

A study on the impact of evaluation on teaching (Weisberg et al., 2009) identifies a lack of feedback as one of the primary problems with evaluation systems. The authors found that "nearly three of four teachers went through the evaluation process but received no specific feedback about how to improve their practice" (p. 14).

Often, when teachers could have received formative or judgmental feedback to help them improve, they get no developmental feedback at all. Here's what one teacher told us about her experience with feedback through a career's worth of evaluative visits from principals:

So I will be completely honest. Like all my evaluations, there wasn't a whole ton. It would just say, "Oh, it was a great lesson." I would give my area that I would want feedback on and then I would just get a one-liner. I wanted more. So it was just like, "I think your transitions were great." The end. OK, what made it great?

Unfortunately, even when supervisors do provide high-quality feedback, it is too infrequent to improve performance (Marshall, 2009; Weisberg et al., 2009). Another teacher who participated in a year-long protocol designed to elicit collegial feedback said that she now felt cheated after being told for years by her supervisor that she didn't have to worry about her evaluations because "everything was fine." After engaging in a year of self-assessment that included analyzing videos of her own teaching and using tools to elicit developmental feedback from her students, she realized that she had the capacity to self-identify opportunities to improve and access enough feedback in those areas to change her instructional practice for the better. She felt empowered by the realization that she no longer had to passively "wait for the principal to come in" and hope for meaningful feedback.

A balanced approach to evaluation, supervision, and reflection honors the fact that a system that helps teachers generate and respond to continuous feedback empowers them as *the active agents* in the growth process. Once a school has established a shared understanding of a model of effective teaching, individual teachers can use a wide range of approaches to generate and receive feedback without the involvement of a supervisor (Knight, 2011; Lewis & Hurd, 2011; Marzano et al., 2011). These approaches include student surveys that ask students about the frequency of effective teaching behaviors, self-directed video analyses of specific components of one's own teaching, and instructional rounds and collegial dialogues that enable teachers to reflect on visits to other teachers' classrooms.

Fallacy 5: Systems of evaluation are a catalyst for teachers to establish meaningful improvement goals.

Observation and evaluation by an evaluator typically occur only a few times a year. A handful of visits and the judgment that follows often result in the evaluator prescribing, or suggesting, areas in which to establish improvement goals. Unfortunately, when others establish goals for us, we are less likely to obtain them (Deci & Ryan, 2000, 2002). Consider this self-reflection from a teacher who engaged in a video-analysis protocol to establish improvement goals:

> In one word, "Boring!" It was my exact thought as I watched myself continue to teach a math lesson for 15 minutes longer than necessary. . . . I need to better identify the critical information to introduce to the students in a shorter amount of time.

Imagine an evaluator telling a teacher his lesson was "boring" and he needed to "better identify the critical information to introduce to the students in a shorter amount of time"! The teacher would surely be defensive after receiving such pointed feedback.

When given the opportunity to reach his own conclusion about an improvement goal, this teacher not only identified the goal but also thought about instructional strategies to add to his repertoire to address this need. Rather than being defensive, he likely never again bored students with an overly lengthy introductory lesson.

Of course, teachers should not direct components of a system of *evaluation*, but they should be empowered through *supervision* to direct their own efforts toward purposeful, meaningful *reflection*. Allowing teachers to generate and monitor data about their own teaching, identify their own areas of focus (with students and colleagues providing developmental feedback), and establish their own improvement goals provides the autonomy support necessary to increase motivation and engagement (Deci & Ryan, 2002). When teachers participate in these self-assessment protocols, they are remarkably adept at identifying specific areas of need and creating clear pathways to improvement (Mielke, 2012).

When reaching self-directed improvement goals becomes a habit of mind that guides teachers' instructional decisions every day, they become their own best supervisor. After engaging in a variety of self-assessment strategies to guide her deliberate practice toward an improvement goal, one teacher told us this:

> The peer observation, combined with the video observation, combined with the group discussion . . . together provided a really powerful experience in terms of being able to say, "There are some really specific things I can do right now, and some things I can do down the road."

For most teachers who engage in these processes, this awareness results in a set of specific—and ambitious—improvement goals. When adult learners are empowered to objectively analyze and understand their own practice and have a clear vision of where they can improve, they are intrinsically motivated to embark on a pathway that leads to growth (Ericsson et al., 2006; Knowles, 1984; Ryan & Deci, 2000).

Moving Beyond the Status Quo: The Answer to *What* Is *Why*

On its own, evaluation does little to improve teaching and may actually undermine teacher growth. How can we reframe our efforts to use comprehensive teaching frameworks in a manner that ensures we are focused on more than just evaluation?

Good journalists know that their stories should tell the reader the basic elements of *who, what, where, why, when,* and *how.* As they gather information to write a story, they begin with the end in mind by revisiting these *Five Ws and How*—again and again—to ensure the final piece not only is factual but also represents the most relevant perspectives of different stakeholders.

Like journalists, effective principals play a critical role in framing events in a manner that helps teachers understand the *Five Ws and How* of different initiatives. They understand that although the facts are essential, it is often stakeholders' perceptions of those facts that are most relevant. As Simon Sinek (2009) states, "Start with why." The meaning that drives our work serves as a powerful catalyst for how well that work gets done. When implementing change, leaders and those they serve need to be clear about the following (Frontier & Rickabaugh, 2014):

- *Why* is the change important/necessary?
- *Who* will be required to adopt new beliefs? Skills?
- *What* are the intended outcomes?
- *Where* in the organization will the change occur?
- *When* will new processes/procedures be implemented?
- *How* will we ensure stakeholders understand why this change is important, and *how* will we support the new beliefs and skills that are required to successfully implement the change?

When we think about change in these terms, it is evident that not all change is created equal. Some changes may require leaders to guide planning and strategy around only a few of these questions, whereas others may be of a much larger magnitude and require leaders to build capacity to address all of these questions.

In the book *Five Levers to Improve Learning,* Tony and his coauthor, James Rickabaugh, argue that leaders need to be attuned to three types of change: *managing the status quo, transactional change,* and *transformational change* (Frontier & Rickabaugh, 2014). Understanding these three types of change is critically important to ensure that an organization's efforts are aligned to intended outcomes. This is particularly true when implementing changes related to something as mission-critical as teacher evaluation. Consider how the *Five Ws and How* would be engaged in radically different ways if changes to a system of supervision and evaluation were intended to maintain the status quo, to manage transactional change, or to create the necessary conditions for transformational change.

Managing the Status Quo

Managing the status quo can be summarized as follows: *Same beliefs, same processes, same skills, same results; repeat as needed.*

When principals or teachers manage the status quo, they expect similar processes to yield results that are similar to past results. Effort is put forth to maintain existing roles, systems, and structures to obtain satisfactory results. Examples could include an administrator rolling over calendar dates for the following year or a teacher using the previous years' lesson plans.

When managing the status quo in a system of supervision and evaluation, the emphasis is on maintaining and managing the processes, procedures, and forms that have worked (or, perhaps, not worked) in the past. For example, in a school that has used the same approach to supervision and evaluation for many years, few people may question *why* the system is used or *how* it could be improved. The emphasis is typically on maintaining clear answers to questions related to *who* fills out *what* forms *when*. Managing the status quo is not a bad thing. If existing systems are efficient and effective, there may be little need for change. However, if the goal is to improve a system, maintaining the status quo and hoping for a better payoff rarely yields desirable results.

The hallmark of efforts to maintain the status quo is that logistical changes in process such as dates and deadlines may occur, but the underlying premise, practices, and payoff are expected to remain the same.

Transactional Change

Transactional change can be summarized as follows: *Underlying premises remain the same, but new processes are implemented with new rewards in order to create incentives for better results.*

When principals and teachers engage in transactional change, the goal is to improve results through an exchange of new skills valued by one group for new rewards valued by another. For example, for a principal, transactional change could include completing a mountain of paperwork to obtain much-needed grant monies.

Transactional change in a system of supervision and evaluation emphasizes implementing processes, procedures, and forms that are different from those used previously. New incentives or consequences may be used to emphasize the importance of the change and to ensure that individuals complete the new processes. Unlike the status quo example, transactional change places *why* and *how* on the table as well as *who*, *what*, and *when*. *How* the supervision and evaluation process was used in the past is no longer pertinent because now there is a new process.

In a transactional implementation of a new system of supervision and evaluation, the reason why supervision and evaluation occur will likely be framed in terms of incentives or consequences. For example, teachers may be told that it is necessary to change the evaluation framework to comply with state mandates, or because of a shift to a system of more accountability or pay for performance. Unfortunately, external motivators toward transactional change can ultimately do more to demotivate rather than motivate individuals' efforts to achieve (Ariely, Gneezy, Loewenstein, & Mazar, 2005; Pink, 2009b).

Most perplexing, transactional change can be implemented in a manner that results in a change in process ("Listen up, everybody," said the principal. "We have a new evaluation framework!") but maintains the status quo for those the system is supposed to serve ("Evaluation is still just a dog and pony show," the teacher thought. "New hymnal, same old psalms."). We expand on the ramifications of this challenge later in this chapter.

The hallmark of transactional change is that the processes and associated payoff may change, but the underlying premises and assumptions about those processes remain the same.

Transformational Change

Transformational change can be summarized as follows: *New premises guide new thought and action; underlying assumptions shift from an emphasis on external rewards and consequences to intrinsic meaning and transformation.*

When principals and teachers engage in transformational change, effort is put forth to empower others to see themselves and their work in new ways.

For example, a principal may shift how he or she uses staff meeting time—from telling teachers about logistics and policies to using protocols to work with teachers to build trust, discuss new instructional strategies, and constructively troubleshoot progress toward a schoolwide improvement plan. For a teacher and students, transformational change could include a teacher working closely with students on setting and achieving goals—both academic and personal—in a way that emphasizes intrinsic motivation rather than external rewards and threats.

When transformational change is underway in a new system of supervision and evaluation, the emphasis is on reframing the *why* and making new decisions about *who, what, where, when,* and *how,* based on each logical extension of that new premise. Unlike transactional change, where external mandates and incentives were the answer to *why* we are implementing this change, a transformational approach to supervision and evaluation might begin with questions such as "*Why is effective teaching critical to our mission?*" or "*Why have existing systems of supervision generated frustration among principals and teachers?*" and truly listening to different perspectives in search of understanding.

The hallmark of transformational change is that existing underlying beliefs change regarding the premise of the system. The new beliefs result in new processes that empower individuals to participate in, and benefit from, entirely different protocols and behaviors that create conditions for an entirely new and different payoff.

When leading or experiencing change, how stakeholders understand *why* the change needs to occur makes a profound difference in *what* is changed, *who* participates, and *how* the change is implemented. We believe these components have been remarkably unclear in the area of teacher evaluation.

Rather than confronting the complex interrelationship among an individual's assumptions, beliefs, and skills associated with transformational change, we often opt for a transactional solution. When homeowners commit this mistake, they ignore the bad furnace and leaky water pipes that have created cracks in the walls and instead simply apply a fresh coat of paint. In teacher evaluation, this approach becomes a process of adopting new frameworks, forms, dates, and deadlines but not addressing the foundational need for clarifying the premises, purposes, and expected payoffs from the implementation of new systems of evaluation.

How Stakeholders' Views Frame Their Reality: Magnitude of Change

Among the most important work leaders do is frame issues (Bolman & Deal, 2010). This means leaders honor, and are responsive to, the fact that individuals bring different mental models to the table when engaged in their work (Senge, 1990). Regardless of the intent of a change within an organization, what ultimately matters is how stakeholders *perceive what the system is and what needs to change.* These mental models are often revealed by the types of questions different stakeholders ask when engaging in change.

This point is significant because depending on one's perception of whether the purpose of the change is to maintain the status quo, to engage in transactional change, or to engage in transformational change, individuals will approach that change process in very different ways. Consider Figure 1.2, which presents perspectives on teacher evaluation from different stakeholders based on the three magnitudes of change we described earlier. The questions in this table are neither good nor bad. What matters most is an awareness of how the questions associated with each magnitude of change can influence a dominant mode of response and action.

For example, consider Mr. Payton, a new teacher with tremendous potential who is struggling in his first months of teaching. At a closed school board meeting, a board member asks for an update on the status of the new teachers. After hearing that Mr. Payton is struggling, consider how board members might frame the situation based on different magnitudes of change:

- A board member focused on the *status quo* may ask for information about the district's legal requirements under state statute and the teachers' contract as related to due process, notification, and termination. If Mr. Payton is focused on the status quo, he may not see any need to change. He may believe that if he was good enough to obtain licensure and get hired, he is good enough to maintain his employment status.
- A board member focused on *transactional change* may ask about incentives and consequences to motivate or punish the teacher into improving. If Mr. Payton is focused on transactional change, he may only see the need to improve if consequences are put in place in the form of an "improvement plan."

FIGURE 1.2

**Key Stakeholders' Questions About Teacher Evaluation,
Depending on Intended Magnitude of Change**

Magnitude of Change *Essential Question* **Stakeholder**	**Status Quo** *What dates and deadlines are required, to be met to ensure compliance?*	**Transactional** *What processes are required, and what are the associated rewards and consequences?*	**Transformational** *How do we continuously build capacity to serve our mission?*
Teacher	What do I have to do to get the same ratings as last year?	What do I have to do to fulfill requirements for employment/fiscal rewards?	How do I improve my expertise in various facets of teaching?
Principal	What do I have to do to get evaluations completed?	What do I have to do to maintain/non-renew staff?	How do we build capacity for teachers to become experts in such a complex field?
District/Board	What dates and deadlines fulfill contractual and legal obligations?	What do we have to do to be in compliance with external requirements for evaluation? What processes ensure valid employment decisions?	How do we ensure improvement of instructional practice and develop autonomous professionals who maximize student learning?
Public	What do we have to do to maintain existing levels of school quality?	What do we have to do to ensure the good teachers are hired/rewarded and the bad teachers are not hired/fired?	How do we ensure teachers can effectively meet the changing needs of future employees/leaders/taxpayers?

- A board member focused on *transformational change* may ask about systems that are in place to mentor new teachers and support their growth in their first years of teaching. If Mr. Payton is focused on transformational change, he may seek opportunities to build expertise by acknowledging his need for growth and learning from colleagues.

Each of these perspectives is valid; however, there are consequences and opportunities associated with a focus on questions that seek to address challenges through these different levels of change. Over time, these questions may become dominant modes of inquiry that result in a culture that tends to perpetuate the status quo, to strive for transactional change, or to seek transformational growth. Consider how differently the culture of evaluation would be in the following contexts:

- If questions about compliance with the status quo become the dominant mode of inquiry, the district will establish a record of being firm and fair with the letter of the law but may alienate teachers in the process and actually create disincentives for teachers to acknowledge the need for improvement.
- If questions about incentives and consequences to entice individuals into transactional change become the dominant mode of inquiry, the board may find itself relying on, and teachers may become dependent on, rewards and punishments as the only way to improve practice or change behavior.
- If questions about how systems are designed and implemented to support the growth of all teachers become the dominant mode of inquiry, administrators and teachers may find themselves analyzing how internal assumptions can be challenged and processes can be continuously improved to build capacity within the organization.

Only by clarifying the premise, purpose, and payoffs expected from evaluation, supervision, and reflection can board members, administrators, and teachers clarify the magnitude of change required to move away from a system that is primarily concerned with ratings, rewards, and consequences and move toward a system that builds capacity to improve teaching.

In this book, we argue for a balanced approach to the use of comprehensive teaching frameworks to support, rather than merely measure, professional practice. The balanced use of these frameworks requires the implementation of a coherent system of evaluation, supervision, and reflection. In this system, these three components serve very different purposes:

- The *purpose* of **evaluation** is to ensure competent teaching in every classroom through a valid, reliable ratings process. The *premise* is that evaluation renders a judgment in a performance environment. The *payoff* comes in the form of accurate ratings of teacher quality on a criterion-referenced scale.
- The *purpose* of **supervision** is to support teacher growth by creating opportunities for developmental feedback that focuses teachers' efforts

and empowers them to achieve goals related to improved professional practice. The *premise* is that supervision creates the conditions for developmental feedback to inform progress in a learning environment. The *payoff* is teacher growth.

- The *purpose* of **reflection** is for teachers to become autonomous in their ability to become expert in their craft. The *premise* is that reflection is the foundation for the meaningful thinking and the purposeful, aware, and responsive actions made by experts. The *payoff* is autonomous teachers who are developing expertise.

If the purpose of evaluation, supervision, and reflection answers the *why* of each component, then *what* should be emphasized to ensure successful implementation? Figure 1.3 presents quality criteria for each component, along with key questions and a set of action steps. These components are described in detail in each chapter of this book.

Because the purposes of evaluation, supervision, and reflection are very different, they require the use of different protocols and processes to ensure that each component functions to its own specific ends. Figure 1.4 lists key protocols and processes for each component.

The Six *P*s

In this chapter and those that follow, we explain the components of a balanced framework by describing important distinctions among evaluation, supervision, and reflection in terms of their purpose, premise, protocols, processes, practices, and expected payoff. Each of these is a key element of the three components and of a balanced system.

Purpose. Moving beyond forms, dates, and deadlines, what is the reason for engaging in each component of the balanced system? Systems designed to measure performance, or achieve performance goals, or make progress toward expertise have different purposes that require the use of different protocols.

Premise. What ways of thinking must all participants understand to ensure alignment between beliefs and actions? The performance orientation that is essential for evaluation has a different premise than the learning orientation and the deliberate practice emphasized in a system of reflection.

FIGURE 1.3
A Balanced System's Criteria for Quality, Key Questions, and Action Steps

Component	Criteria for Quality	Key Question	Action Steps
Evaluation	Valid	*Are ratings valid?*	• We use a valid, research-based framework to determine ratings. • We ensure valid ratings and credible evaluators. • We provide timely, accurate judgmental feedback.
	Reliable	*Are raters and ratings reliable?*	• We focus on collection of quality data, not just quantity. • Teachers are actively involved in data collection. • We have high levels of interrater reliability; different raters produce similar ratings.
Supervision	Empowering	*Is the context empowering?*	• We strive to create and support a learning environment where errors are welcomed and questions are honored. • We strive to build teacher autonomy through autonomy-supportive practices. • We use frequent, high-quality, developmental feedback from a variety of sources to support teacher growth.
	Focused	*Are goals focused?*	• Teachers use a comprehensive teaching framework to establish and guide efforts toward specific improvement goals. • Teachers' goals are rooted in, and supported by, continuous data collection and modification of practice. • Teachers collaborate to calibrate.
Reflection	Meaningful	*Is reflection meaningful?*	• Teachers operate from an internal locus of control; they believe their classroom practices matter profoundly to influence student learning. • Teachers have a growth mindset; they believe they can make dramatic improvements in any area they choose. • Teachers are metacognitive in their efforts to clarify the gap between current and ideal performance.
	Purposeful	*Are reflection and action purposeful?*	• Teachers are increasingly purposeful about, aware of, and responsive to the relationship between student learning and effective teaching. • Teachers embrace dissonance; they develop a nuanced view of the gap between current and expert practice. • Teachers use the framework of effective instruction and structured processes to accurately clarify areas for specific, deliberate practice and incremental growth.

FIGURE 1.4

Purposes, Protocols, and Processes

Component	Purpose	Key Protocols and Processes
Evaluation	The purpose of **evaluation** is to ensure competent teaching in every classroom by measuring teacher performance through a *valid, reliable* ratings process.	• Clinical observations • Walkthroughs • Judgmental analysis of artifacts • Judgmental analysis of achievement data • Judgmental feedback • Summative conferences • Summative ratings
Supervision	The purpose of **supervision** is to support teacher growth by creating opportunities for developmental feedback that *focuses* teachers' efforts and *empowers* teachers to achieve goals related to improved professional practice.	• Formative conferences • Formative ratings • Developmental feedback • Goal setting • Instructional rounds • Student surveys • Video analysis of exemplary teaching • Video analysis of others' practice • Monitoring/supporting teachers' efforts to improve
Reflection	The purpose of **reflection** is for teachers to become autonomous in their ability to make *meaningful* connections between their efforts and student results as they purposefully engage a pathway toward expertise.	• Teaching inventories • Metacognition and self-reflection through PAR (purposeful, aware, responsive) framework • Structured reflective writing • Deliberate practice • Video analysis of own practice • Data collection of student perceptions • Collegial dialogue • Fishbowl

Protocols. What are the specific protocols—strategies used to ensure valid measurement for evaluation, high-quality developmental feedback for supervision, or purposeful metacognition for reflection—that allow for a strategic approach to gathering data, responding to feedback, and improving one's professional practice? Protocols include classroom walkthroughs, video analysis, reflective peer visits, and reflective journaling, to name a few.

Processes. Across a school year, what are the processes to be used to successfully implement comprehensive systems of evaluation, supervision, and reflection? Although these processes are typically clearly defined for evaluation, systems of supervision and reflection require similar levels of clarity and intentionality.

Practices. What are the specific skills professionals should practice in order to move the entire system toward more effective teaching and learning? While evaluators should continually hone their ability to evaluate accurately and provide high-quality judgmental feedback, teachers require copious amounts of developmental feedback from a broad range of sources, as well as focused practice to develop their skills as reflective practitioners on a path toward expertise.

The payoff. If each component of the balanced system is used to maximum effect, what is the ultimate benefit for teachers? Students? Administrators? The purpose of these processes is not to create a paper trail of evidence to justify ratings but to collectively improve the capacity of the system to improve student learning.

The purpose of all three components of an effective system—evaluation, supervision, and reflection—answers the question "Why are we doing this?" Although the comprehensive teaching framework is a constant across the three components, the who, where, and when that drive how that framework is used need to be different to align with each component's unique purpose and payoff. Figure 1.5 articulates some of the key differences among these unique attributes.

As we've shared the table in Figure 1.5 in our work with schools and districts, we're struck by how often we hear three comments: *Can you show this to my principal? Can you show this to my teachers?* and our favorite, which is something along the lines of *We've been asking people to play the violin and giving them a pair of cymbals; no wonder everyone is so frustrated.*

FIGURE 1.5

Comparison of Key Elements of Evaluation, Supervision, and Reflection

	Evaluation to Ensure Competence	Supervision to Influence Growth	Reflection to Support Deliberate Practice and Expertise
Purpose	The purpose of evaluation is to ensure competent teaching in every classroom through a *valid, reliable* ratings process.	The purpose of supervision is to support teacher growth by creating opportunities for developmental feedback that *focuses* teachers' efforts and *empowers* teachers to achieve goals related to improved professional practice.	The purpose of reflection is for teachers to engage in *meaningful* thought processes that result in *purposeful* action that results in growth toward expertise.
Premise	Evaluation renders a judgment in a performance environment.	Supervision creates conditions for growth in a learning environment.	Reflection is the foundation for the purposeful, aware, responsive decisions and actions made by experts.
Owned by . . .	State/district	Teacher with the support of supervisor	Teacher
Payoff	Accurate measurement	Improved performance toward growth goals	Expert performance
Primary Effort	Trained evaluators and observation conducted by principals	Teachers gather data, establish goals, and engage in practices and protocols to help better understand, and close, the gap between current and ideal performance.	Meaningful reflective and purposeful, deliberate practice by teachers to support intentional change
Processes	A series of classroom visits and collection of data by an evaluator that culminates in a valid rating	An ongoing process designed to affirm strengths, identify opportunities for growth, create dissonance, and generate developmental feedback	Continuous, recursive, internal process of meta-cognition, reflection, and deliberate practice
Informed by . . .	Walkthroughs, clinical visits, achievement data, artifacts	Observation, data, reflection, discussion	Student data, teacher data, collegial dialogue, modification, and intentionality

	Evaluation to Ensure Competence	Supervision to Influence Growth	Reflection to Support Deliberate Practice and Expertise
Purpose of Comprehensive Teaching Framework	*Comprehensive teaching framework* used to create common language of evaluation and expectations for competence.	*Comprehensive teaching framework* used to create common language to focus efforts toward improved professional practice.	*Comprehensive teaching framework* used to inform shared language of reflection and deliberate practice.
Type of Feedback	Summative, judgmental	Formative, developmental	Formative, developmental, self-generated
Frequency of Feedback	Feedback is given occasionally.	Feedback is accessed frequently through as many sources as possible.	Feedback is continuous.
Disposition	Performance Orientation	Learning Orientation	Growth Mindset + Internal Locus of Control + Learning Orientation
Active Participants	Evaluator and teacher	Teacher, supervisor, colleagues, coaches, mentors, students	Teacher, colleagues, students
Primary Users	Principal/district	Teacher, supervisor, coaches, colleagues	Teacher/colleagues
Leadership Role	Evaluating	Coaching	Supporting
Focus	General teaching behaviors, professional behaviors, student outcomes.	Specific teaching behaviors	Metacognition and modification of specific teaching behaviors based on student response to teaching.
Controlled by	State/district/board	Administration and teachers	Teacher
Key Process Question	How will we ensure evaluations are valid and reliable?	How will we create feedback that focuses teachers' efforts in a way that empowers them to move from their current level of performance to the next level of performance?	How will teachers use continuous feedback in meaningful ways to ensure the autonomy support, ownership, and purposeful, deliberate practice associated with developing expertise?
Key Outcome Question	How good is good enough to maintain or improve employment status?	What is the current level of performance, and how can we support growth toward next levels of performance?	How will I develop expertise in the complex craft of teaching?

Supporting the Walls of the Pyramid: The Foundational Components

Earlier in this chapter, we presented an analogy that compared the current state of evaluation, supervision, and reflection to the experience of a group of nomads from three regions who convened in order to trade. As they discussed a distant pyramid, they each erroneously claimed that their perspective represented the entire pyramid. Amid their debate about which of the walls of the pyramid was the most important, they failed to realize that the most important component was not a wall but the foundation upon which each wall was built. This point reminds us that as we describe the three "walls" that must be in place to use comprehensive teaching frameworks for effective instruction in a way that both measures and improves professional practice, the foundation is also critically important.

A balanced system of evaluation, supervision, and reflection must be built upon a solid foundation of trust and credibility. These components create the conditions upon which the premise, purpose, processes, and protocols of a balanced system can pay off in valid measurement of teaching *and* empower teachers to grow. Without trust and credibility, efforts to implement a balanced system will fail to realize their potential to improve, rather than merely measure, teacher performance.

Trust

In a seminal study of 400 schools in Chicago, Tony Bryk and Barbara Schneider (2002) found that a key ingredient in school improvement is relational trust among teachers, parents, and school leaders. Unfortunately, "the need to improve the culture, climate, and interpersonal relationships in schools has received too little attention" (Bryk & Schneider, 2003, p. 40). In their study (2002), relational trust is defined as clarity around each individual's role as related to the personal obligations and expectations of others. Relational trust can flourish when four components are present:

- Respectful exchanges among individuals, active listening, and valuing the perspectives and contributions of others.
- Personal regard to extend efforts to serve others in a way that transcends only using one's job description as the criterion for supporting someone in need.

- Competence in core responsibilities that ensure that the building is managed appropriately and teachers use strategies to effectively meet students' learning needs.
- Personal integrity in the belief that individuals within an organization will keep their word and decisions will, ultimately, be made based on an analysis of what is considered the best course of action to serve each child's learning needs.

Relational trust will be mandatory if, as a field, we are going to (1) transcend the traditional hierarchy of using comprehensive frameworks of instruction solely for evaluative purposes, (2) overcome the notion that teachers require a principal to be in the room to receive thoughtful feedback, and (3) develop systems where teachers are willing to say to a colleague, "I need your help to get better." Relational trust will be central to ensuring that this latest round of teacher evaluation doesn't land in the education-reform dustbin as another transactional fix that failed. As Bryk and Schneider state in the conclusion of their 2002 study:

> Absent more supportive social relations among all adults who share responsibility for student development and who remain mutually dependent on each other to achieve success, new policy initiatives are unlikely to produce desired outcomes. Similarly, new technical resources, no matter how sophisticated in design or well supported in implementation, are not likely to be used well, if at all. . . . Good schools are intrinsically social enterprises that depend heavily on the cooperative endeavors among the varied participants who comprise the school community. (p. 144)

We agree with this statement wholeheartedly. Valid, reliable evaluation can occur between an evaluator and a teacher, but developing individual and collective expertise is a social endeavor that cannot occur without trust. Ground rules for establishing and maintaining trust read a bit like a kindergarten report card; articulating the components is simple. Implementing them requires attention and energy to ensure they become a series of cultural norms. We've adapted a list of behaviors that author Margaret Wheatley articulates in her book *Turning to One Another: Simple Conversations to Restore Hope in the Future* (2002, p. 145) as a starting point for thinking about the types of behaviors that foster and support a solid foundation of relational trust that can accelerate an organization's progress toward serving the common good:

- Ask "What is possible" rather than merely pointing out what is wrong.
- Be brave enough to engage in meaningful conversations with a broad range of people across the organization.
- Be intrigued by differences; embrace curiosity and not just certainty.
- Invite input; creative solutions come from new connections.
- Recognize that real listening brings people closer together.
- Trust that meaningful conversations matter.
- Acknowledge that serving the common good is challenging work; stay together.

Trust is important, but trust alone is not enough. A balanced system of evaluation, supervision, and reflection is a professional endeavor that also needs to be credible with teachers, administrators, board members, and the community.

Credibility

Credibility is the extent to which something is accepted as truthful or accurate. Implementing a balanced system of evaluation, supervision, and reflection requires the community's and board's belief that administrators can evaluate accurately. Boards and superintendents need to believe that principals and coaches can design and support engaging systems of supervision. Principals and coaches need to believe that teachers can engage in reflection that improves their teaching and better supports each student's learning. Here, credibility comes in a variety of forms.

The credibility of the comprehensive teaching framework itself. Other than the researchers who generate regression models that demonstrate the validity of evaluation frameworks, no one understands regression models that demonstrate the validity of evaluation frameworks. Joking aside, we've seen too many presentations from statisticians trying to convince teachers that the new rating process must be credible because of the number of Greek symbols used to validate the framework. Different types of validity are important when researchers validate an evaluation tool, but the most important type for practitioners is face validity. Face validity means, quite simply, that the evaluation tool makes sense simply by looking at it. If a teacher were to look at an evaluation tool with a high level of face validity, he might say something like "Yep, this explains why I love teaching so much and why I go home exhausted at the end of every day."

To be credible with administrators and teachers, the comprehensive teaching framework needs to be adopted and implemented in a way that helps build collective understanding of its premise, purpose, and payoff, and how it will be used. To these ends, the goal of a district's professional development associated with a comprehensive teaching framework should not be to merely explain how the framework will be used to justify ratings for evaluation. In a balanced system, a comprehensive framework of effective instruction can be used to guide supervisory and reflective components such as orientation and mentoring for new teachers, articulation of individual growth goals, establishment of building and districtwide professional development goals, and a shared language to guide collaborative protocols among departments and teams.

The credibility of how the organization uses the comprehensive teaching framework. Here, credibility refers to the *transparency, consistency,* and *clarity* of the processes related to the use of the comprehensive framework to evaluate, set goals, and build expertise.

Transparency includes clear communication of how the tool will be used to make employment decisions and support growth; how frequently formal evaluations, evaluative walkthroughs, or various teacher-led protocols will be used; and all pertinent dates and deadlines associated with the processes.

Consistency refers to the extent that the framework produces valid ratings across the entire organization, and the extent that teachers use protocols in a way that exemplifies the relational trust essential for the collaborative and reflective processes required for one to visit other classrooms and seek feedback from a variety of sources. If teachers believe their rating and accompanying feedback have less to do with the evaluation framework and more to do with the administrator assigned to give the evaluation, the system lacks the consistency across raters to be credible. Likewise, if some teachers do not honor the norms of the protocols related to confidentiality, internal locus of control, and personal accountability, then the protocols will lack the consistency required to serve as a catalyst for teacher growth.

Clarity refers to the extent of shared understanding among all stakeholders. Teachers, administrators, board members, and the community should be clear about the fact that rigorous processes are in place to ensure evaluation is taken seriously by administrators and rigorous protocols to support reflective practice and professional growth are taken seriously by teachers. We're more accepting of judgmental feedback when we understand how it is generated and how it will—and will not—be used.

The credibility of the system and the credibility of all who use it are equally important. Throughout this book, we focus on specific practices that support the credible implementation of a balanced system of evaluation, supervision, and reflection.

2

Evaluation as a Component of a Balanced System

A Case Out of Balance: When Evaluation Works Poorly

It was the final Thursday in May. Students could barely contain themselves. Exams loomed—a final hurdle to be cleared before summer. Teachers walked into the building with their typical year-end level of excitement, but some anxiety as well, because this was the day each year when evaluations appeared in their mailboxes. After saying good morning to the office secretary and grabbing their mail, they scurried to their rooms and closed their doors to look at their evaluations.

Teachers who had Principal Smith opened their evaluations slowly. Principal Smith was notorious for being a tough evaluator. He rarely gave the highest marks, and if any parent complained—about anything—at any point in the year, you could be sure he would note the complaint on the evaluation and give a low rating in that area. As teachers looked through their evaluations, they were occasionally pleased that the evaluation score in some areas aligned to their own perception of their level of competence. But more often than not, scores were lower than teachers thought they should be.

The ratings were defensible. Principal Smith was always in classrooms for walkthrough visits and diligently arranged three formal observations a year. Unfortunately, he seemed to keep a running list of everything that didn't go perfectly. Because he was a former math teacher, it was the math teachers who were more anxious than any others. His one-sentence explanations for his ratings often read something like "Demonstrates potential in this area, but missed many opportunities to utilize strategies that I might have used while teaching this content." Comments like these made teachers shake their heads in disbelief.

After reviewing their evaluations, teachers who had "Stickler Smith" would convene in the teachers' lounge and express a chorus of complaints: *He never tells us about parent concerns until they appear in the written evaluation. He spends most of his time during post-conference meetings talking about what he would have done. He has a model of effective instruction in his head that was cutting-edge a full generation ago.* The complaints went on and on. Despite their concerns, the teachers knew there was no point in bringing them to the director of human resources. He would say the same thing he always said: "Our principals are professionals; it is not my job to tell them how to evaluate teachers."

A second group convened in the teachers' lounge. These teachers didn't talk about their evaluations. They were evaluated by Assistant Principal Everett— "Excellent Everett," as they called him. He gave nearly the highest ratings possible on every category to every one of his teachers—even those whom others knew were struggling. "Excellent job this year. You are truly an excellent teacher!" was the standard line at the end of everyone's evaluation. When new teachers saw this on their first evaluations, they felt great about the recognition. It wouldn't take long, however, before a veteran teacher would ask, "How was your eval? Did he tell you that you did an excellent job this year and you are truly an excellent teacher?" Inevitably, the new teacher's heart would sink. Teachers appreciated the high ratings—one less thing to worry about in a stressful profession where the challenges always exceed the time allotted. But teachers were also torn. Assistant Principal Everett's evaluations were based on a couple of walkthroughs. He never did formal observations. He never had post-conference discussions with teachers about their lessons. He never mentioned specifics in his evaluations, only glowing generalizations.

Several years ago, a well-regarded veteran teacher—who was tired of getting the exact same ratings as the struggling teachers and the brand-new teachers— went to the superintendent to express his concerns about the "low bar" that Everett had set for everybody. The next year, the veteran teacher was assigned to Stickler Smith as his supervisor. Since then, no one else has expressed a single concern about Excellent Everett.

The Purpose of Evaluation in a Balanced System

The purpose of evaluation is to judge teacher performance using a reliable process that results in a valid measure of competence in every classroom. The payoff is the school's or district's assurance that it is making ongoing personnel decisions that maximize student learning and allow the school or district to fulfill its mission.

As uncomfortable as many educators are with being evaluated and evaluating others, it helps to remember that we evaluate students all the time. When we ask students to take a classroom assessment, a state test, or a college entrance exam, the need to evaluate is clear. We need to quantify their current level of learning or achievement. We acknowledge the imperfection of these assessments—they capture only a small portion of each student's performance, interests, and abilities—and then we administer them anyway. The reason we do so is to gather some empirical evidence that allows us to communicate with others —students themselves, parents, colleagues, colleges, employers—about each student's academic strengths and needs. The primary obligation of educators is to ensure the tests are as valid and reliable as possible and to ensure that the data generated from them are used in a manner that informs sound decisions about each child's current educational status, strategic opportunities to maximize next levels of learning, academic standing, and even life opportunities in the form of college admissions and scholarships.

When teachers are evaluated, the purpose should also be clear: we need to quantify their current level of professional practice. We acknowledge the imperfection of evaluation frameworks—they capture only a small portion of each teacher's performance, skills, and abilities—and then we evaluate them anyway. The reason we do is so that evaluators can gather empirical evidence that allows them to communicate with others—the teachers themselves, board members, state agencies, fellow administrators—about each teacher's professional strengths and needs. The primary obligation of the evaluator and the board is to ensure the process is as valid and reliable as possible and to ensure that stakeholders respond to the resulting data in a manner that informs personnel decisions, strategic professional development opportunities, employment status, and even life opportunities in the form of compensation.

Neither student testing nor teacher evaluation is bad. They are tools. When used mindfully in a system that spends the majority of time building capacity—and pauses occasionally to evaluate performance—they can provide meaningful data that illuminate current and next levels of performance.

Evaluation that serves as a component of a balanced system of evaluation, supervision, and reflection is most likely to align the purpose to the payoff of evaluation when there is a clear link among premise, protocols, processes, and areas of practice. Figure 2.1 illustrates this relationship and recalls the pyramid analogy we introduced in Chapter 1.

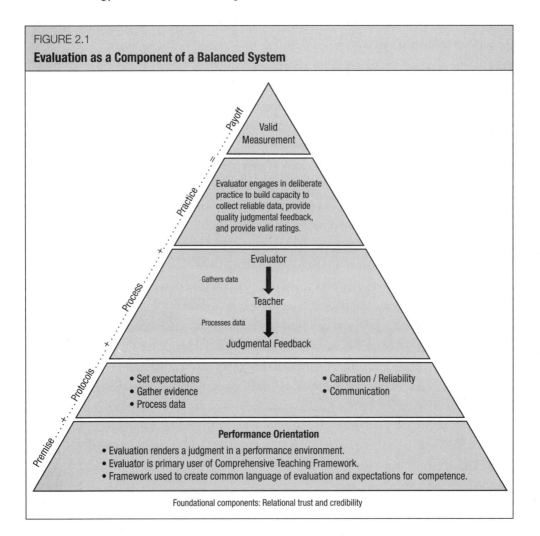

FIGURE 2.1

Evaluation as a Component of a Balanced System

Payoff: Valid Measurement

Practice = Evaluator engages in deliberate practice to build capacity to collect reliable data, provide quality judgmental feedback, and provide valid ratings.

Process +

Evaluator
Gathers data
Teacher
Processes data
Judgmental Feedback

Protocols +
• Set expectations
• Gather evidence
• Process data

• Calibration / Reliability
• Communication

Premise +
Performance Orientation
• Evaluation renders a judgment in a performance environment.
• Evaluator is primary user of Comprehensive Teaching Framework.
• Framework used to create common language of evaluation and expectations for competence.

Foundational components: Relational trust and credibility

The Premise: Evaluation Renders a Judgment in a Performance Environment

Given the parallels between student evaluation and teacher evaluation, it is accurate to think of evaluation as a summative assessment. Summative assessments are designed to render a judgment about an individual's performance at the end of a specific period of time. Summative assessments require both the individual taking the assessment and the person administering or scoring the assessment to adopt a performance orientation toward the process. A performance orientation stands in stark contrast to a learning orientation, which we describe in detail in the next chapter.

A *performance orientation* occurs in an environment where (1) the data generated from the process are used to make a judgment, (2) the evaluator wields the sole power to judge the quality of the performance, and (3) the result of the evaluation serves the information needs of an external source. As difficult as these facts are to hear for some teachers, understand that the processes and assumptions of effective systems of supervision and reflection occur in a *learning orientation,* which is governed by a completely different set of assumptions. A metaphor used by Rick Stiggins and his colleagues (2004) to describe summative assessment, which occurs in a performance environment, is that it is like an autopsy conducted by a coroner. The information is useful to the coroner but not the patient. The metaphor is a bit morbid but apt!

Make no mistake about the premise and purpose of evaluation. The goal of the process is to render a judgment. Anyone who tells you otherwise is either being disingenuous or, as we discussed in Chapter 1, trying to play a violin concerto with a pair of cymbals. It is important for evaluators and teachers to remember that this process is not personal, but it will result in an objective evaluation of the individual's personal performance. It feels personal because it reflects your work. This is why relational trust and credibility are essential foundational components. To open yourself to judgment requires trust in others that they ultimately have the best interest of the organization and you in mind. Being open to the results of that judgment requires a belief that the framework, the process, and the evaluator are credible.

Consider the following anecdotes that speak to why trust and credibility are such essential elements in a performance environment.

If you've ever been to the first day of a child's swim lessons, you understand the interrelationship of a performance orientation, trust, and credibility. The stakes are high, the water is deep, and the child is anxious, but you hand her over anyway. You trust the instructor has your child's best interests in mind. The instructor spends some time with the child to get a sense of how her skills relate to pre-established criteria. If the child is fearful and hesitant to get into the water, that does not mean she is good or bad; it means she is not comfortable in the water yet. The instructor will not try to help her quickly overcome this fear but will note her current level of performance to determine where she should be placed on the established continuum of proficiency. This judgment will ensure the child is placed in a credible system by a credible evaluator who has identified her strengths and needs. At the end of the six-week session that is designed to address the child's learning needs, she will be reevaluated to be properly placed in the next level. Clearly, the evaluation is about the child's skills—not about the child. The fact that she is a great kid does not automatically mean she should be swimming laps in deep water. Rendering a judgment based on anything other than the most relevant, objective data about the child's performance undermines trust, destroys credibility, and prevents the system from effectively serving her learning needs.

A second characteristic of a performance environment is that someone other than the performer renders the final judgment. For example, we adopt a performance orientation in athletics and the performing arts all the time.

We practice a sport during the week, but come game day, it is time to perform. The game will be played in the context of the rules, and only one team will win. We trust that the referees are credible; they will interpret evidence from the game evenly for every player. In the end, there will be a final score. We agree that those data points will be the judgment that matters. The losing team can rationalize or attempt to justify why they are, in fact, the better team, but that is irrelevant to the judgment. The final score is the final score. Although everyone likes to win, a victory feels hollow when we know it is based on misinterpretation of the criteria in place (the rules) or misinterpretation of the evidence (what actually happened during the game).

In the arts, we may rehearse a play for months, but come opening night it is time to perform, and the audience will respond accordingly. If the audience includes a credible critic, she will write an analysis and render a judgment about what she saw. The actors can disagree with the critic's judgment, but the review that appears is simply *what it is*. The actors don't write it. If we receive a harsh review, it is easier to accept if the critic is credible and offers valid criticism. And if the critic is credible and the review is great, it feels amazing to know that the hard work, the rehearsals, and the practice were noticed by someone with high standards of excellence.

The parallels to teacher evaluation are clear here. In a balanced system of evaluation, supervision, and reflection, evaluation is unapologetically about judging.

The Payoff: Valid, Reliable Measurement of Teacher Performance

The payoff of a system of effective evaluation is a valid, reliable, summative measure of teacher performance. Teaching is a complex, challenging, and important profession. Effective teaching matters. Therefore, it should be valued based on high standards of excellence. When a valid, reliable system of evaluation yields accurate results, it creates clarity for teachers regarding their current and next levels of performance, builds credibility in the community, and supports efforts to focus resources on fulfilling the school's purpose to meet each student's learning needs. Figure 2.2 summarizes the key elements of an evaluation system that ensures competence.

Aligning Protocols, Processes, and Practice to Purpose: Valid, Reliable Evaluation

Validity is about accuracy. Reliability is about consistency. In any system of measurement, attention to validity and reliability is essential to ensure accurate measurement. The quality of any evaluation system is determined by the extent to which it uses reliable raters, processes, and protocols to gather valid data related to valid criteria, resulting in a valid judgment of each teacher's teaching. We know that's a mouthful of validity. Let's apply those concepts to a scale at a physician's office to further clarify the importance of each of these types of validity.

FIGURE 2.2

Key Elements of Evaluation to Ensure Competence

Purpose	To ensure competent teaching in every classroom through a *valid, reliable* ratings process
Premise	Evaluation renders a judgment in a performance environment.
Owned by . . .	State/district
Payoff	Accurate measurement
Primary Effort	Trained evaluators and observation conducted by principals.
Processes	A series of classroom visits and collection of data by an evaluator that culminates in a valid rating
Informed by . . .	Walkthroughs, clinical visits, achievement data, artifacts
Purpose of Comprehensive Teaching Framework	To create common language of evaluation and expectations for competence
Type of Feedback	Summative, judgmental
Frequency of Feedback	Occasional
Disposition	Performance orientation
Active Participants	Evaluator and teacher
Primary Users	Principal/district
Leadership Role	Evaluating
Focus	General teaching behaviors, professional behaviors, student outcomes
Controlled by . . .	State/district/board
Key Process Question	How will we ensure evaluations are valid and reliable?
Key Outcome Question	How good is good enough to maintain or improve employment status?

The scale must be calibrated to ensure it provides a valid measure of weight. This requires attention to the accuracy of the tool (the scale) and its use to reach valid conclusions about what it was designed to measure (body weight). A few times a year, a technician may come in and calibrate the scale. The technician places exactly 150 pounds of weight on the scale, but the scale reads 152 pounds.

He removes the weight and places it on the scale 10 times, and every time the scale reads 152 pounds.

The scale is clearly reliable because it produces consistent results. However, it is invalid because it is not measuring weight accurately. So the technician calibrates the scale to ensure it accurately produces a valid and reliable measure of weight. The scale is now calibrated; it has been validated as a tool that accurately measures what it has been designed to measure. Remember the importance of form and function here: a perfectly calibrated scale is useful only for measuring body weight; it will provide a completely invalid measure of blood pressure every time.

Calibration of the scale is not enough to ensure accuracy. Even if the scale is valid, the conditions under which it is used can produce dramatically different results. A reliable process needs to be used to gather valid data. Should the patient remove his keys from his pocket? Take off his shoes? Be weighed in the morning or the evening? Stand on the front, middle, or back of the scale? The answers to these questions result in uniform processes and protocols that ensure the validated scale is used in a consistent manner that produces valid results.

This interrelationship between validity and reliability is critically important for teacher evaluation as well. Unless a system of teacher evaluation is reliable and valid, it will not be credible.

For example, a system of evaluation that is reliable but not valid would use the same processes year after year, but the ratings may not be accurate or may not accurately discern strengths and needs of individual teachers. Or, in a worst-case scenario, the ratings would consistently but inaccurately identify differences in quality among groups of teachers; struggling novices would always have higher ratings than teachers on the cusp of excellence!

An evaluator who was reliable but not valid would be diligent about doing exactly seven walkthroughs and three extended classroom visits, and completing all of the necessary forms on time and in triplicate—but the ratings would still be inaccurate. This inaccuracy could occur because the evaluation framework failed to identify valid, research-based components of effective practice. Or, as in the opening case study about Stickler Smith and Excellent Everett, the consistent inaccuracy could occur because evaluators were not sufficiently trained to use the evaluation rubric in a way that produced valid scores.

A system that was valid but not reliable would use a high-quality framework for effective instruction, but the evaluators would be all over the map in their ability to rate in a reliable manner. So, three evaluators would watch the same lesson but produce wildly different scores.

A high-quality system of evaluation, supervision, and reflection begins with the assumption that the evaluation system is reliable and will produce accurate ratings. However, validity and accuracy do not occur by chance. We contend that there are three action steps that must be in place to ensure validity and three action steps that must be in place to ensure reliability in a high-quality system of evaluation.

Figure 2.3 summarizes the areas of focus for a system of evaluation that is both valid and reliable. We discuss these attributes in detail in the sections that follow.

FIGURE 2.3

Areas of Focus for a Quality System of Evaluation

Criteria for Quality	Key Question	Action Steps
Valid	*Are ratings valid?*	• We use a valid, research-based framework to determine ratings. • We ensure valid ratings from credible evaluators. • We provide timely, accurate judgmental feedback.
Reliable	*Are raters and ratings reliable?*	• We focus on collection of quality data, not just quantity. • Teachers are actively involved in data collection. • We have high levels of interrater reliability; different raters produce similar ratings.

Valid Ratings as a Component of Effective Evaluation

A system that balances evaluation, supervision, and reflection includes a high-quality system of evaluation that results in ratings that are valid. Valid evaluation occurs in systems that emphasize the following beliefs and practices:

1. We use a valid, research-based framework to determine ratings. There are numerous research-based frameworks for effective teaching practice; select one. Ultimately, the quality of a balanced system of evaluation, supervision, and reflection will have less to do with which framework you select and more to do with how that system is implemented and used.

2. We ensure valid ratings from credible evaluators. An effective system of evaluation invests significant time, effort, and energy to ensure that all evaluators have access to high-quality professional development and certification in rendering valid judgments that result in accurate scores. This process requires evaluators to practice and hone their ability to provide accurate ratings.

3. We provide timely, accurate judgmental feedback. Despite hundreds of research-based instructional practices associated with an increased effect size in student learning (Hattie, 2009), teaching cannot be reduced to a mere checklist (Marzano, 2007). Expertise is about deploying the right strategy in the right way at the right time. Valid measurement of teaching requires that the evaluator understand the nuance and complexity of the intentional use of strategies to respond to each class's—and each student's—emotional, behavioral, and cognitive needs.

In the sections that follow, we describe these beliefs and practices in more detail. We refer to them as "action steps" and include specific information about how to develop a system that incorporates all of the elements necessary to ensure validity.

Valid Evaluation Action Step 1

We use a valid, research-based framework to determine ratings. If the purpose of evaluation is to accurately assess teacher performance, then it is critical that the assessment process be based on a valid framework that captures the essence and complexity of high-quality teaching that improves student learning. Fortunately, a number of frameworks have a strong research base for articulating what high-quality teaching looks like and how those various levels of quality should be valued on a judgmental continuum (e.g., Danielson, 2007; Marzano et al., 2011; Pianta, LaParo, & Hamre, 2008; Stronge, 2013).

When selecting an evaluation framework, it is critical to consider both the qualitative and quantitative components of that system.

Qualitative components describe the components of effective practice and should be used for evaluation, supervision, and reflection. They articulate what effective teaching looks like. These descriptors need to be general enough to capture the broad range of knowledge, skills, and dispositions associated with high-quality teaching yet specific enough to identify the complex range of practices and strategies that need to be prioritized and acted upon "in the moment of teaching," throughout a lesson, and across a unit of study.

When considering the merits of the qualitative components of a research-based comprehensive framework, it is important to strike a balance between a framework that has so much information that the evaluation tool is unwieldy and one that has oversimplified the elements of effective teaching to a mere checklist (Marzano et al., 2011). A framework with 100 components—all of which appear to be equally important—will consume large amounts of each evaluator's time and will merely result in information overload when communicating results to teachers. Conversely, effective teaching cannot be reduced to a simple checklist. In the 1980s, Madeline Hunter's seven components of an effective lesson were maladapted as an evaluation framework that mistook the elements of *an approach* to lesson design for the *only approach* to teaching. The "Hunterization" of teaching resulted in a reliable way to determine the quality of a lesson: *Are the seven components present or not?* But using the seven components as a checklist to determine teacher quality was not valid, was not Hunter's intent, and resulted in frustration for teachers and evaluators throughout an entire era (Hunter, 1985).

If qualitative components of a framework comprise the language of quality, quantitative components discern the levels of quality. Quantitative components are the numerical scores and associated ratings derived from those scores. We believe there are four important points to consider when analyzing a framework's evaluative rating scale.

Acknowledge the reality and limitations of reducing a complex set of skills and understandings to a numerical score. Teaching is a complex profession. Mutual funds are complex financial instruments. Hospitals are complex organizations. However, all of these are routinely evaluated using numerical scales that result in a summative rating. These ratings systems aren't perfect; in the world of assessment, perfection doesn't exist. What matters most is that these systems are as accurate as possible, can be used to clarify next steps for improvement, and are used fairly. While acknowledging the imperfection and limitations of ratings systems, we believe that a balanced approach to evaluation, supervision, and reflection is the best way to ensure that these systems are fair and are used to empower, rather than undermine, educators and their work.

Use the numerical score exclusively for purposes of evaluation. An emphasis on numerical scores for evaluation *and* supervision *and* reflection implies that the process exists solely for transactional measurement and is "all about the score." Too often, conversations about scores related to a teacher's performance are typically about the rater (*He's not fair; He doesn't like me; He rates everyone too high or too low*) or the teacher (*She's always gotten high ratings in the past; She's been teaching for 15 years, so she should always receive the highest ratings*). More productive conversations focus on the evidence that warranted the rating. The qualitative language of a framework is what must be used to inform mean-ingful reflection and dialogue about the effect of a person's teaching on each student's learning.

To put this another way, a teacher and a student can use the words on a well-designed writing rubric to talk about how the student might use a different approach to more effectively organize an essay. The purpose of this conversation is to help the student reflect on his learning, the quality of his work, and goals for improvement. However, conversations about the numerical value obtained on a component of a rubric tend to result in haggling over a grade.

Use enough levels when using categorical descriptors to identify and discern different levels of quality in the profession and discern growth. At a minimum, we recommend five levels ranging from Novice to Expert. This range creates enough evaluative "space" to acknowledge differences in practice across one's career. Systems that ultimately merely categorize teachers as "acceptable" or "unacceptable" fail to tap the power of systems that acknowledge, and allow for, the attainment of challenging goals and celebrate progress toward expertise (Toch & Rothman, 2008).

The semantics of different levels of descriptors for evaluation (such as Novice, Proficient, Accomplished) matter profoundly. As we discussed in Chapter 1, an evaluation system that equates low ratings with "needs improvement" paints teachers into a semantic corner that is impossible to escape. *If needing improvement means I am a poor performer, why would I ever acknowledge the need to improve? If I can't acknowledge the need to improve, how will I ever get better?* Everyone needs improvement. In education, science, business, athletics, and the arts, the individuals at the top of their field will all tell you they "need improvement." If improvement is associated with an evaluative liability, the potential of balancing evaluation with supervision and reflection is severely undermined.

The quality of a balanced system of evaluation, supervision, and reflection begins with the adoption of a research-based framework. Attention must be paid to both the qualitative and quantitative components of that framework to ensure it can be used in a manner that produces valid ratings.

Valid Evaluation Action Step 2

We ensure valid ratings from credible evaluators. A valid evaluation framework requires raters who can observe lessons and produce valid ratings. If this doesn't occur, the evaluation framework is irrelevant.

Training evaluators to produce valid ratings typically requires them to watch video clips of lessons that have been anchored to specific levels of quality. Over time, they develop an understanding of the specific behaviors and practices in the lesson that warranted specific, criterion-referenced scores. In general, these processes include the following steps:

- Experts identify videotaped anchor lessons related to the rating scale.
- Evaluators are trained to discern which components of a lesson (for example, the evaluator sees a teacher effectively asking higher-order questions) are associated with various components of the evaluation framework (the evaluator knows that those behaviors are relevant for the component associated with "challenging and supporting students' critical thinking").
- After evaluators have observed enough anchor lessons, they should be able to demonstrate competence in their ability to produce a valid rating by watching other videotaped anchor lessons, discerning which components of effective practice were most relevant to that particular segment, and generating an accurate score for the relevant indicators or domains.
- With enough feedback and deliberate practice, the evaluator can look into any classroom and discern what is happening, what is relevant, how what he or she sees is relevant to which criterion, and determine the appropriate level of quality for that criterion.

There is a wide chasm between "being familiar" with an evaluation framework and being able to use it to produce valid ratings. The recent emphasis on evaluation has created greater interrater reliability among raters and more valid ratings. Overall, this is good for the profession because it builds credibility with teachers and establishes relational trust. Internet-based training and assessments to become a "certified rater" are now standard practice for the most frequently used frameworks.

For districts that have developed their own framework, the process of validating the framework and ensuring raters can provide valid ratings is no less important. This local approach requires additional work because the district needs to capture anchor lessons on video or pull clips of teaching from the Internet and establish anchor scores for those lessons.

The days of different evaluators in the same district (or sometimes even the same building) observing the same lesson and producing wildly different ratings should be behind us. However, we still see significant challenges to ensuring accurate ratings, which we will discuss in more detail on the topic of reliability.

Valid Evaluation Action Step 3

We provide timely, accurate judgmental feedback. Effective judgmental feedback allows those who receive it to fully understand where they stand relative to organizational expectations for quality. Judgmental feedback is the most difficult type of feedback to deliver and receive (Stone & Heen, 2014). It is also the reality check that is essential to creating the conditions for improved practice (Bransford, Brown, & Cocking, 2000). Both the giver and the receiver need to clarify intent and expectations when delivering or receiving judgmental feedback.

Educators place a high value on developmental feedback to support student learning. Developmental feedback is essential because it helps learners understand where and how they need to invest their efforts to improve. We will describe the characteristics and the critical role of developmental feedback when we discuss systems of supervision and reflection. Evaluation, however, is about judgmental feedback. This type of feedback has a single, objective purpose: to clarify an individual's standing relative to specific criteria for quality.

Giving Judgmental Feedback

Have you ever applied for a grant? Typically, on the cover page of the application are criteria that explain how the application will be scored. The criteria could include components such as "evidence of your successful completion of projects of a similar scope in the past" or "includes a minimum of four letters of reference from nongovernmental agencies to whom you have provided services for a minimum of three years." Then it explains a scoring process, with points allocated for the amount or strength of evidence provided for each criterion. Finally, the application explains who will review the application: "Applications will be reviewed by an independent panel of individuals with extensive experience with program implementation in the field."

After weeks of waiting, the notification of the decision arrives. Typically, the letter starts with a "Congratulations! Our independent panel has reviewed your application and . . ." or a "Thank you, we're sorry . . ." that is then followed by an objective analysis of your application as related to the criteria.

If you received the grant, the judgmental feedback may state, "You provided evidence of successful completion of four projects that are similar to the scope of this project" and "Your five letters of reference from nongovernmental agencies exceeds the criterion for this component." If you did not receive the grant, the judgmental feedback may state, "You provided evidence of successful attainment of two projects that are similar to the scope of this project, but you did not provide evidence that these have been completed" and "You included three letters of reference from nongovernmental agencies, whereas the minimal criterion for this component was four."

Although you and your team are happier receiving the "Congratulations!" letter, if you do receive the "Thank you but sorry" letter, the quality of the judgmental feedback takes away the sting of not being awarded the grant because the process and the feedback are credible; you know exactly where you stand relative to the criteria.

Whether for a grant application or for teaching performance, the characteristics of high-quality judgmental feedback are the same: it is criterion referenced, objective, specific, and credible. (See Figure 2.4 on page 58.)

Criterion referenced. The premise for high-quality, judgmental feedback is that it is based on clearly articulated, published criteria. Rubric descriptors in comprehensive frameworks for effective practice provide the criteria upon which all feedback should be based. If an evaluator is giving judgmental feedback about a teacher's ability to set instructional outcomes, then the feedback should be stated in terms of the criterion. Comparisons to other teachers or to how the evaluator might have done the lesson stray from the intent of a criterion-referenced system and should not be used.

Objective. Evaluation is an objective—never a personal—process. An objective system of evaluation ensures the alignment and interpretation of a teacher's observable behaviors with published criteria. The evaluator is the conduit that connects the relevant data to the relevant criterion. High-quality, judgmental feedback objectively connects the observable evidence and relevant data to rubric descriptors.

Specific. A critical component of any type of feedback is specificity. General platitudes such as "Nice work" or "Good job" ring hollow and fail to help the teacher focus specific efforts to maintain quality in those areas. Furthermore, they distract the learner from focusing on areas to improve (Brophy, 1981). Conversely, general criticisms such as "Weak communication skills" or "Poor job teaching the lesson" invite defensiveness and confusion. Specifying the link between the criterion and specific behaviors associated with that criterion ensures clear alignment between the attributes of the performance that led to the specific conclusion about the individual's performance.

Don't confuse specificity with accuracy. A numerical value by itself does not provide adequate feedback. For evaluative purposes, a rating of 3 is a rating of 3. The specificity of *why* it is a 3 is what is most useful to the individual being evaluated. The feedback should clarify what it was about the performance that was most relevant to justify the obtained rating.

Credible. The components of credibility for evaluation are so central to a balanced system that they were described as a foundational component in Chapter 1. In the area of judgmental feedback, credibility means the evaluators clearly and accurately provide feedback that is aligned to the most relevant components of the comprehensive teaching framework.

FIGURE 2.4

Judgmental Feedback: Nonexample and Examples of Characteristics of Quality

Danielson Framework for Teaching—3C Engaging Students in Learning
Proficient—Level 3
The learning tasks and activities are fully aligned with the instructional outcomes and are designed to challenge student thinking, inviting students to make their thinking visible (Danielson, 2013, p. 51).

	Nonexample	Example
Criterion referenced	I might have started the lesson differently. When I *(reference to self rather than criteria articulated in the descriptor)* was a teacher	The learning activity of having students identify where they are on a kindergarten through 12th grade timeline was fully aligned with the learning goal of having students accurately place geologic periods on a timeline of the Earth.
Objective	I really liked this lesson! *(subjective and vague)*	Three students asked clarifying questions, and for each student you restated their question and provided a specific clarifying response as well as a follow-up question to confirm and challenge student thinking.
Specific	At 10:26, you asked your fourth question. *(specific, but not necessarily relevant to the criterion)*	20 of 25 students completed the in-class activity.

Marzano Observational Protocol—Design Question 1
8. Previewing New Content
The teacher engages students in activities that help them link what they already know to the new content about to be addressed (Marzano et al., 2011, p. 118).

	Nonexample	Example
Criterion referenced	The teacher didn't use previewing activity as well as other teachers I've seen this year. *(norm referenced)*	The teacher used a "hook" activity about dividing a pizza as a preview to help students access prior knowledge about fractions.
Objective	Some students had no idea what was happening. *(too subjective)*	25 of 28 students gave an answer to the preview question on their mini-whiteboards.
Specific	Good job! *(too vague)*	Evidence of student engagement included full participation in choral responses, all groups engaged in each pair share, and each student wrote at least 5 relevant examples during the brainstorming activity.

Receiving Judgmental Feedback

Receiving judgmental, or evaluative, feedback invokes fear in most people. In their seminal article in the *Harvard Business Review* on the fear of feedback, Jay Jackman and Myra Strober (2003) describe the procrastination, denial, jealousy, and self-sabotage that people use as coping mechanisms to avoid receiving or hearing judgmental feedback. This kind of reaction is unfortunate, because judgmental feedback can alleviate stress when it serves as an affirmation that lets us know we are doing our work well or as a catalyst that pushes us out of our comfort zone and helps us improve.

To respond to judgmental feedback more productively, Jackman and Strober (2003) contend that individuals should do five things: recognize emotions and responses, get support, reframe the feedback, break up the feedback, and use personal incentives. Here, we describe examples of these action steps through the lens of teacher evaluation.

Recognize emotions and responses. Evaluation occurs in every profession. Remember, the principal who evaluates you probably feels anxiety when he or she is being evaluated by the superintendent. If you feel fear and anxiety before an evaluative classroom visit, acknowledge that reality and talk to a trusted colleague or mentor. Alternatively, talk to your evaluator before a formal observation or post-conference. You might be pleasantly surprised at your evaluator's response when you articulate your concerns.

After you receive judgmental feedback, you may feel excited and affirmed if the feedback is positive or frustrated and angry if it is negative. The key is not to ignore or dismiss the feedback but to accept it with a humility that can build your awareness of opportunities for continued growth. Temper and balance your emotions. You may be as good as your strongest supporters believe you are, but you are never as bad as your detractors may claim.

Get support. All of us take pride in our work—and all of us can improve. Sometimes the feedback we receive strikes us particularly hard. We feel as though *we* have been judged more than *our work* has been judged. If you feel blindsided by a difficult evaluation, tell someone. Tell a confidant who can help you put the evaluation into a broader perspective and perhaps help you consider ways to confront the evaluator if the feedback was unfair. However, the most productive support is likely to come from an individual who helps you interpret, rather than dismiss, the feedback as an opportunity to improve.

Reframe the feedback. When we receive judgmental feedback, we may be overly sensitive to words we don't want to hear. This is a human response; we want to protect our ego. However, it is a response that severely limits our capacity to improve. Give yourself some space and look at the feedback objectively. Being told to "pay more attention" to something or that you used an "interesting approach" may seem like a personal criticism at first, but ultimately such feedback may provide guidance related to a growth strategy. It is important to really listen to the feedback. The fears we hear in our head are often irrational and far removed from the evaluator's intent. It is always appropriate to ask clarifying questions about feedback.

Break up the feedback into manageable tasks. If you receive too much feedback to respond to, break it up into smaller, more actionable chunks. Jackman and Strober believe that it is difficult to manage more than one or two improvement goals at any given time. Focus on a component of feedback that may require little change to improve and perhaps another area that is high leverage but will require some focused time, effort, and strategy.

Use personal incentives. Create small incentives that are of value to you as you make progress in responding to the feedback. For example, you might circle a date on the calendar and treat yourself to a personal reward if you successfully modify your practice by that date. Or you can create a social incentive such as telling your colleagues what you are working on and why, and then keeping them updated and hearing their affirmations as you make progress.

It is beneficial to all stakeholders to ensure that evaluations are valid. The adoption and appropriate use of a comprehensive teaching framework, trained evaluators who understand their role in connecting relevant data to aligned criteria, and the appropriate use of—and response to—judgmental feedback are essential areas of focus to ensure evaluation is a component of a balanced system.

Reliable Processes as a Component of Effective Evaluation

In a system that balances evaluation, supervision, and reflection, reliable processes for evaluation ensure that ratings are accurate and conducted efficiently.

Reliable evaluation occurs in a system that emphasizes the following beliefs and practices:

1. *We focus on collection of high-quality data, not just quantity.* Too often, systems of evaluation can turn into a transactional paper chase. The system is perceived to be about frequency of visits and number of forms rather than evidence and accuracy. "How many visits are required?" is the wrong question. "How much evidence is enough?" ensures the reliability of the process because it attends to the ultimate goal of generating a valid rating.

2. *Teachers are actively involved in data collection.* Evidence of effective teaching does not only occur while teachers are teaching. Artifacts such as assignments, assessments, examples of feedback teachers have given to students, and written reflections for the purpose of evaluation are all reliable ways to improve the validity of specific ratings.

3. *We have high levels of interrater reliability; different raters produce similar ratings.* If all evaluators have been trained and certified as having the ability to provide valid ratings, then all of them should have a high level of interrater reliability. This means five evaluators could watch the same lesson and all provide nearly identical scores for the relevant portions of that lesson. High rates of interrater reliability build credibility in the system because teachers understand the system is consistent and not arbitrary.

In the sections that follow, we describe these beliefs and practices in more detail. As with the beliefs and practices related to validity, we refer to them as "action steps," and we include specific information about how to develop a system that incorporates all of the elements necessary to ensure that an evaluation system uses reliable processes.

Reliable Evaluation Action Step 1

We focus on collection of high-quality data, not just quantity. A reliable system of evaluation uses processes that emphasize consistent collection of relevant, high-quality data. A comment we've heard hundreds of times in our work supporting the implementation of valid, reliable systems of evaluation is that principals are completely overwhelmed by time requirements related to evaluation. Although the goal of ensuring valid, reliable ratings is clearly important, we've seen too much emphasis on the number of visits to classrooms and not nearly enough on the quality of data collection about teaching. The recent emphasis on teacher evaluation in federal grant programs and state legislation has created an even greater urgency for principals to invest time and effort in the evaluation process. This situation has merely exacerbated the challenges faced by principals who were already stretched too thin.

According to Kim Marshall (2005), "most principals are too busy to do a good job on supervision and evaluation" (p. 731). This reality results in three types of principals that Marshall describes as saints, cynics, and sinners.

The saints spend countless hours on the technical components of the evaluation process. They follow the letter of the law, intentionally engage in the clinical evaluation process like clockwork, and complete every form on time, producing defensible, detailed, accurate ratings. Unfortunately, they are so focused on the process that they forget to include teachers in the formative opportunities that could lead to genuine improvement.

The cynics complete the evaluation process by putting forth as little effort as possible to produce a defensible rating. However, they don't believe the process matters much in terms of improving teacher quality or supporting student learning.

The sinners don't bother much with evaluations unless they are trying to get rid of an ineffective teacher. They operate on the premise that if there are no complaints, then everything must be fine. Clearly, this is inexcusable. Failure to fulfill their obligation to ensure a high-quality teacher in every classroom is a violation of principals' core responsibilities and should be dealt with severely. Furthermore, this is precisely the approach that results in evaluation being seen purely as punitive in some schools.

Marshall's "coping" mechanisms resonate with what we've seen in the field. The imbalance between the number of evaluators and the number of people being evaluated means there is not enough time for principals to gather enough data to ensure flawlessly reliable ratings, let alone to provide enough feedback to support each teacher's growth. The net effect is that some principals may find themselves driven by the frequency of visits and number of forms rather than mindfully engaging in reliable processes to gather data that ensure a valid rating.

To ensure the reliable implementation of a valid evaluation process, evaluators need to begin by acknowledging that they are likely powerless to improve teaching through the evaluation system. Consider the following example.

If a typical middle or high school teacher has five classes a day, he or she will teach approximately 900 classes a year. If an evaluator visits three of those classes for nearly an entire period and does five or six 10-minute walkthroughs, then he or she has collected a sample of about 0.3 percent of the teacher's total teaching. This ratio does not provide enough data to improve teacher practice. Given this fact, we argue that principals should spend less time thinking that evaluation will improve teacher performance and more time ensuring they can reliably produce valid ratings.

Reliable processes for data collection require principals and other evaluators to consider the length and frequency of data collection, the type of data collected, and focused efforts to gather specific types of data. Let's look more closely at each of these.

Length of data collection. In studies to determine how the length of visits contributes to validity of ratings, researchers found that "shorter observations can yield scores that are highly predictive of scores based on a whole-lesson observation" (Joe, McClellan, & Holtzman, 2014, p. 439). Although they caution that exclusive use of a few short observations will not afford valid ratings, the findings justify considering a focus on high-quality data collection rather than time spent collecting data, as a discerning factor.

Frequency of data collection. In a longitudinal study of teacher evaluation in four districts ranging in size from 25,000 to 100,000 students, researchers found that three to five formal observations were required to ascertain acceptable levels of reliability (Whitehurst, Chingos, & Lindquist, 2014). Reliability did not increase significantly after the third observation.

Type of data collected. Although most components of frameworks for effective practice are related to classroom teaching, elements such as the planning and preparing of lessons, communication, and collaboration are better discerned through various artifacts. (See the next action step for more on this topic.)

Strategic data collection. Random data collection processes yield random results. There is nothing random about the outcomes that evaluators need to measure; they must make specific judgments about specific facets of teaching. Given the amount of time evaluators have available, random data collection processes (e.g., an evaluator randomly popping into a class and quickly looking around with the hope that enough data will be collected to complete a good chunk of the evaluation form at a later time) are a waste of valuable minutes. In their analysis of evaluators' use of the Measures of Effective Teaching (MET) framework, researchers found that focusing observation on a few dimensions of teaching produced more reliable scores than when evaluators looked for evidence of the full set of dimensions in the MET framework (Joe et al., 2014).

Robert Marzano argues that evaluators need to be explicitly purposeful in gathering data for evaluation. If an evaluator needs evidence of a teacher's ability to ask higher-order questions, then the evaluator should be explicit about that fact. Guessing at a score without any evidence of performance related to that score is unacceptable. A principal might say, "I don't have any evidence related to how effectively you engage students with higher-level questions. Is there a class period next week when I might see you use some questioning strategies?"

Objectivity and randomness are two different things. Reliability requires the focused, strategic collection of data.

That said, consider this possibility. Despite the fact that almost all teachers (and students) carry a video and recording device with them everywhere they go, we rarely think of using smartphones to record evidence of effective teaching. Could a teacher submit a video clip of a lesson segment in lieu of a walkthrough? If the goal is conducting five walkthroughs, the answer to this question is no. However, if the goal is to gather valid evidence that results in a reliable score, then why not?

Reliable Evaluation Action Step 2

Teachers are actively involved in data collection. A reliable evaluation framework acknowledges the fact that while the final, evaluative judgment comes from an evaluator, the data-collection process can be made more efficient by trusting teachers to provide credible evidence of their professional practice. If we are gathering data to make a judgment about someone, shouldn't that individual play a key role in the process to ensure consistently accurate ratings?

Artifacts. Too often, teachers themselves—the most reliable source of information about their own practice—are kept out of the process. Teachers should actively gather artifacts—assessments, lesson plans, examples of feedback given to students, evidence of student learning—to build a portfolio of evidence related to their competence. Cynics may say that teachers will simply gather samples of their best work, but isn't it useful to know what work teachers believe to be their best? If it is exemplary, the evaluator better understands the level of quality the teacher should be able to produce with greater consistency. If it is emerging, the evaluator better understands the teacher's strengths and needs.

A study of the influence of teacher portfolios on the evaluation process found that teachers and administrators believed that portfolios created "a more accurate and more comprehensive reflection of teacher performance" than observations alone (Attinello, Lare, & Waters, 2006, p. 140). This does not mean that teachers should be given significantly more work by engaging in a transactional, haphazard documentation process. However, a measured approach adds to the reliability of the data-collection process, fosters relational trust, and builds credibility. As the authors of the study on portfolios state,

> Teachers valued the opportunity to showcase their achievements to administrators who demonstrated they cared about what was taking place in the classroom. . . . Therefore, teachers felt that evaluation was not only fairer; they also sensed empowerment and control over their professional development as their work was shared with their administrators. (Attinello et al., 2006, p. 146)

Teacher voice. In addition to giving teachers the opportunity to provide artifacts, their voice needs to be honored in dialogue about various facets of effective practice throughout the evaluation process. Too often, the principal does most of the talking during a post-observation conference. We believe the teacher should engage in a written analysis of the lesson after it has occurred, answering questions such as these: What went well? What would you do differently next time? How did you know the students were learning?

These are powerful questions that provide insight into the extent that teachers are purposeful, aware, and responsive. These questions can serve as a catalyst for thoughtful conversation about the lesson that occurred. For these questions to be effective, the written reflection needs to occur before the post-observation conference. Furthermore, during the post-conference, the teacher should do most of the talking. Too often, the specter of judgment shuts down the reflective process. If the teacher believes that a few moments after the principal asks, "How do you think the lesson went?" the principal will simply provide the only answer that matters, then the teacher has little incentive to provide insight about the quality of the lesson, especially if relational trust or credibility is not present.

Reliable Evaluation Action Step 3

We have high levels of interrater reliability; different raters produce similar results. Interrater reliability is the extent that different evaluators produce similar scores after observing the same teaching. If evaluators have a low level of interrator reliability, ratings are not valid because the scores have more to do with this miscalibration of the evaluators than the teaching they were supposed measure. Too often, evaluators are assigned a group of teachers for whom they have primary responsibilities, and then they proceed as though there is no one else who can assist in the evaluation process. Having multiple evaluators allows for additional pathways for a teacher to access judgmental feedback and allows for the evaluators to access developmental feedback about their skills in evaluation. In fact, pairing new evaluators with an experienced evaluator to engage in the process with two or three different teachers is an excellent way to build the capacity and confidence of the new evaluator. A recent study by the Brown Center on Education Policy (2014) suggests that outside evaluators are able to rate teachers with a higher degree of accuracy than school administrators.

In a report published on the culminating findings from a three-year study on the Measures of Effective Teaching Project (Bill & Melinda Gates Foundation, 2013), researchers found that "given the same total number of observations, including the perspectives of two or more observers per teacher greatly enhances reliability" (p. 5). The study also found that "adding observations by observers from outside a teacher's school . . . can provide an ongoing check against in-school bias" (p. 5).

Protocols to Align the Purpose of Effective Evaluation to the Payoff

As we have previously stated, the purpose of evaluation is to accurately assess teacher performance using a reliable process that results in a judgment that is a valid measure of quality. Valid evaluation occurs in systems that emphasize the following beliefs and practices:

- Using a valid, research-based framework to determine ratings.
- Developing credible evaluators.
- Providing timely, accurate judgmental feedback.

Reliable evaluation occurs in systems that emphasize the following beliefs and practices:

- Focusing on quality of data collected, not just the quantity.
- Actively involving teachers in the data-collection process.
- Ensuring different raters produce similar results.

The protocols listed in the Evaluation section of the matrix in Appendix E can be used to help ensure that the evaluation process is both valid and reliable. Each protocol is categorized by main users, purpose, and outcome. See Appendix A for more detailed explanations of the specific purpose and process for each protocol, as well as the actual protocols.

A Case in Balance: When Evaluation Works Effectively

It is the second week of September. Staff members file into the multipurpose room for the first of four quarterly meetings about the district's evaluation process.

A packet of information is distributed that outlines the purpose and process of the evaluation system and how the system supports students, teachers, and the district's mission and goals. New teachers are already familiar with the language of the rubrics because exemplary practices aligned to that shared language are the focus of the district's induction program. Principal Connor and Assistant Principal Franklin discuss the ongoing certification work they engaged in over the summer to ensure their ratings were both valid and reliable. They also discuss the ongoing work being done across the entire district to ensure calibration in the use of the rating system. The union representative and four instructional coaches from the building talk about what they learned over the summer while sitting alongside Principal Connor and Assistant Principal Franklin during the training that allowed them to receive their certification in using the evaluation framework.

Giving students more effective developmental and judgmental feedback is a strategic district goal. Principal Connor discusses how some of those practices will be applied to her work in giving feedback to teachers. The professional development committee reviewed teachers' professional growth goals that had been established in the previous year and determined that student engagement and questioning were two areas of need identified by teachers. During a staff meeting each quarter for the remainder of the year, video of classroom teachers will be used to train staff in understanding the relationship between specific classroom behaviors and their corresponding accurate ratings. The training will include the same modules for these two areas that the principals, coaches, and union representative had as they engaged in the certification process.

The evaluation process is clearly laid out for all staff, including frequency of visits and the use of specific forms and web tools. Principal Connor talks about her primary responsibility to the board in evaluating teachers: to ensure valid, reliable ratings that guarantee a baseline of quality teaching in every classroom, for every student—no exceptions. She explains how this work is no different than the administration of summative assessments or final exams. "My job is to support you as much as possible in a manner that results in a strong—and accurate—rating." She then states her mantra: "No surprises."

As Principal Connor engages in the evaluation process, she communicates clearly about the strengths and opportunities she sees. When she does a walkthough, she follows up that day about specifics that she saw and provides clear judgmental feedback about strengths and needs. Furthermore, her formal observations are meticulous: the teacher submits a lesson plan and describes the lesson in terms of the broader unit. Additionally, the teacher submits a copy of the assessment that will be given at the end of the unit. Principal Connor reviews these documents before visiting the classroom. After the observation, the teacher completes a fairly lengthy reflection document and submits that document before the formal post-observation conference.

Principal Connor keeps it real; she discusses areas of need in a respectful manner. She is clear about the strengths of the lesson. What is most interesting is how she does this. As a teacher who transferred from a nearby district notices, "She did more listening than talking, but when I left, I'd had all of my questions answered, I knew where I stood on the evaluation front, and I felt empowered to do what I needed to do to get even better."

When the final Thursday in May arrives, there is little anxiety. Teachers grab their evaluations. They open their envelopes in the office and scan the ratings quickly—no surprises—and read a narrative that seems to capture exactly where they are in their professional journey. A short line forms outside the offices of Principal Connor and Assistant Principal Franklin. A teacher pokes her head in Principal Connor's doorway and says, "I just wanted to say thanks for all the feedback. I am thrilled that I went up in the engagement domain. I really learned a lot of different strategies this year, and I was amazed at how my students responded. Thanks for your support throughout the year, and thanks for noticing."

3

Supervision as a Component of a Balanced System

A Case Out of Balance: When Supervision Works Poorly

In the third week of September, the link to the website for the annual goal-setting process was sent to all teachers. It included the following e-mail from Principal Thompson:

> Teaching Staff:
>
> As you know, state statute and board policy require you to set two instructional improvement goals and one student growth goal each school year. Please use the template provided on Teacher Link to complete your two professional growth goals. For your student growth goals, given the district's focus on improving achievement in mathematics and reading, all teachers are required to establish a growth goal of 10 scale-score points on the state math or reading assessment. Additionally, you are required to attend at least five professional development sessions annually. Sessions can only be counted if you have your certificate signed the day of the workshop and scan and upload your certificate of attendance to Teacher Link within one week of the session; no exceptions. Goals are due October 15. Your End-of-Year Inventory form is due May 30. If you need any help accessing or completing these forms on Teacher Link, let me know.
>
> Thanks,
> Principal Thompson

The teachers dutifully complete the forms. Those who teach something other than mathematics or reading/language arts feel some resentment about having to set student learning goals built around the state test, but they do so, as requested. The professional growth goals that they set range widely. Some talk about better meeting the needs of struggling learners, others about wanting to increase student engagement; a few talk about a workshop they want to attend around a topic of interest to them, but not necessarily directly connected to teaching and learning. Some teachers have set the same goal each year for the last seven years. Many select a goal based on instructional skills or strategies that they already see as areas of strength.

As the year progresses, teachers upload their certificates of completion for the professional development sessions they've attended. During Principal Thompson's evaluation conferences, he does a "supervisory check-in" by asking how many certificates they've uploaded and how their progress is going toward their goals. "Very well" is the typical response. "Good to hear" is the typical reply.

Before May 30, teachers work on their End-of-Year Inventory form. They write a list of workshops attended and articles read. Some scramble through their files to check what their goals were. Each teacher dutifully writes a short reflection of three or four sentences about whether or not they met their professional practice goals and their student growth goal. If they did not meet their student growth goal, they have to explain what they will do differently next year.

The following week, evaluations appear in teacher's mailboxes. Near the top of the form are three boxes:

☐ Professional growth goal completed.

☐ Minimum of five professional development sessions attended.

☐ Student learning goal met, or submitted explanation why goal was not met.

All three boxes are checked on nearly every teacher's evaluation.

The Purpose of Supervision in a Balanced System

The purpose of supervision is to support teacher growth by creating opportunities for developmental feedback that *focuses* teachers' efforts and *empowers* teachers to achieve goals related to improved professional performance. This occurs in the form of a series of learning opportunities whose *function* is to ensure teachers understand the gap between expert use of skills and strategies, their current use of skills and strategies, and the practice that will help them achieve goals for growth.

Despite more than 60 years of literature advocating for a distinction between evaluation and supervision (Burton & Brueckner, 1955; Sergiovanni & Starratt, 1979), too often these terms—and systems—are still used synonymously. This is a decidedly anachronistic use of very different processes with very different purposes. Although the word *supervision* implies a subordinate relationship between a principal or department chair and a teacher, a more contemporary use of the term implies a teacher-centered process that supports teacher growth. As we discussed in Chapter 2, systems of evaluation that focus solely on performance may unintentionally punish individuals for efforts to move beyond their comfort zone and take risks. When this occurs, supervision and evaluation are in direct conflict: *How can I improve when merely acknowledging the need to improve will be held against me?*

A system of supervision that serves as a component of a balanced framework of evaluation, supervision, and reflection is most likely to align the purpose to the payoff of supervision when there is a clear link among the premise, protocols, processes, and areas of practice, as shown in Figure 3.1.

The Premise: Supervision Creates Conditions for Growth in a Learning Environment

The quality of any system of supervision is determined by the extent to which it focuses teachers' efforts on areas to improve and empowers them to chart a path to do so. Although we've characterized evaluation as being done "to" teachers, supervision is intended to be done in partnership: a teacher "with" a supervisor or coach. In a system of effective supervision, the emphasis is not on what the individual supervisor does; it is on how that supervisor creates the conditions for teachers to uncover and close the gap between their current performance and the next level of performance. When this occurs, teachers become intrinsically motivated to access the continuous feedback necessary to improve.

The Payoff: Improved Performance Toward Growth Goals

The payoff of a system of effective supervision is that it helps teachers focus their efforts on meaningful improvement goals and empowers teachers to access, and act on, feedback necessary to improve. Teaching is a complex profession that requires the understanding and use of hundreds of specific skills and strategies. When teachers are freed from the isolation that often characterizes the profession, are empowered to make informed decisions about opportunities for improvement, and have access to the developmental feedback necessary to improve, they can make tremendous progress in acquiring and developing new skills and strategies. Figure 3.2 summarizes the key elements of a supervision system to support growth.

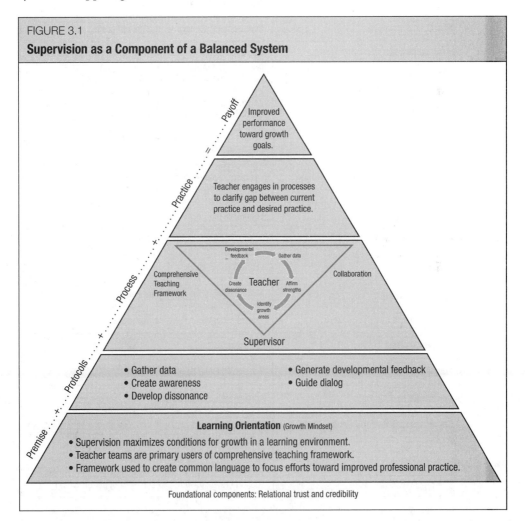

FIGURE 3.1

Supervision as a Component of a Balanced System

FIGURE 3.2

Key Elements of Supervision to Support Growth

Purpose	To support teacher growth by creating opportunities for developmental feedback that *focuses* teachers' efforts and *empowers* teachers to achieve goals related to improved professional practice
Premise	Supervision creates conditions for growth in a learning environment.
Owned by . . .	Teacher, with the support of supervisor
Payoff	Improved performance toward growth goals
Primary Effort	Teachers gather data, establish goals, and engage in practices and protocols to help understand, and close, the gap between current and ideal performance.
Process	An ongoing process designed to affirm strengths, identify opportunities for growth, create dissonance, and generate developmental feedback
Informed by . . .	Observation, data, reflection, discussion
Purpose of Comprehensive Teaching Framework	To create common language to focus efforts toward improved professional practice
Type of Feedback	Formative, developmental
Frequency of Feedback	Frequently, and through as many sources as possible
Disposition	Learning orientation
Active Participants	Teacher, supervisor, colleagues, coaches, mentors, students
Primary Users	Teacher, supervisor, coaches, colleagues
Leadership Role	Coaching
Focus	Specific teaching behaviors
Controlled by . . .	Administration and teachers
Key Process Question	How will we create feedback that focuses teachers' efforts in a way that empowers them to move from their current level of performance to the next level of performance?
Key Outcome Question	What is the current level of performance, and how can we support growth toward the next levels of performance?

How Supervision Is Different from Evaluation

For supervision to fulfill its potential as a process to improve teacher capacity, we believe three primary differences between evaluation and supervision need to be addressed.

First, whereas evaluation is a series of events completed by an evaluator, supervision is a process—not a position—that is designed to support teachers' efforts to improve. Too often, the words *evaluation* and *supervision* are used interchangeably with *evaluator* and *supervisor*. In the context of evaluation, this makes sense because the evaluator is the active agent, gathering evidence that determines a valid rating. However, if the supervisor is the active agent in the supervision processes, teachers find themselves watching from the sidelines; the supervisor makes the visits, uses the instructional framework, establishes the goals, and generates the feedback. *This is problematic.* When this occurs, supervision is merely being used as an extension of the evaluation process.

An apt metaphor to students' schooling experience helps clarify the distinction between evaluation and supervision. *Evaluation* is like the state accountability assessment, and *supervision* is like the curriculum that students engage in to do well on the state assessment. All educators understand these are two very different processes. Just as the state assessment is designed to allow others to render a judgment based on a sampling of student performance, evaluation is designed to render a judgment based on a sampling of teacher performance. It is obvious that taking the state assessment doesn't transform kids into better students, and evaluation will not transform those being judged into better teachers. To help students improve, you need a curriculum that has clear targets for quality, provides focused exposure to new skills and understandings, and allows students to try those new skills, receive feedback, and monitor their growth toward improved learning. Effective systems of supervision afford teachers these exact same opportunities for learning.

Second, whereas evaluation is primarily concerned with validity to ensure accurate ratings across a broad spectrum of performance, supervision is concerned with supporting teachers' capacity to focus their efforts toward specific opportunities for growth. Ideally, these efforts are focused in areas that will best leverage their capacity to better support their students' learning needs. In other words, evaluation is driven by the question "Is the evaluator's rating accurate?" whereas supervision is driven by the question "Is the teacher empowered to focus on data, opportunities, and feedback required to develop important new skills and strategies?" This difference requires a significant shift away from the evaluative, quantitative dialogue of justifying scores and ratings to a formative approach that allows each teacher to take a "deep dive" that allows for better understanding of the nuanced strategies expert teachers use to support student learning.

This shift from *evaluation as valid* to *supervision as focused* occurs through two very different habits of mind. The holy grail of evaluation is developing and implementing an iron-clad, infallible, completely accurate rating system. *We have defined what good teaching is and can measure it accurately every time.* (We agree with you that this system doesn't exist, and the people who develop such tools know this isn't possible, but they are expected to strive for it anyway.) Ironically, a high-quality system of supervision attempts to do the opposite—to create ambiguity through dissonance. Here, the goal is to help teachers see their practice in new ways, to move them out of their comfort zone. *I thought I was really good at asking higher-order questions, but I was in a classroom today and saw a teacher ask higher-order questions that completely blew me away. I wonder what strategies I could learn that would allow me to ask questions like that some day?* This is a statement from a teacher who has identified a specific gap between current and ideal practice. Statements like these are catalysts for focused growth. Effective systems of supervision elicit statements like these from teachers all the time.

Third, whereas it is essential that evaluators can reliably use a valid evaluation tool, supervision is concerned with empowering teachers to be autonomous in their ability to continuously find new ways to improve. This is analogous to the distinction between teachers who see themselves as either the "sage on the stage" or the "guide on the side." A teacher in the first group seeks fulfillment through the sound of *her* voice; a teacher in the second group seeks fulfillment in helping students find, and trust, *their* voice. To paraphrase John Hattie's (2009) observation that the most effective educators help *students* to see themselves as their own best *teacher*, we assert that the most effective systems of evaluation, supervision, and reflection help *teachers* see themselves as their own best *supervisor*.

According to Malcolm Knowles's theory of andragogy (1984), adults and children have unique learning needs. Immersed in ongoing professional responsibilities, adults want to improve their ability to face the challenges they encounter each day. Rather than gravitating toward "just in case" opportunities to learn skills and concepts that might be relevant in an authentic context at some point in the future, adult learners gravitate toward learning opportunities that honor their rich skills and experiences while simultaneously acknowledging new learning needs.

Knowles (1984) describes four key premises:

- Adults need to be involved in the ongoing planning and evaluation of their learning. Self-direction and relevancy precede authentic engagement.
- Experience (including mistakes) provides the basis for next learning.
- Adults are most interested in learning about subjects that have immediate relevance to their job or personal life.
- Adult learning is problem centered rather than content oriented.

Subsequent research supports these principles (e.g., Cochran-Smith & Lyte, 2001; Haslam & Seremet, 2001); adults learn best when they are empowered by opportunities to learn new skills and understandings and apply solutions to the challenges they face.

Aligning Protocols, Processes, and Practice to Purpose: Focused Goal Setting and Empowered Teachers

The concept of *focus* as a key to growth is found in influential works by Kerry Patterson and Peter Senge. In *Influencer: The Power to Change Anything*, Patterson and his coauthors claim that "enormous influence comes from focusing on just a few vital behaviors. Even the most pervasive problems will often yield to changes in a handful of high-leverage behaviors." (Patterson, Grenny, Maxfield, McMillan, & Switzler, 2007, p. 23). Senge (1990), who coined the phrase *learning organization*, describes how "small, well-focused actions can sometimes produce significant, enduring improvements, if they're in the right place" (p. 64). Both authors see focusing on specific, high-leverage skills and strategies as the pathway toward meaningful growth. Anders Ericsson uses the term *deliberate practice* to define the focused process by which expertise is reached (Ericsson, Krampe, & Tesch-Romer, 1993). We describe deliberate practice in more detail in our discussion of reflection in Chapter 4.

Empowerment means teachers, not the supervisor, are the active agents in the supervision process. Teachers need to make insights, use data, and engage in protocols that support their understanding of their own professional growth. The *teachers* are visiting other classrooms, watching video of their own practice, surveying students to better understand their classrooms through their students' eyes, writing reflections about the lesson that just occurred, and writing insights related to the gap between where they are, what they hope to become, and how they will close the gap to get there. The supervisor facilitates the system and supports a culture of relational trust and credibility that creates opportunities for teachers to accurately appraise their own teaching.

Whereas a system of effective evaluation requires significant effort addressing validity and reliability to ensure that the purpose and the payoff are aligned, a system of effective supervision requires processes that empower teachers to focus on important growth goals. Figure 3.3 summarizes the areas of focus for a system of supervision that is both empowering and focused. We discuss these attributes in detail in the sections that follow.

FIGURE 3.3		
Areas of Focus for a Quality System of Supervision		
Criteria for Quality	**Key Question**	**Action Steps**
Empowering	*Is the context empowering?*	• We strive to create and support a learning environment where errors are welcomed and questions are valued. • We strive to build teacher autonomy through autonomy-supportive practices. • We use frequent, high-quality, developmental feedback from a variety of sources to support teacher growth.
Focused	*Are goals focused?*	• Teachers use a comprehensive teaching framework to establish and guide efforts toward specific improvement goals. • Teachers' goals are rooted in, and supported by, continuous data collection and modification of practice. • Teachers collaborate to calibrate.

Empowered Teachers as a Component of Effective Supervision

In a system that balances evaluation, supervision, and reflection, supervision empowers teachers. Empowerment is exemplified in systems that emphasize the following beliefs and practices.

1. **We strive to create and support a learning environment where errors are welcomed and questions are valued.** A high-quality system of supervision emphasizes a learning orientation rather than a performance orientation. If a system of supervision is intended to inform teacher growth, it must be owned by the individuals who are engaged in the learning process and not simply implemented as an extension of the evaluation system. Acknowledging the need for growth, asking clarifying questions, and saying *I don't know* are essential processes in a learning environment.

2. **We strive to build teacher autonomy through autonomy-supportive practices.** In a high-quality system of supervision, teachers are the central agents and the supervisor facilitates the system to benefit and empower teachers. Teachers need to actively use protocols that clarify their current level of practice, the desired level of practice, and how to close the gap in between.

3. **We use frequent, high-quality, developmental feedback from a variety of sources to support teacher growth.** Meaningful, actionable feedback is the fuel that generates learning. If the goal of a supervisory system is to generate growth, then it is not possible for a single supervisor to provide enough feedback to support that system. Developmental feedback can also come from students, colleagues, artifacts, and video.

In the sections that follow, we describe these beliefs and practices in terms of "action steps" that include specific information about how to develop an empowering system of supervision.

Empowering Supervision Action Step 1

We strive to create and support a learning environment where errors are welcomed and questions are valued. In Chapter 2, we discussed the characteristics of a performance environment. In a performance environment, the function of the system is to render a judgment. Key processes and assumptions of a performance environment are that (1) the evaluator wields the sole power to judge the quality of the performance, (2) mistakes are counted and count against you, and (3) the data generated from the process are used to make a summative judgment and serve the information needs of an external source.

A learning environment is entirely different. In a learning environment, the purpose of the system is to support growth and create opportunities for actionable feedback. Here, individuals (1) work with others as they strive to close the gap between current and next levels of performance, (2) use mistakes as a catalyst to inform the next steps in the learning process, and (3) use data generated from the process to serve the information needs of the learner. Figure 3.4 shows some of the key distinctions between a performance environment and a learning environment.

For a clear example of the difference, consider the process of getting ready to perform a play. The goal is clear: by opening night the cast needs to be ready

FIGURE 3.4

Performance Environment Versus Learning Environment

Performance Environment	Learning Environment
• Is evaluation centered.	• Is learner centered.
• Judgmental data justify a rating.	• Actionable data inform the learner's efforts.
• Mistakes count, and count against you.	• Mistakes are a part of the learning process.
• Trying new skills and strategies may be viewed as admission of the failure of existing skills.	• Trying new skills and strategies is a sign of ongoing growth.
• Questions may be deemed as evidence of ignorance.	• Questions are a pathway to deeper understanding.
• Feedback justifies a rating.	• Feedback is embraced as a pathway to growth.
• Is an occasional, summative event.	• Is a process to navigate the ambiguity and struggle of the learning process.
• Results in a judgment.	• Results in growth.

for *the performance.* The audience will come and judge. Glaring mistakes will count and will be counted against the cast or crew. The number of laughs, the amount of applause, or the number of times audience members find themselves confused will be data that the audience uses to render a judgment. The director's job is to create a learning environment that maximizes the likelihood that the performance will go well.

In this scenario, the director supports a learning environment by giving the cast members their script in advance of rehearsals to help develop a shared understanding of the plot, the characters, and the setting. Then each cast member focuses specifically on his or her character's lines. The initial run-throughs focus on specific scenes with specific actors. Here, the director creates opportunities for rehearsal and a lot of developmental feedback. The same sequence of lines may be repeated over and over again. If a mistake is made, the actor may simply pause and self-correct, or the other actor in the scene may simply suggest they try it again. Rehearsals may be videotaped and scrutinized by the director *and* the actors—not to cast judgment, but to focus efforts.

Additionally, the director collects data and feeds that data back to the actors and crew: *The scene should take four minutes and it's taking five. How can we pick up the pace? The lighting in that scene was too dark; next time let's try it with another spotlight.* The director welcomes mistakes and troubleshooting: *Every mistake we make during rehearsal is one we can correct before opening night.* The director understands he cannot fix every error; he needs to support a culture where everyone is empowered to access and respond to feedback in a manner that helps each individual engage in the right work that will, ultimately, make the entire production better. As opening night draws closer, the feedback from each rehearsal gets more detailed and specific. In this learning-environment scenario, everyone understands that the goal of the process is to improve. Individuals work collaboratively to address weaknesses and affirm strengths in order to clarify and then close the gap between *what is* and *what will be.* In theater, there is a clear understanding about the distinction between rehearsal in a *learning environment* and opening night in a *performance environment.* But what if this distinction didn't exist?

If the director and cast adopted a performance orientation during rehearsals, a very different scenario would unfold. The director might watch rehearsals and silently keep tabs on strengths and errors but not communicate any of those until after opening night. An actor who does not know his lines for a scene may deny the need to rehearse because he doesn't want to be judged. The director may chastise the actors and crew during the first rehearsal for not knowing all their cues or hitting all their marks—leaving the cast and crew feeling distrustful and alienated. Or, conversely, the director may settle for mediocrity after the first rehearsal by simply declaring, "Really great! Nice job!" and in doing so, fail to facilitate the challenge and support required to help everyone improve. And to be completely absurd, the actors may never rehearse together for fear of being judged by one another; the director watches each of them rehearse individually and gives them feedback about their level of proficiency for various facets of acting just before the curtain rises.

This performance-environment scenario is fraught with abundant risk and little reward to acknowledge the need to improve. The director is the only individual empowered to make decisions about quality. Feedback is almost nonexistent or is given only after it is too late to do anything about it. Individuals are isolated from one another and, in turn, miss opportunities to learn. The failure of the system in this scenario is glaring. But for many educators, changing the word "director" to "supervisor," "actor" to "teacher," and "rehearsal" to "observation" results in a scenario that feels suspiciously like systems of supervision that are stuck in an evaluative, performance-oriented context.

The shift from a performance environment to a learning environment requires the following actions:

1. Determine the extent to which teachers view the existing systems of evaluation and supervision as primarily serving the information needs of evaluators to justify ratings, as compared to the information needs of teachers to guide their efforts toward growth.
2. Collaborate to articulate the distinctions between the purpose and processes intended for evaluation as compared to those intended for supervision. Publish the results, and build credibility by honoring the distinctions.
3. Emphasize relational trust and continuous improvement as key values of the organization through genuine dialogue (talking the talk), actively

addressing concerns (listening, not just hearing), and acting in ways that model a learning orientation (walking the walk).

4. Clarify which processes, protocols, and forms must be completed and submitted for evaluation as compared to the processes, protocols, and forms that are required, or optional, for supervision.

5. Clarify the purpose of data collection: who accesses the data and whose information needs does data collection serve? Acknowledge that any data that must be collected and turned in to an evaluator are evaluative.

6. Celebrate learning by creating time in staff meetings and board meetings to describe a problem that was addressed in a novel way or an opportunity that was created through new ways of thinking and doing.

7. Use autonomy-supportive practices that emphasize choice, purpose, and opportunity to create the capacity for each teacher to be his or her own best supervisor (we discuss this in detail in the section that follows).

8. Create pathways for high-quality, developmental feedback from a variety of sources to support teacher growth (we discuss this in detail in the next action step).

When looking at a list like this, you may say, "We have established a learning environment already!" If you believe that is the case, ask teachers these questions and mindfully listen to their answers:

- Do you trust that your principal is competent in all facets of her job? Do you believe this about your colleagues?
- Do you believe your principal is a credible source to provide high-quality feedback about your teaching? Do you believe this about your colleagues?
- Is the primary purpose of the district's comprehensive teaching framework to make judgments about teacher quality or to inform teacher growth?
- If the existing goal-setting process were not required as a part of your evaluation, would you do it anyway?
- If you had a question about curriculum, instruction, or assessment in your classroom, would you ask it aloud at a staff meeting?
- Do you trust that your colleagues have your best interests in mind and that they want to see you become an expert teacher?

- Would you be willing to have other teachers visit your classroom to inform their professional practice and raise questions about your professional practice without fear of being overtly judged or criticized?
- If you were struggling with a component of curriculum, instruction, or assessment, would you tell an administrator?
- If your principal is made aware of a concern about your practice, do you believe it would be brought to your attention as a productive learning opportunity, or do you fear it might be held against you?

Empowering Supervision Action Step 2

We strive to build teacher autonomy through autonomy-supportive practices. Self-determination theory seeks to explain human motivation as related to our basic needs to be autonomous and productive. Edward Deci and Richard Ryan (1985, 2000, 2002) have spent their careers researching and documenting how choice, purpose, and opportunity are more effective teaching tools than the behaviorist's arsenal of rewards and threats. They describe two types of motivation: autonomous and controlling.

Controlling motivation is based on the premise that a transactional reward or punishment needs to be present to get a learner to complete a task. Although the task may get done, this approach can lead to haphazard work, tension, and anxiety. Furthermore, Deci and Ryan argue that these controlling behaviors often alienate the learner from engaging in the task in the future when the reward or punishment is not present. So when students don't do a formative assignment because it is not worth any points, or when teachers ignore a principal's recommendations for improvement when he is not sitting in the back of the room, Deci and Ryan are not surprised. The learners do not own, and therefore are not interested in, acquiring these processes or skills; they've been coerced and conditioned to value the reward or consequences rather than the work itself.

Autonomous motivation, on the other hand, is based on the premise that when learners find the work to be interesting, believe their efforts will result in positive outcomes, and feel a sense of control over how the work is completed, they will not only get the work done but do it with greater quality and care. Furthermore, autonomously motivated learners take more measured risks, tend to be more creative, and are more likely to persist when they encounter obstacles. Therefore, if teachers and leaders want to create learners who are intrinsically motivated, they need to use leadership or teaching behaviors that support each learner's independence and need for autonomy. As Daniel Pink (2009a) states, "Management works, but self-direction works better; when people are self-directed, engagement goes up."

Therefore, when autonomy-supportive leaders want to build capacity in their organizations, they don't ask *"How do I motivate people?"* Instead, to paraphrase Edward Deci, they ask, *"How do I create the conditions in which others will motivate themselves?"*

In a recent TED Talk, Edward Deci (2012) described four key components to support individuals' autonomy: (1) look at the situation from their perspective; (2) give individuals choice in tasks and goals; (3) encourage and affirm initiative; and (4) provide individuals with the meaning of the work they are asked to do so they relate its importance to their own values. The payoff benefits teachers and students alike. Deci states that when teachers are given opportunities to thrive in an autonomy-supportive environment, they are more likely to create autonomy-supportive environments for their students as well. Figure 3.5 shows how Deci's components of autonomy support can be used in a system of supervision of teaching.

Motivation in adult learners is improved if the work is self-directed and the goals are self-generated (Pink, 2009b). Structured protocols such as written reflections, video analysis of one's own or another's teaching, and collaborative dialogue paired with the use of a comprehensive framework can provide the autonomy support necessary to maximize efficiency and effectiveness of a learning experience.

Controlling and Autonomy-Supportive Behaviors

For example, consider how a controlling principal as compared to an autonomy-supportive principal might use video in a staff meeting. The controlling principal may return from a conference interested in a new strategy, briefly explain the strategy to his teachers in a staff meeting, and then play a video clip of a teacher using the strategy. Before he plays the video clip, he says the following:

I was just at a conference on effective questioning, and I think this technique will help raise test scores. Here is what this looks like. Please take some notes. The next time I am in your classroom, I want to see you doing more of this.

FIGURE 3.5

How Autonomy Support Relates to Supervision of Teaching

Key Components of Autonomy Support	Examples Related to Supervision of Teaching
Look at the situation from their perspective. (What is their internal frame of reference?)	• Consider how the history of supervision and evaluation from teachers' perspectives may undermine, or support, trust and credibility. • Consider if forms and protocols are designed to fulfill requirements for evaluation or authentically serve teachers' needs to improve. • "Stand in their shoes" and acknowledge perspectives other than that of the evaluator or supervisor.
Give individuals choice in tasks and goals. (Support active engagement in the decision-making process.)	• Ensure that improvement goals come from the *teacher's* analysis of the *teacher's* reliable data and the *teacher's* use of protocols to move from current to next practice.
Provide individuals with opportunities to see their practice in new ways by encouraging and affirming initiative.	• Use the framework for effective practice as a shared language for teachers to talk about teaching and learning, not just for evaluators to justify ratings. • Acknowledge isolation as a limiting factor in improving teacher capacity. Create a culture, and provide opportunities, where teachers can discuss teaching and learn from observing one another. • Use protocols and provide resources necessary to create healthy dissonance between current practice and what is possible. • Develop a growth-mindset culture that does not punish mindful attempts at learning: not *"Why did you do that!"* but *"What did you learn from that?"* • Encourage and affirm creativity.
Provide individuals with a meaningful rationale so they understand the importance of the work they are being asked to do as related to their own values.	• Frame initiatives in terms of shared goals, values, and vision rather than in terms of contractual requirements and mandates. • Frame opportunities in terms of the individual's personal goals, values, and vision.

Note: Key components in Column 1 are from Edward Deci, "Promoting Motivation, Health, and Excellence: Ed Deci at TEDxFlourCity," 2012.

In this frame, it is likely that the only change the principal will evoke is greater frustration and longer parking-lot conversations. Without components of choice, purpose, and opportunity, the principal resorts to external accountability as the carrot and veiled threats as the stick to obtain compliance.

Consider a very different approach from the autonomy-supportive principal. The autonomy-supportive principal looks at his staff's improvement goals and notices that nearly 60 percent of teachers have an improvement goal that is related, in some way, to effective questioning techniques. He goes out of his way to learn more about effective questioning and identifies a resource that he believes may be of interest to many of his teachers. Before the staff meeting, he asks teachers to bring a copy of their goals and the school's framework for effective instruction. He guides teachers' attention to the improvement goals and the aligned portion of the framework and asks them to discuss the interrelationship between these two documents with a colleague. Before he plays the video clip, he says the following:

> *I am going to play a video clip of a teacher using a questioning technique that I thought would interest many of you because I know it's a specific area where many of you already have some great strategies and are trying to get even better. We'll look at it twice. The first time, I simply want you to look for strategies the teacher uses so you can do a pair-share and articulate them to a colleague in terms of our instructional framework. The second time I play the clip, I want you to answer these questions:*
>
> - *What did the teacher do?*
> - *How did the students respond?*
> - *What questions does this raise about my own teaching?*

The controlling principal issues a directive to teachers to fulfill *his* interests and needs. The autonomy-supportive principal invites his staff to engage in a way that honors their capacity as self-directed learners; he empowers teachers to engage in the analytical thinking that will create some reasonable dissonance and get them thinking about their own professional practice. By "standing in their shoes," the autonomy-supportive principal empowers teachers to build their capacity to be their own best supervisors.

Context for Autonomy-Supportive Coaching: Four Essential Components

Four components are required to create a context for successful coaching relational trust, choice, a learning environment, and a shared language of effective practice.

Relational trust. There needs to be a culture of honesty and integrity: *I will be honest with you because I respect the work that you do, and I will hold our discussions in the strictest of confidence.*

Choice. Giving someone a coach feels a bit like giving someone a book about how to dress with style or a self-help book on how to make friends. Regardless of intent, giving advice that isn't asked for can create defensiveness rather than openness. Creating a culture where coaching is widely accessible and valued extends a powerful opportunity for professionals invested in the complexities of teaching.

Learning environment. The collective beliefs that *everyone can improve* and *we are all here to learn from one another* need to permeate the school culture. In schools where past practice assigned coaches only to teachers who were struggling, mindful attention to implementation is especially important.

Shared language of effective practice. When everyone, not just evaluators, uses the framework to guide discussions about current and next practice, it creates a shared language for professional dialogue. This shared language ensures that coaching is productive and does not devolve into miscommunication, confusion, and a guessing game in which the "coach" articulates some version of *I saw how you did it; now tell me how I would have done it.* A shared language of effective practice empowers teachers to help one another get better because it clarifies the purpose for having the conversation in the first place. It places parameters around, and clarifies the direction of, powerful coaching conversations that guide efforts to improve professional practice.

Autonomy Support via the "Seven Caps" of Coaching

If we are going to empower teachers to be their own best supervisors, we need to harness the collective expertise and skills of anyone on staff who can help a colleague move from current to next levels of practice. Those individuals will need a general understanding of a shared framework for effective teaching, have experience teaching in a classroom, know how to state observations, and know how to ask a few specific types of questions. Individuals who meet these criteria are qualified to engage in powerful coaching practices. Fortunately, this description fits almost everyone on staff. Just as we advocate for less of a focus on *supervisor* as a position and a greater emphasis on *supervision* as a process, we believe there should be less emphasis on *coach* as a position and more emphasis on *coaching* as a process that should be taught to all teachers.

But how can we afford to provide professional development for coaching for all teachers? Isn't coaching a specialized, autonomy-supportive role? Our response to these questions comes in the form of more questions: If the role of a coach is to motivate, challenge, and support others to attain a goal, wouldn't students benefit from a cadre of teachers who had strong coaching skills? How can we afford *not* to improve our collective capacity for coaching?

According to Robert Hargrove, whose seminal book *Masterful Coaching* (2008) has influenced coaches across dozens of disciplines, effective coaching requires individuals to understand seven different types of conversations, or wear seven different "caps." Each of these conversations can be matched to the needs of individuals seeking support. As Hargrove states, "Once people can distinguish among the seven coaching caps, they can become effective with using them fairly quickly" (p. 98). Here we describe each of Hargrove's roles and how they look through a lens of balanced evaluation, supervision, and reflection.

1. *Declaring new possibilities.* Educators can become deeply entrenched in what teaching and learning has to look like and what a classroom "is." A coach who declares possibilities pushes people beyond their own self-imposed limits by helping them brainstorm a new "what if?" reality. Hargrove advises using this cap when people "say they have no choice but to pursue conventional options" (2008, p. 99). One of Tony's favorite questions to start a conversation about new possibilities is this: "What would you do differently if you had to hold all kids to high standards, you couldn't give grades, and kids could come and go as they pleased?"

2. *Serving as thinking partner.* Educators are faced with hundreds of problems each day, most of which cannot be "solved" but can certainly be improved upon to benefit students and learning. Simply ask, "What do you think?" as an invitation to thinking together with someone else. If the other person is stuck, we like this question: "I know you don't know the answer now, but if you did, what advice would you give to yourself?"

3. *Drawing others out.* Telling people the answer disempowers them to find solutions for themselves. "Instead, start with the premise that the answer is within the person and your job is to draw it out by listening for brilliance," says Hargrove (2008, pp. 99–100). By stating "I am curious to hear what you are thinking" and "I think you are on to something; tell me more about that," we've found that teachers articulate profound insights. Too often, the best ideas go unstated and unattempted because of the assumption that they are not worthwhile.

4. *Reframing thinking and attitudes.* According to Hargrove, reframing can be a matter of asking "Will the way you have framed the problem give you the results you want?" (2008, p. 100). Reframing can be very powerful when teachers are frustrated and coming from a perspective of helplessness or expressing limited beliefs about what children are capable of doing. We've found questions that reestablish locus of control, which we talk about in more detail in Chapter 4 on reflection, can provide a powerful reframe. For example, consider these statements and questions: "It sounds like you feel like the new reading program is limiting how you can teach. What are some things you still have control over in your classroom, and how might you focus on those practices?" Or "It sounds like you have an energetic group of students in that class. What are some ways you could harness that energy into some active learning?"

5. *Teaching and advising.* Coaching comes from a perspective. A framework for effective instructional practice articulates a set of values that, regardless of the details, educators can rally behind. Statements such as "The energy in a highly engaged classroom is contagious," "All kids are capable of doing amazing things," or "Teaching is a complex process and requires purposeful planning" capture the essence of why many of us went into this profession in the first place. These statements require expertise to move from value to action. If someone wearing the *teaching and advising* hat has advice to share, it can be done when relational trust and credibility have been established with another. The advice, however, must be thoughtful. As Hargrove states, "Give advice that is caring and candid, practical, wise, and well timed" (2008, p. 101). In other words, draw from a common base of values, but give advice with quiet confidence that honors the intelligence and strengths of the people you want to listen.

6. *Forwarding action.* Coaching can create the conditions in which an individual says, "I can see the possibility, but what do I do next?" This is a powerful point in any coaching conversation because the coach can help an individual move from identifying a need to closing a gap with thoughtful action. Here we agree completely with Hargrove's advice to "focus on small, high-leverage steps that move the ball forward without overwhelming people" (2008, p. 101). This is the time to consider an action plan to begin learning about and implementing a new instructional strategy or a new approach to curriculum or assessment. Focus is essential to engage in the deliberate practice that results in growth.

7. *Giving honest feedback.* High-quality developmental feedback is critically important to any system of growth and learning. Hargrove reminds us that "we cannot see ourselves as others see us, detect our strengths or gaps, or recognize the unintended consequences of our actions . . . the feedback cap is essential to helping people become more aware" (2008, p. 102). Collegial feedback can be tremendously powerful in a peer-to-peer coaching relationship. However, it is essential that the feedback be objective and based on a shared set of objectives for quality. Objective feedback that holds up a mirror to one's own practice can harness the capacity of a shared framework by creating parameters around what "better" looks like. (Effective, nonjudgmental feedback is so important, and so difficult to do well, we discuss it in detail in the section on the next action step.)

These seven modalities of coaching are not intended to be followed as a set of steps. As any good teacher knows, the approach taken depends on the learner's needs. The same strategy doesn't work every time. The goal is to harness these conversations in a manner that moves individuals in a direction that helps them see what is possible, believe they can address any challenge or opportunity they choose, and move from vision to action.

If the purpose of supervision is to support teacher growth, then autonomy-supportive practices that help all teachers become their own best coach can build unlimited capacity to help teachers grow. When teachers have identified a clear sense of purpose related to how they can improve and are given choices that honor their needs as autonomous learners, they are more likely to seek out, listen, and value opportunities that support their own growth.

Empowering Supervision Action Step 3

We use frequent, high-quality, developmental feedback from a variety of sources to support teacher growth. In Chapter 2 on evaluation, we described the importance of high-quality, *judgmental* feedback to clarify learners' understanding of their current level of performance. The purpose of *developmental* feedback is to help clarify how to close the gap between current and next levels of performance in support of an individual's efforts to grow. Consider the following anecdote.

One of the reasons Paul loved coaching high school football was because it helped him learn how to be a better teacher. In fact, one of his favorite teaching stories did not occur in a classroom but on a football field with a linebacker named Daryl.

Like all good coaches, Paul put in a lot of time developing scouting reports, practice plans, and practice drills to ensure his players were successful. During one game, the opposing team was successfully running a specific type of offensive play called a *play-action pass*. In a play-action pass, the offensive team fakes a running play and then passes the ball downfield to a wide-open receiver. On multiple occasions, he and the other coaches knew the play-action pass was coming, but they still couldn't stop it. The coaches realized that their middle linebacker, Daryl, was in the wrong place each time.

Early in the game, before the other team started using the play-action pass, the coaches saw Daryl hustling. "Great work out there, Daryl!" one of the coaches yelled to affirm his effort. Daryl flashed a smile. It felt good to be noticed.

As the game progressed, the other team started to take advantage of the fact that Daryl was in the wrong position each time on the play-action pass. "Daryl," another coach called out onto the field. "You've got to try harder to stop the play-action pass." The opponents ran the play again, Daryl was nowhere to be found, and they racked up even more yards.

"How can the coaches say *try harder*?" Daryl muttered under his breath. "I'm killing myself out here."

On the next play, Daryl was taken out of the game. Paul pulled Daryl aside, walked him away from the other players, looked him right in the eye, and, in his best inspirational voice, said, "Daryl, if we're going to win this game, you've got to stop the play-action pass."

Daryl nodded, gave his coach a thumbs-up, and ran back onto the field. The next play was a play-action pass. The receiver caught the ball for a long gain. Again, Daryl was nowhere near the receiver.

Once again, Paul pulled Daryl aside, looked him right in the eye, and asked, "Daryl, do you know what a play-action pass is?"

"I have no idea, Coach," Daryl replied.

Paul grabbed a small whiteboard, drew a few quick *X*s and *O*s, and gave Daryl a succinct explanation of a play-action pass and why they weren't able to stop it. When Paul paused to catch his breath, Daryl grabbed the pen.

"So I've been here"—Daryl scribbled an *X* on the whiteboard and then crossed it out—"and I should be all the way over here?"

"Exactly," replied Paul.

"That makes a lot more sense," said Daryl.

Back in the game, Daryl was a different player. Not only was he able to stop the play-action pass for the rest of the game; he also was able to read the offense more effectively in other kinds of plays and seemed to be in on every tackle.

Initially, the coaches thought they were giving Daryl the feedback he needed to be successful. In reality, they were simply communicating information that was meaningful to *them*. How often have we felt like Daryl? We're told to try harder despite feeling exhausted by our current efforts. We're told to change something without having any time to learn something new. We're told to do something that we do not understand—and rather than acknowledge our ignorance, we pretend to know exactly what a coach, or a supervisor, or a principal means. Understanding the components of developmental feedback can support our efforts to help others dramatically improve.

The Components of Developmental Feedback

There are six components in an effective system of development feedback. If you've ever been lost and asked for help to arrive at your destination, the presence or absence of these components probably determined the ease or frustration you experienced in arriving at your destination. Consider the following scenario.

You are driving to a family wedding in a rural community where you have never been. You drive over a hill, and your cell phone, which you've been using to navigate to the church, is suddenly out of service. You realize you will need to ask for directions. You see a farmer and you pull over to ask for help. There are likely six components that will need to be present if the farmer is able to guide you to your destination.

First, you have to have a specific destination in mind, and you need to be able to articulate where you are headed. If you don't know where you are going, you are not really lost; you are just out wandering.

Second, you have to clarify your current position. You cannot get useful information about how to get to your destination unless you know the starting point. If you're asking for directions in person, this is a fairly clear process; but if you're calling for directions, this can be very challenging (*"I see a field on my left and a field on my right"* will be of little use to the person on the other end). This is a critical step because the directions to guide your way are different if you're coming from the east than if you're coming from the west.

Third, you need to establish a general understanding of the gap between your current position and your desired destination with the person who is trying to help you. You need to know about how far you are from the intended destination and the nature of the terrain you will need to cover to get there.

Fourth, the feedback must be given and sought continuously in a manner that is understood by the learner. If the farmer tells you to drive until you see the Smith farm and then turn north, that information is of little use to you unless you know what the Smith farm looks like and you know which way is north. Without a shared understanding of the terrain and landmarks, this part of the process can be the most difficult and frustrating for both individuals.

Fifth, the information you are given needs to be timely. This means you need to access the information while it is still useful to inform your efforts. Being told the route you *should have* taken well after you arrive late for the wedding is not useful. In fact, hearing the "obvious" route after you've been lost usually only adds to the frustration.

Finally, the information you are given needs to be developmental and not judgmental. Imagine the farmer simply giving you a rating for orienteering (*"Son, I've rated your navigation skills to be minimal"*), judging your effort (*"You must not be trying very hard"*), sharing a general platitude *("Nice try! Keep up the good work!"),* or being sarcastic *("You city folk don't know much about getting around, do you?").* None of these forms of judgmental feedback would help you get to the destination. In fact, they would alienate you from seeking further assistance. On the other hand, developmental feedback would focus on the components of the first four items: *You are going north on Highway C, and the destination is to the east on Pioneer Road. The church is a few hundred yards away from that water tower at the top of that hill. You'll know you're close when you go over the railroad tracks."* This feedback provides specific, objective information that you can use to guide your efforts as you move forward in the process.

More important, once you arrive at the church, you can get the final and most important piece of developmental feedback to clarify your next steps in learning. When your aunt asks, "So, what did you learn from the experience and what will you do differently next time?" she is working with you to create a pathway for what John Hattie (2009) calls *feed forward*. Feed forward clarifies the link between your strategy and results the next time you face a similar situation.

This scenario provides a rich metaphor for understanding the components of developmental feedback that we've identified from a variety of sources (Black & Wiliam, 1998; Hattie & Yates, 2013; Stiggins et al., 2004; Wiggins, 1998). Figure 3.6 illustrates how these components relate to effective supervision.

Feedback of this level and depth does not need to be given all the time. But awareness of these components and of the learner's interests and needs can help a supervisor, coach, or colleague give feedback that is more purposeful and useful.

Giving and Receiving Developmental Feedback Effectively

Although much has been written about *giving* effective feedback, far less has been written about *receiving* feedback effectively. Harvard's Douglas Stone and Sheila Heen (2014) argue that how people receive feedback is as important as how it is given. A skilled receiver of feedback can create value from feedback even if it is poorly delivered, inaccurate, or ill timed. Stone and Heen separate feedback into three categories to help those receiving the feedback better discern how to act on it: feedback as appreciation, feedback as coaching, and feedback as evaluation.

FIGURE 3.6

Components of Effective Developmental Feedback to Support Learning

1. Recognizes the desired goal. The feedback provides a clear, concise picture of the learning that is to be developed or the skill that is to be demonstrated.

> **Yes:** *"You are working on stating clear learning goals to empower students to establish action plans to demonstrate proficiency in identified goals."*

> **No:** *"You need to do a better job letting the kids know what they're supposed to do."* (Too vague)

2. Shows evidence of present position in relation to the goal. The feedback provides clear, unambiguous information about the qualities or attributes of the current performance, the desired performance, and the gap between the two.

> **Yes:** *"You clearly stated the learning goals. This was evidenced by the goal being articulated, appropriately, on top of the assignment sheet. Student evidence of use of the goal was clear when students restated the goal in their own language, discussed two ways they would accept evidence from a learner who successfully obtained the goal, and wrote one goal-related thing they already do well and one goal-related thing they are still learning."*

> **No:** *"It would be better if the kids were clearer about what they were working on."* (Unclear and ambiguous)

3. Includes a shared understanding of how to close the gap between current and desired goal. The feedback focuses the learner on effective efforts and strategies required to develop the specific skill or understanding.

> **Yes:** *"Some of the students didn't articulate the goal correctly; they stated an activity. I wonder if giving them a T-chart with examples and nonexamples might clarify their understanding of the difference between the two."*

> **No:** *"The kids didn't know the learning goal. You need to be sure they do."* (No strategy referenced)

4. Is given and sought continuously in a manner that is understood by the learner. A continuous process that guides and modifies the learner's efforts will most efficiently build skills and understanding associated with the goal.

> **Yes:** *"In today's lesson I noticed the learning goal was posted, you referenced it several times, and students were able to accurately identify how the homework supported their efforts to obtain the learning goal."*

> **No:** *"I've been reading a lot by [name of author] lately, and her ideas on motivation theory seem pertinent here."* (No shared understanding)

5. Is timely. Timely feedback allows learners to adjust their behavior before going too far off course or adopting bad habits. Feedback after a summary judgment has been made is of little use to the learner.

> **Yes:** *"I noticed that you called on the same two students repeatedly for answers during the lesson on improper fractions this morning. I know they were the only ones raising their hands, but how could you involve more students in the discussion?"*

> **No:** *"When I visited your classroom in October (seven months ago), I saw students responding with interest and persistence as you engaged them in an authentic problem-solving task."* (Not timely)

6. Is developmental, not judgmental. Feedback should be targeted toward the specific performance and strategies that may improve the understanding or skills of the learner. Statements of judgment about intentions or innate ability are rarely effective.

> **Yes:** *"It was clear that students could articulate the goal in their own words. This clarifies the fact that the learning goals are for the students, and not just the teacher, to use to guide their efforts."*

> **No:** *"That was really good"* or *"That was awesome"* or *"Are you kidding me?"* or *"That clearly didn't work."* (Judgmental and ambiguous)

Feedback as appreciation is used to "acknowledge, connect, motivate and thank individuals" (Stone & Heen, 2014, p. 35). Appreciation is essential because it helps others feel connected and valued. Of the three types of feedback, appreciative feedback is the easiest to receive, but not all appreciative feedback is created equal. The most effective feedback given as appreciation is specific, is valued by the person receiving it, and is conveyed in an authentic manner. *"Good job on the science fair"* will not resonate as well as *"Your effort in preparing the science fair this year resulted in a well-attended, exciting learning experience for students and parents. I saw kids just beaming with pride. Thank you!"* Unfortunately, we often take the "good" for granted and focus on giving feedback about needs and deficits. Giving appreciative feedback is essential to ensure that when giving coaching and evaluative feedback, those on the receiving end are actually willing to listen.

Feedback as coaching is used to "expand knowledge, sharpen skills or improve capabilities" (Stone & Heen, 2014, p. 35). Receiving this kind of feedback is essential because it is information that helps us improve. Coaching feedback occurs in two forms. The first form is providing specific information to help the receiver learn new knowledge and skills. For example, *"You mentioned that you thought some of the projects weren't well organized. What might you do differently next year to help students be better organized?"* This coaching feedback directs the receiver's attention to address a deficit that she has acknowledged.

The second type of coaching feedback includes information about a gap that the *giver* believes needs to be filled. This is a more difficult type of coaching because you are imposing your will on another. *"I think there needs to be more of an emphasis on high-quality design of student displays. How did you help students plan and arrange their layout and design?"* Clearly, this is more complex; the teacher may counter by answering your question or challenging your premise. Awareness of components of Deci and Ryan's autonomy support and Hargrove's coaching hats, described earlier in this chapter, can support informed decisions about what type of coaching feedback is best suited to the learner's needs.

Feedback as evaluation is used to "rank against a set of standards, to align expectations, to inform decision making" (Stone & Heen, 2014, p. 35). Evaluation is essential because it helps individuals know where they stand relative to expectations for quality. Evaluative feedback can be positive: *"Your work on the science fair demonstrates an exceptional level of professionalism in communicating clearly with families and being an active member in school and community events."* Or it can be negative: *"Your inability to collaborate with colleagues in an open-minded and timely manner created confusion and resentment among faculty and staff."* Here, the feedback is given in a manner that creates a direct link between the individual's performance, expectations for quality, and the results.

According to Stone and Heen, when giving feedback, it is critical to remember three things: (1) strive for balance, (2) consider the receiver's perspective, and (3) know that regardless of the giver's intent, evaluative feedback is what the receiver pays the most attention to. Specific strategies for how to give and respond to judgmental, evaluative feedback were discussed in detail in Chapter 2.

Striving for balance in feedback for affirmation, coaching, and evaluation is difficult, but essential, for the following reasons:

- *To be constantly evaluated but never affirmed* can paint teachers into a corner of learned helplessness. Anything short of attaining the highest ratings often leaves teachers feeling as though nothing they ever do is good enough, they are given little or no support to improve, and they are not appreciated.
- *To be continually coached but never evaluated* can leave teachers feeling as though they are running on a treadmill with a broken LED display: they are endlessly asked to exert more effort to improve but don't know where they are in the learning process. Does their supervisor keep asking for even more because he thinks they are nowhere near their destination, or because he thinks they have unlimited potential and have almost accomplished something exceptional?
- *To be endlessly affirmed but never coached* can communicate a message of low expectations, leaving teachers feeling as though there is no expectation for improvement or learning new skills, because the supervisor doubts improvement is possible.

Considering the feedback from the receiver's perspective is critical to avoid what Stone and Heen call "cross transactions" (2014, p. 38), which occur when there is a mismatch between the type of feedback given and the type of feedback that was expected. For example, Tony recalls an experience as a district office administrator when he was asked to do some clinical evaluations of teachers in an elementary building with many new teachers.

After engaging in a traditional clinical cycle with a teacher through a supervisory pre-conference, observation, and post-conference, he wrote the post-conference summary report and sent it to the teacher. A few minutes later the principal from that school called. "What did you say in Sally's post-conference summary report? She's outside my office crying!" On the post-conference evaluation form, in addition to some affirmation and words associated with high levels of evaluation, Tony had written copious amounts of coaching feedback, much of it in the form of questions: *How might you . . . ? I wonder if . . . ? How will you . . . ?* The teacher had grown accustomed to receiving primarily affirmation in her first two years of teaching. She had expected affirmation, instead received coaching, and assumed it was evaluative: *If he is asking me to think about other ways of teaching, then he must think I am a horrible teacher.*

To avoid cross transactions, Stone and Heen (2014) recommend two important steps. First, ensure clarity between the giver and the receiver about the purpose of the feedback. Second, work to separate evaluative feedback from feedback that is designed for coaching and appreciation. This is particularly important given research that implies that when given evaluative feedback and affirming feedback at the same time, some individuals will completely ignore the evaluative feedback and only process the affirmation. Conversely, other research implies that negative comments are given the greatest weight by the receiver even if negative, evaluative comments were only a small portion of the feedback. We believe these conflicting findings mean there are other variables involved. Perhaps relational trust and credibility between the giver and receiver are variables that influence how feedback is interpreted.

A balanced system of evaluation, supervision, and reflection provides opportunities for high-quality developmental feedback that supports each individual's efforts to grow. We've relied too heavily on evaluation as the only source of feedback for teachers. By identifying and communicating the distinctions among systems designed to measure and evaluate, supervisory systems to inform progress toward goals, and systems that strive for self-reflection to inform an individual's path toward expertise, all stakeholders can better deliver and receive feedback aligned to its intended purpose.

Focused Goal Setting as a Component of Effective Supervision

In a system that balances evaluation, supervision, and reflection, effective supervision creates and supports focused efforts to achieve challenging improvement goals. Focus is exemplified through an emphasis on the following beliefs and practices.

1. Teachers use a comprehensive teaching framework to establish and guide efforts toward specific improvement goals. If teachers are to establish valid growth goals and monitor their progress toward those goals, they need to understand and use comprehensive frameworks for effective instruction just as well as evaluators do. In a slight twist on John Hattie's (2009) synthesis of meta-analysis of student learning, we argue that teacher growth is best supported by a system in which all teachers see themselves as their own best supervisor.

2. Teachers' goals are rooted in, and supported by, continuous data collection and modification of practice. Teachers establish goals only after they have collected formative data, from a variety of sources, that explicitly connect their classroom practice to student perceptions and student performance. Three truths about goal setting impede individuals' progress toward their goals. First, when goals are given to someone rather than developed autonomously, that person is less likely to obtain those goals (Locke & Latham, 1990). Second, when goals are established in a performance environment solely to obtain external rewards or avoid external consequences, individuals are less likely to achieve those goals (Ariely et al., 2005). Third, when goals are developed by an individual but are established without data related to a framework for quality, individuals tend to establish goals in areas where they already excel, preventing them from demonstrating much improvement through the goal-setting process. When individuals are empowered to gather data about their performance and use that data in an objective manner to establish growth goals, they are more likely to flourish.

3. Teachers collaborate to calibrate. Teachers work together to calibrate their perception of current performance and next levels of performance. Comprehensive frameworks for instruction provide a shared language not only for evaluators to justify ratings but also for teachers to guide collaboration, professional dialogue, and goal setting. These frameworks contain a rich language for talking about teaching, learning, assessment, engagement, and planning.

In the sections that follow we describe each of these beliefs and practices in terms of "action steps" that include specific information about how to develop a focused system of supervision.

Focused Supervision Action Step 1

Teachers use a comprehensive teaching framework to establish and guide efforts toward specific improvement goals. A week before an annual golf outing, the best player in your foursome bows out. Although the real purpose of the outing is to raise funds for a good cause, you've been talking to all the other participants about how great your group will be. You need to find the best player possible, and you need to do it fast.

You approach an old friend who you know plays golf. "How is your golf game these days?" you ask.

"I want to improve, so I'm playing a lot and trying to get better," he replies. You note your old friend as a possible participant but aren't ready to decide yet.

You call an acquaintance from work. "How is your golf game these days?" you ask.

"For the last couple of months I've been working on changing my backswing on uphill putts that break to the left, and I've noticed a remarkable difference in my short game," she replies.

Which player do you ask to join you for the golf outing?

According to psychologist Edwin Locke, who has spent his career understanding the link between goal setting and improvement (Locke & Latham, 1990), the player you should ask to join you is obvious. Locke contends that people don't do their best when simply trying to *improve*. Vague goals are often approached in a haphazard manner and end with minimal, or merely random, results. For the first golfer, *playing more* may simply mean repeating the same mistakes with greater frequency. The second player has articulated a much more specific approach to improvement. She has analyzed her game, established a targeted area of need, and is working on a specific set of strategies to improve. Edwin Locke would not be surprised that her results are remarkable and would advise you to select her as the better player. Understanding the components of effective goals can support our chances of improving in any area we choose.

Locke's assertions, which were supported by psychologist and collaborator Gary Latham, can be applied to teaching as well. Consider the teacher working to improve "my students' understanding of important content" as compared to a teacher who is working to "increase my frequency of stopping at strategic points throughout presentations so students can use sentence stems to summarize main ideas and ask clarifying questions." Based on Locke and Latham's (1990) seminal theory of goal setting and improved performance, the second goal is more likely to be attained because it includes five critical components that link improvement to goal setting. These components are (1) specificity, (2) challenge, (3) commitment, (4) feedback, and 5) task complexity. Let's take a closer look at each of these.

Specificity. Specific goals reduce variance in performance because they leave little room for interpretation. Vague goals such as "differentiate instruction" or "improve student engagement" have limited value because they fail to provide specific guidance to link the teacher's behaviors to intended outcomes. Questions such as *"What specific strategies will you use to differentiate instruction?"* or *"How will you increase their engagement?"* have to be addressed or nothing will change. Additionally, vague goals can be too easily redefined to accommodate low performance. *"I tried some strategies to increase engagement, but the students didn't really respond to them. I think these students just don't want to be engaged, but I might try the engagement strategies with next year's class."*

Experts set very specific goals because they can envision outcomes based on the use of specific processes or strategies (Zimmerman, 2006). They plan to address the nuance of those strategies in a way that nonexperts might not even be aware of. For example, an expert teacher might articulate a goal of "asking challenging questions to low-expectancy students in a supportive and nonthreatening manner through cueing," whereas nonexperts tend to focus on general goals such as "have high expectations for all students."

Challenge. Surprisingly, Locke and Latham found that the more difficult the goal, the more likely it is to be obtained, provided that individuals are committed to it and have the ability, knowledge, and resources to achieve it. We want to be challenged. The thrill of obtaining a goal that was only recently beyond one's reach provides an intrinsic feeling of reward and satisfaction that cannot be matched. The key here is to set a goal that is challenging enough to require concentrated effort but not so unrealistic that it results in frustration. Setting a goal that is either too easy or too difficult can limit professional growth.

Commitment. If goals are specific and challenging, they will require effort to be attained. Therefore, commitment is crucial for success. People are likely to increase their commitment when they believe a goal is important and attainable. Where the goal comes from is also critical. Locke and Latham found that goals set collaboratively by a supervisor and an employee lead to higher commitment than those set by a supervisor curtly telling someone what to do. Interestingly, if a supervisor does need to be directive in setting a goal for an employee, a clear rationale as to why the goal is important improves the employee's commitment.

Fortunately, commitment can be improved by leaders who can articulate a vision of excellence, have high expectations for themselves, model effective goal-setting behaviors through their own professional practice, express confidence in employee capabilities, and provide the training and support necessary for employees to obtain their goals.

If individuals do not believe a goal is attainable, their commitment will likely be low. Fortunately, a leader can work with those individuals to address one of three factors and raise their level of commitment (Bandura, 1986). The goal can be adjusted to better align to the individuals' present capacity; specific training or learning opportunities can be provided to build that capacity; or the leader can work to build individuals' perceptions of what they are capable of through affirmation of their current strengths.

Feedback. Feedback allows people to check and track their progress toward the goal. What is most important about feedback is that it allows the learner to modify strategies in a manner that actually yields different results. As Locke says, "Feedback alone is just information" (1996, p. 121). Both the quality of feedback (such as that described earlier in Figure 3.6) and the learner's perception of the intent of the feedback are critical factors for increasing the likelihood that a goal is obtained.

Task complexity. The more complex the goal, the more time will be required to achieve it. Teaching integrates a complicated set of understandings, strategies, and dispositions. In the context of the hundreds of decisions that teachers make every day, addressing specific improvement goals in meaningful ways can become overwhelming. To make the task complexity more manageable, teachers need to be given (1) sufficient time to meet the goal and (2) opportunities and resources to visualize, practice, and learn specific components of the strategies they are trying to attain.

The ultimate purpose of goal setting is not to complete a set of forms, placate a superior, or knock some transactional requirements off your to-do list. The purpose is to identify a valued outcome that is currently unattainable and create a plan to add new skills and strategies to your repertoire. Articulating a worthwhile goal requires commitment to attain a specific, challenging goal, by reflecting and acting on feedback about very specific components of a complex craft. Figure 3.7 shows goals that do—and do not—exemplify Locke's and Latham's attributes.

Focused Supervision Action Step 2

Teachers' goals are rooted in and supported by continuous data collection and modification of practice. In the initial roll-out of new systems of evaluation, significant time and effort are put forth to ensure that principals are trained to use the comprehensive framework for instruction in a manner that ensures valid, reliable ratings of teacher performance. If the purpose of the framework is purely evaluative, this approach will yield valid ratings. But if another purpose is to improve professional practice, then teachers must also be able to use the framework to objectively assess the relationship between their teaching and student learning in order to support their efforts to establish, monitor, and make progress toward meaningful improvement goals.

The importance of teachers understanding the relationship between the framework for effective instruction, their teaching, and student learning cannot be emphasized enough. Consider this exchange from Lewis Carroll's *Alice in Wonderland*, as Alice comes upon the Cheshire Cat:

"Would you tell me, please, which way I ought to go from here?"

"That depends a good deal on where you want to get to," said the Cat.

"I don't much care where—" said Alice.

"Then it doesn't matter which way you go," said the Cat.

FIGURE 3.7

Using Components of Effective Goal Setting to Establish Focused Improvement Goals

Locke and Latham's Components of Effective Goal Setting	Nonexemplar	Exemplar
Specificity—Specific goals focus efforts on the actionable components of a complex process. *Prompt: The goal is to . . .*	. . . Have students use graphic organizers at the start of every unit. (Goal is too transactional; just pass them out and you're done! No link exists among teacher, strategies, students, and improved learning.)	. . . Expand my understanding of, and ability to use, K-W-L strategies and graphic organizers in a manner that builds students' anticipation for unit content, acknowledges their questions as a pathway to engagement, and supports students' conceptual understanding of new content.
Challenge—The more difficult the goal, the more likely it will be attained, given commitment to the goal and access to the knowledge, practice time, and resources to achieve it. *Prompt: This goal will challenge me to strive toward my ideal classroom because . . .*	. . . I already use K-W-L a lot, and my students really like it. (Goal implies teacher is already comfortable with, and has already successfully used, this strategy.)	. . . This goal will challenge me to focus my efforts to ensure that students are taught how to use tools to preview new content. Students should be able to adapt the K-W-L and graphic organizers to other learning situations, which will help them become more independent learners.
Commitment—If goals are specific and challenging, they will require effort to be attained. Therefore, commitment to the goal is crucial for success. *Prompt: I will demonstrate my commitment to develop the strategies required to obtain this goal by . . .*	. . . Making sure I preview new content with my students every week. (Focus is on outcome only, not on openness to the need to be purposeful, aware, and responsive to students and to engage in deliberate practice to acquire this skill.)	. . . Reading two articles/chapters on using K-W-L, video-recording myself three times this year during lessons where I focus on introduction of new content, then analyzing the recording and comparing it with our teaching framework to better understand my strengths and weaknesses.
Feedback—Feedback allows people to check and track their progress toward the goal and to modify strategies in a manner that actually yields different results. *Prompt: I will obtain feedback on my progress toward this goal by . . .*	. . . Seeing how well students do on end-of-unit quizzes and tests. (Feedback does not connect teacher use of strategy and understanding to instructional practice.)	. . . Surveying my students about the extent that I used best practices when I previewed new content with them. I will also ask them how I can make K-W-L activities more successful and what graphic organizers work best for them. I will arrange for a colleague to do a collaborative protocol in my room on three days when I kick off a new unit. I will modify my use of the strategies accordingly.

continued

FIGURE 3.7
Using Components of Effective Goal Setting to Establish Focused Improvement Goals (*continued*)

Locke and Latham's Components of Effective Goal Setting	Nonexemplar	Exemplar
Task Complexity—The more complex the goal, the more time will be required to achieve it. In addition, people need opportunities and resources to visualize, practice, and learn specific components of the strategies they are trying to attain. *Prompt: Because of the complexity of the skills and strategies required to attain this goal, I will need . . .*	Time: September 1–June 1 Resources: Graphic organizers (There is no articulation or connection between reflection and deliberate practice.)	Time: September 1 to January 15, with monthly check-in on progress with supervisor and collaborative team. Resources: Graphic organizers, minimum of once-a-month collaboration with peers to discuss how they preview new content with their students, articles, teaching framework, Video Analysis of Own Teaching protocol, formal observations, and Mirror Protocol.

"—so long as I get SOMEWHERE," Alice added as an explanation.

"Oh, you're sure to do that," said the Cat, "if you only walk long enough."

This exchange is the epitome of a process that lacks focus. There is a sense that *something* must be done, but little clarity around where to go and the best way to get there. Furthermore, because Alice has little investment in the destination, she is ambivalent about the process. As long as she is doing something, she is comfortable with her efforts.

Unfortunately, this conversation mirrors many thoughts we've heard from teachers as they articulate their perception of the evaluative goal-setting process. As long as the teacher is working on something, the transactional requirement of setting and attaining an improvement goal is fulfilled. *The teacher is Alice. The evaluator is the Cat. As long as some data are collected and the goal-setting forms are completed, the walk is long enough.* Whether or not real learning and growth occur seems beside the point.

With Alice and the Cat in mind, consider these excerpts from a speech given by Graham Nuthall, who has been credited with completing the longest series of classroom studies on teaching and learning in the history of the field of education (see Nuthall, 2007). Explaining the complexities of acquiring understanding and the need for high-quality educational research, he states:

. . . teaching is a kind of cultural ritual, like many religious rituals. We do it that way because we have always done it that way. . . . The breakthrough came when we started to look at the classroom through the eyes of individual pupils. We did it by having pupils wearing their own individual microphones, and setting up sets of miniature video-cameras in the ceilings of the classrooms. . . . What we discovered was that what teachers thought was going on in their classrooms was quite different from what was actually happening. . . .

The pupils knew how to give the appearance of being attentive and involved, but their main concern was their participation in their relationship with their peers. . . . In many classrooms, what matters is not learning but the production of visible products: completed worksheets, well-written and presented reports, sets of answers to problems. When you listen closely to what teachers and pupils say about their work, it is about how long it will take to finish, does it all have to be done before Friday. . . .

What the teacher needs to know about the minds and experiences of pupils is much more subtle and complex [than medical sciences], but nevertheless necessary to genuinely effective practice. And our research makes it clear that it is never going to be achieved except through careful pupil- or student-focused research in classrooms. (Nuthall, 2004)

If we are to heed Nuthall's words, we need to reconsider the importance of data to inform teachers' efforts to improve their professional practice.

Establishing meaningful, focused improvement goals requires a shared understanding of the present position in terms of student learning and a teacher's teaching, the ideal destination, and the path between the two. *If you don't know where you are going, any road will get you there.* If the improvement goal is focused, it requires each teacher to have the capacity to accurately identify—and focus upon—specific skills and strategies that can be added to that teacher's instructional repertoire to more effectively meet the learning needs of every student. Without this clear focus, little growth is likely to occur.

Learning is an incredibly complex process. When we only consider data that are collected every few months or every year, we miss a lot. These summative measures fail to provide insight into the formative, day-to-day process of meaning making that supports students' efforts to integrate content, concepts, understandings, and misunderstandings into learning.

Teaching is also an incredibly complex process. When we are in the act of teaching, we miss a lot. Our focus on delivering the lesson can prevent us from seeing how students are, or are not, responding in ways that are merely compliant as compared to ways in which they are integrating content, concepts, understandings, and misunderstandings into learning.

Although improvement goals can be articulated in terms of student achievement or student growth, merely monitoring achievement data does not create a clear enough link between how we teach and what students learn. We need better ways to collect data in our own classrooms in a manner that illuminates the intersection between teaching and learning.

Shifting from data collection for evaluation to data collection for growth begins by asking ourselves, *Who uses the data and how are the data used?*

For example, we know of many schools that are using a protocol that asks students three questions:

- What is the learning goal for the day?
- How does the work you are doing right now support your efforts to achieve the learning goal?
- How will you know if you are successful?

These questions are powerful because they are focused on the learner, not just the teacher. However, consider the following scenarios to better understand how the purpose for collecting data results in very different responses from teachers to guide their efforts to improve.

Scenario 1: An evaluator comes in and asks 10 students the three questions. The evaluator notes that only three students knew all the answers. Two months later, the evaluator asks the students the questions again, with similar results.

The data are articulated in the narrative portion of the teacher's evaluation at the end of the year: "Communicates learning goals" is noted as "Basic."

Scenario 2: As a part of the school's coaching program, a coach comes in and asks 10 students the three questions. He notes that only three students knew all the answers. The data are articulated in a meeting later that day between the coach and the teacher. The coach asks a series of coaching questions to help the teacher see some alternative approaches to communicating the learning goal to students. Their meeting ends with an agreement to revisit the topic next quarter.

Scenario 3: A teacher is working on "communicating learning goals and clarifying success criteria" as a growth goal. The teacher asks five students the three questions on an exit slip every day for a week and records responses on her phone using the following scale:

> 0—Student did not know.
> 1—Student had a general idea/described task or grade.
> 2—Student explained accurately/described criteria for quality.

At the end of the week she notices that students can articulate the learning goal (45 of 50 possible points by the end of the week), but they don't see the connection between their classwork and the learning goal (25 of 50), and only three students could discuss success criteria in terms of anything other than a grade (5 of 50). The teacher is surprised at the gap in how students can, or cannot, respond to the three questions. The next week, she strategically opens the floor to a discussion about the three questions and why they are important. The students start asking her questions about her questions—at which point she realizes that sometimes she is not clear about how she'd expect the students to answer the three questions. If she is not clear in her own mind, how could they possibly be? She continues to do the exit slips. She continues to talk to her students about what works—and does not work—to best support their learning.

Only the third scenario is likely to result in meaningful change. The teacher owns the data. She has made her own meaning of the problem and is considering more mindful solutions. She doesn't have to wait months or weeks for feedback. She doesn't have to wonder what her students do and don't understand about this powerful set of guiding questions that are designed to help students and teachers join in a collaborative effort to clarify where they should invest their efforts for learning.

What if teachers strategically and actively gathered data *from students* on these types of questions to monitor their progress toward their growth goals? Exit slips, student surveys, student interviews, and video analysis (with the camera in the back of the room or the front of the room, pointed at the students) can provide valuable, "in the trenches" data that do not require a teacher to wait weeks or months for a principal or a coach to intervene. As one teacher told us after using student surveys to identify areas of strength and areas of need in her teaching, "The survey opened up communication with me and my students. I realized they don't always know why I am asking them to do certain things to help their learning." The real power is not in the data but in the conversations that result in more focused efforts to modify and improve one's instructional practice.

Data that inform efforts toward improvement goals need to be informative and actionable. Real-time perception data obtained directly from students provide useful, focused information that can accelerate teachers' progress toward growth goals.

Focused Supervision Action Step 3

Teachers collaborate to calibrate. Put two people at a table. You've doubled the capacity to learn something new. We are social beings. We learn by observing and talking with others. Unfortunately, teaching is one of the most isolated professions in the world. We rarely engage in professional practice with, or in front of, others. When we do collaborate, it is often about everything *but* teaching. Teams collaborate about schedules, curriculum, assessment, students, and logistics, but they rarely talk about the specifics of instructional strategies.

Collaboration occurs when individuals with common needs work together to build their capacity to be successful. A truly collaborative relationship is based on an openness to the possibility of what might be. It requires careful observation and deep listening (Scharmer, 2009).

We've seen the most powerful collaboration occur when teachers observe one another's practice and talk about their teaching. Unfortunately, due to the specter of observation as judgment, this rarely happens in any field. In an interview for this book, Anders Ericsson shared the following insight about the net effect of isolation in professional practice:

> In a lot of jobs, people keep doing what they are doing because it is what they have always done. We don't know if we are doing as well or better than if someone else was in our exact same job. There is very little feedback as to how well you do your job compared to other people in similar situations.

Ericsson's insights are critically important. Imagine an artist or a musician or a surgeon who never watched another person engage in that area of practice once attaining professional status. There could be no growth. You would quickly become boxed in by your existing habits of practice. *Your own practice would become the entire field of practice.* Oblivious to what you don't know, you would be completely unaware of the opportunities that await to improve your practice.

The process of collaborating with others begins with a shared language of effective practice (Marzano et al., 2011). Imagine you are about to have surgery and just as you are drifting off from the anesthesia you hear the following exchange:

> Voice 1: "Scalpel."
> Voice 2: "What do you mean by *scalpel*?"
> Voice 1: "The sharp thing over there; no, not that one; no, no, no; yes, that one."
> Voice 2: "You call that a *scalpel*? I usually just call that a *knife*."
> Voice 1: "Whatever."

If you are in this situation, no matter how groggy you are, run! Without a shared language, it is nearly impossible to engage in meaningful professional dialogue. A shared language of effective instruction creates a shorthand to discuss what we are doing in our classrooms to meet students' learning needs.

For example, if we are going to talk about what it is students should learn as a result of a lesson, how do we talk about that with colleagues? Is it an outcome? A learning goal? A learning target? A learning intention? Without a shared language of instruction, we can spend as much time defining terms as we do discussing practice. As in the surgery example, time is too limited to spend haggling over definitions. When comprehensive frameworks for effective instruction are used by teachers for collaborative dialogue, they can turn to one another and engage in focused conversations to improve their professional practice.

With a shared language and a shared framework for effective practice, I can observe, reflect on, and discuss my own practice with anyone else who shares that language and framework. Even if my goals for professional growth and your goals are different, our shared language allows us to focus our attention on the opportunities and needs that we've identified through that framework. Most important, I can now get developmental feedback from *anyone* who has the same shared language and understands the same instructional framework. I don't need to wait for my principal, mentor, or instructional coach. I can access developmental feedback from any colleague.

How Affirmation Leads to Growth

Affirmation of skill is what happens when we receive positive feedback about our current level of performance. Hearing affirmation feels good; it tells us that the effort we're putting forth is worthwhile and productive. When a colleague compliments us on our work, it fuels us to know that our efforts are on the right track and those efforts are noticed. Given the isolated nature of the teaching profession, we can go weeks or months without being affirmed by another adult. This reality needs to be remedied. Affirmation is critically important because it supports our basic human need to feel competent and productive.

Sometimes we receive affirmation that is not about skill but about our anxiety. We've all experienced a student who is particularly challenging or a unit that is particularly difficult to teach. When we hear that a colleague is also challenged by the same student or also struggles with that particular unit, it puts our mind at ease. We may say to ourselves, *She's a really great teacher and she also has a hard time with that unit; I'm glad it's not just me.* This type of affirmation helps us trust our ability to accurately focus on what is working and what is not working.

When our skills are affirmed, we are empowered to grow. A teacher who has received specific, accurate affirmation of specific areas of practice develops the confidence to believe in her own efficacy: *I'm good enough to take risks to*

innovate; as great as this is going right now, I know I can make it even better.
Affirmation of anxiety can also help us grow. A teacher who is confident that she is worried about the right things can step away from the voices of self-doubt and move toward solutions: *I'm struggling with this student, and others are, too; it's good to know that I'm not the problem. I wonder what other strategies I might try?*

Affirmation of skills and practice focuses us on what we do well and supports the basic human need to feel competent. Affirmation of anxiety helps ensure we are worried about the right things. However, if we only receive affirmation, our growth can become severely limited. Dissonance also helps us improve.

How Dissonance Leads to Growth

Dissonance is what happens when we hold two conflicting ideas in our mind at the same time. When we've been told to watch our cholesterol and we're offered a piece of cheesecake, we experience dissonance. We firmly believe that our health is important, *and* we firmly believe that cheesecake tastes good! If we wrestle with this dissonance in a productive way, we skip the cheesecake: *I used to eat cheesecake, but I now understand how that can affect my health, and my health is more important.* Dissonance is a powerful psychological principle because dissonance lays seeds for change and growth.

If we are isolated from seeing others teach, we cannot experience dissonance. If we do not experience dissonance, not only do we not see the need for change, we're not even aware that options beyond our own practice exist. We are blissfully unaware.

Dissonance helps us calibrate our lens to focus on even more effective ways of teaching.

How Collaboration Calibrates Affirmation and Dissonance

Teachers typically experience dissonance about their professional practice when students are struggling, or an evaluator points out a need for growth, or an instructional coach or mentor guides them down a path to make them aware of a need for change. Each of the pathways to dissonance presents a unique challenge. Negative feedback from students often results in frustration (*What else can I try?*), an evaluator's comment often results in defensiveness (*How does she expect me to do that?*), and the coach's suggestion often results in ambiguity (*How am I supposed to do that?*).

A different approach is to put ourselves in a position to access information about others' practice to let ourselves experience affirmation and dissonance. This can occur through observing and analyzing video of a teacher from another school (van Es, 2010), visiting other teachers' classrooms for instructional rounds (City, Elmore, Fiarman, & Teitel, 2009), or deep collaborative dialogue with colleagues about professional practice. The purpose of this collaboration is not evaluation. It is to gain insights into our own teaching and to further—and focus—our own professional practice. Protocols such as these are described in detail in the appendices of this book.

Protocols to Align the Purpose of Effective Supervision to the Payoff

As we have previously stated, the purpose of supervision is to support teacher growth by creating opportunities for developmental feedback that *empowers* teachers to achieve goals related to improved professional performance and *focuses* teachers' efforts. Teachers are *empowered* in systems of supervision that emphasize the following beliefs and practices:

- Creating a learning environment by welcoming errors and encouraging questions
- Building teacher autonomy through autonomy-supportive practices
- Using frequent, high-quality, developmental feedback from a variety of sources to support teacher growth

Focused goal setting occurs in systems of supervision that emphasize the following beliefs and practices:

- Using a comprehensive teaching framework to establish and guide efforts toward specific improvement goals
- Ensuring that individual teacher goal setting is based on continuous data collection and modification of practice
- Creating opportunities for teachers to collaborate and calibrate around current and next levels of performance

The protocols listed in the Supervision section of Appendix E can be used to support systems of supervision that empower teachers to focus their attention on specific instructional strategies. Each protocol is categorized by the purpose, the process, and the payoff. See Appendix B for more detailed explanations of each protocol.

A Case in Balance: When Supervision Works Effectively

It is the third week of school, and Principal Sanchez has just sent his annual e-mail to the teachers he supervises and evaluates. Four years ago, he and his staff started a process of teaching teachers how to use the district's comprehensive framework for effective practice to engage in a variety of protocols to support their efforts to set meaningful improvement goals, receive developmental feedback from a variety of sources, engage in deliberate practice, and focus on their professional growth.

> Colleagues,
>
> As your principal, I will be completing your annual evaluation at the end of the year. It is my responsibility to ensure your evaluation is an accurate reflection of your current level of performance. Between now and the end of the year I will be in your classroom frequently, and we will meet for several pre- and post-conference meetings. Thank you in advance for welcoming me into your classroom to ensure I can complete this process with fidelity.
>
> Just as important, as your lead supervisor it is my responsibility to create opportunities and resources that support your learning and growth. In the same way that the principalship requires that I continue to learn about the full range of skills and strategies used by outstanding principals, teaching is a challenging profession that requires our best, collective efforts to continue to develop and hone the skills and strategies used by expert teachers.
>
> To support one another's efforts on this path toward growth, we will use the following process again this year:

- September, December, April—Data collection (academic achievement, initial video analysis, and student perception surveys) and analysis of your class's academic achievement and engagement.

- October—
  - Goal setting based on September data collection, including identification of areas of strength and need for yourself and your students.
  - Collegial dialogue meeting about resources and needs to support your growth.
  - Professional Growth and Student Learning Goals forms due. Goal summary statements published for all staff to see who might be working on similar goals.

- November, January, April—Video analysis of your own teaching for purposes of better understanding your use of specific instructional strategies aligned to your growth goals.

- December, February—Instructional rounds (teams of four visit one another's classrooms for purposes of reflecting on your own teaching) and collegial debriefing meetings.

- January—
  - Goal progress check-in; narrative reflection forms and midyear data analysis due.
  - One-on-one supervisory meetings scheduled to discuss progress and needs.

- First week of May—Collegial dialogue on individual synthesis and summary of lessons learned, analysis of relevant data, and next steps for continued growth.

- Third week of May—Professional Growth and Student Learning Goals summary and synthesis narratives due.

Thank you in advance for your efforts to further develop the skills and strategies that you use to meet each student's learning needs. If I can provide resources, time, or simply chat with you as a thought partner while we navigate the pathway toward becoming an expert teacher, do not hesitate to let me know what I can do to support you.

Thanks,
Principal Sanchez

As the year progresses, teachers find themselves talking about their goals frequently with students, colleagues, and Principal Sanchez. The surveys open a dialogue with students about their perceptions and needs in the classroom. Many teachers tell their students their goals. Collegial teams know what one another's goals are as well. They talk about their goals and their progress when doing instructional rounds and during collegial dialogues as related to their data or their self-assessment of their video. Furthermore, their conversations are not focused broadly on topics like "student engagement" or "classroom environment" but are focused on specific instructional strategies like using academic games as a launch activity, or scaffolding to ask students open-ended, higher-order thinking questions and then using think-write-pair-share strategies to improve classroom dialogue related to those questions.

In March, a veteran teacher knocks on Principal Sanchez's door. "I was wondering if I can show my latest classroom video to a teacher who is not in my collegial dialogue group and was asking me about what I'm doing to get more kids actively participating in discussions."

"Of course," Principal Sanchez replies. "I know another teacher who might be interested in seeing what you're doing as well. Can I ask him to contact you? He might want to visit your classroom."

4

Reflection as a Component of a Balanced System

A Case Out of Balance: When Reflection Works Poorly

At the start of the school year, Mrs. Bell was ready to move from teaching 3rd grade to 5th grade. When goal-setting forms were due, she already knew what her goal for the year was going to be: "To increase student engagement in my 5th grade classroom." She underlined "5th grade" as an inside joke to her principal; for the last five years her annual goal had been to increase student engagement. She was eager to do this because she felt that she was good at keeping kids engaged.

For Mrs. Bell, engagement meant she could keep her 3rd graders busy doing a variety of tasks and hands-on activities. Kids created posters for projects, went to the computer lab to work on slide presentations, and did a project board and presentation in math, science, language arts, and social studies each year. Kids had to buy new markers each quarter because they used them so frequently. The bookshelf in the back of the room held dozens of books kids liked; *Believe It or Not!*, *Amazing Facts*, and *World Records* were student favorites. In addition, piles of word searches for math, science, and social studies were on the back shelf. Students knew that if they finished their work early, they should grab a book or do a word search. Fridays were always game days. Mrs. Bell would do Around the World in math class, a spelling bee in language arts, and Jeopardy in science or social studies. She had never had any discipline problems.

The school year started well. Mrs. Bell had many of her same students from 3rd grade. By the end of the first quarter, however, things were different than in previous years. Students started asking why they were still doing "3rd grade stuff." The Friday game days had grown very competitive and somewhat chaotic; arguments would break out over which team had how many points in Jeopardy. Many kids made no effort whatsoever in Around the World. As one student told her, "Darius and Hannah win every time anyway; why should I waste my time?" When students were given class time to work on their project boards, many used it wisely. Some of the boys, however, simply played around with their markers—throwing them at one another, writing on one another. She started giving referrals. By March, she'd sent seven kids to the office.

After a formal evaluative visit from her principal, he asked how things were going in grade 5. "This group is a handful," she replied.

"I know," said her principal. "Don't worry about it. Fifth graders are always testing limits. You just keep up the great work."

Frustrated, Mrs. Bell spent more time than ever in the teachers' lounge. She would tell anyone who would listen to her about the "out of control" 5th graders. When the 4th grade teachers weren't in the lounge, she would openly ask colleagues, "What do the kids do in 4th grade? It's like their skills have gotten worse rather than better."

By April, she was struggling. She decided to do something about it. She made an appointment with her principal to talk about concerns she had about the 4th grade curriculum and the 4th grade teaching team.

The Purpose of Reflection in a Balanced System

The purpose of reflection is to develop each teacher's capacity to engage in an ongoing internal dialogue that results in purposeful action to improve professional practice. Meaningful reflection ensures that teachers consider even more effective ways to provide meaningful learning experiences for students, continuously demonstrate higher levels of awareness of how students respond to those learning experiences, and respond to student learning needs in increasingly sophisticated and nuanced ways. Those ways may include modifying the use of instructional strategies during lessons or developing and deepening the repertoire of strategies teachers use as they progress toward professional expertise.

The word *reflection* is derived from the Latin *reflexion em*, which means to bend back or bounce light from. The root of the word, *flex*, means to be flexible. Both of these conceptualizations are relevant here. A reflective teacher is always considering how students are responding to what has been taught. In this conceptualization of the word *reflection*, teaching is not shining a light on students and assuming they can see more clearly. It is more like using a light meter before taking a photograph of students to better understand what areas of the photo will require more or less light to ensure a high-quality result. The notion of flexibility is relevant because to be flexible means to adapt and change as necessary. In the context of teaching, it means teachers are constantly adjusting their strategy to suit learners' needs.

A process that values reflection takes a decidedly cognitivist, rather than a behaviorist, approach to learning. The early 1900s were dominated by Edward Thorndike's (1931) and B. F. Skinner's (1953) research on behaviorism. In the behaviorist framework, desirable behavior is elicited through reward and undesirable behavior is extinguished through punishment.

For the behaviorist, the path to developing a more effective teacher would consist of praise when something is done well and punishment when something is done poorly. Therefore, enough evaluative cycles of praise and punishment would improve teacher quality. For simple tasks that require skills the learner already possesses, such as submitting attendance data on time, this behaviorist approach works. But for complex processes, such as asking higher-order questions, giving students effective feedback, or designing valid assessments, the behaviorist approach is too crude a tool. The behaviorist assumes the teacher can accomplish the task but simply lacks the incentive to do so.

By the 1950s, a new group of researchers led by psychologists such as Jean Piaget (1936; Piaget & Cook, 1952), Carl Rogers (1961), and Albert Bandura (Bandura & Walters, 1963) sought to clarify the nuanced processes required of individuals to develop skills and understandings. They focused on the cognitive processes that make us distinctly human and argued that learners come to the task with a series of beliefs about the nature of the work at hand, the value of the work, the meaning of the work, and their ability to be effective. To develop new, complex skills and understandings requires learners to be attuned to the nuance and sophistication of making decisions about the specific behaviors most likely to result in effective practice. Complex processes, such as analyzing historical documents, playing a piano concerto, or demonstrating the skills associated with teaching, require the learner to actively process information and make nuanced decisions in real time. When explaining how learners develop skills and understandings, these cognitivist and humanistic approaches were able to account for a more complex explanation of how people learn than the carrot-and-stick approaches espoused by behaviorists.

For example, drawing on cognitivist and humanist perspectives, Jack Mezirow's (1990) transformative theory of adult learning argues that the central component of the learning processes is reflecting on prior learning to determine if what has been learned is applicable in the current context. We call on a set of skills that have worked in the past and apply them accordingly. This is validating because our experience tells us what should work again, but it is limiting because we often rely on the same few skills. According to Mezirow, "By far the most significant learning experiences in adulthood involve critical self-reflection—reassessing the way we have posed problems, and reassessing our own orientation to perceiving, knowing, believing, feeling, and acting" (1990, p. 13).

In 2000, the National Research Council convened a group of experts to synthesize research on how people learn (Bransford, Brown, & Cocking, 2000). Their findings, listed in the left-hand column of the table in Figure 4.1, describe the importance of meaningful reflection and purposeful action in one's efforts to learn. In the right-hand column we've framed these findings in terms of how teachers learn. The findings, as applied to teachers and teaching, can serve as guideposts for the implementation of a system that supports meaningful, purposeful reflection.

A system of reflection that serves as a component of a balanced framework of evaluation, supervision, and reflection is most likely to align the purpose to the payoff of reflection when there is alignment among the premise, protocols, processes, and areas of practice, as shown in Figure 4.2.

FIGURE 4.1
National Research Council Findings Applied to Teachers and Teaching

Synthesis of Findings from the National Research Council's *How People Learn*	Application to Teachers and Teaching
1. Students come to the classroom with preconceptions about how the world works. If their initial understanding is not engaged, they may fail to grasp the new concepts and information that are taught, or they may learn them for purposes of a test but revert to their preconceptions outside the classroom. (pp. 14–15)	1. Teachers come to the classroom with preconceptions about how teaching works. If their initial understanding is not engaged, they may fail to grasp new concepts and information, or they may learn for the purposes of evaluation but revert to their preconceptions when an evaluator is not present.
2. To develop competence in an area of inquiry, students must: (a) have a deep foundation of factual knowledge, (b) understand facts and ideas in the context of a conceptual framework, and (c) organize knowledge in ways that facilitate retrieval and application. (p.16)	2. To develop competence in an area of teaching, teachers must (a) have a deep foundation of factual knowledge about teaching, (b) understand facts and ideas in the context of a comprehensive framework for instruction, and (c) organize knowledge in ways that facilitate retrieval and application.
3. A "metacognitive" approach to instruction can help students learn to take control of their own learning by defining learning goals and monitoring their progress in achieving them. (p. 18)	3. A "metacognitive" approach to balanced evaluation, supervision, and reflection can help teachers learn to take control of their own growth by defining learning goals and monitoring their progress in achieving them.

Note: Excerpts in Column 1 are from *How People Learn: Brain, Mind, Experience, and School* (expanded edition), by J. D. Bransford, A. L. Brown, and R. R. Cocking (Eds.), 2000, Washington, DC: National Academy Press. Copyright 2000 by National Academy Press.

The Premise: Reflection Is the Foundation for the Purposeful, Aware, Responsive Decisions and Actions Made by Experts

Over time, reflective practitioners become expert in their ability to support student learning. They are able to make *meaningful* connections between their efforts and students' learning needs as they *purposefully* engage a challenging pathway toward expertise.

Although many practitioners in complex fields such as teaching, medicine, or music achieve competence, expertise is difficult to obtain. Expertise does not simply mean being good at something; nor does it mean that someone has done the same thing for a long time. Expertise means that someone has mastered the complexity of a chosen domain by developing the ability to deploy the right strategy, in the right way, at the right time, to obtain intended results.

Anders Ericsson is the world's foremost expert on how individuals develop expertise. His research gained prominence when it was discussed in Malcolm Gladwell's book, *Outliers* (2008). Gladwell details the "extraordinary

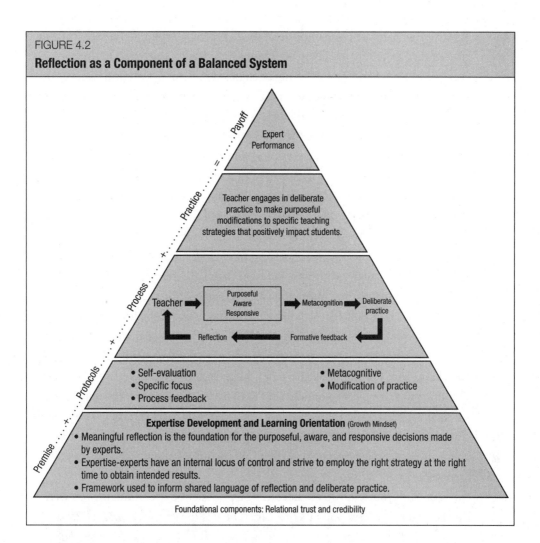

FIGURE 4.2

Reflection as a Component of a Balanced System

Expert
Performance

Teacher engages in deliberate
practice to make purposeful
modifications to specific teaching
strategies that positively impact students.

Teacher ➡ Purposeful
Aware
Responsive ➡ Metacognition ➡ Deliberate
practice

Reflection ⬅ Formative feedback

- Self-evaluation
- Specific focus
- Process feedback

- Metacognitive
- Modification of practice

Expertise Development and Learning Orientation (Growth Mindset)
- Meaningful reflection is the foundation for the purposeful, aware, and responsive decisions made by experts.
- Expertise-experts have an internal locus of control and strive to employ the right strategy at the right time to obtain intended results.
- Framework used to inform shared language of reflection and deliberate practice.

Foundational components: Relational trust and credibility

Payoff · · · · · Practice · · · · · Process · · · · · Protocols · · · · · Premise

opportunities," and not simply talent, that need to be afforded to an individual, as well as the disciplined, focused effort that needs to be put forth to obtain expertise in a particular field. According to Ericsson, expertise "refers to the characteristics, skills, and knowledge . . . [of those] who are consistently able to exhibit superior performance for representative tasks in a domain" (Ericsson et al., 2006, p. 3).

Obtaining expertise in a field is rare. Experts develop a broad enough repertoire of strategies to be successful with the most difficult cases under the most difficult conditions. Obtaining expertise is elusive because it is counter to how we learn almost everything else in life. Typically, when people are learning something new, they initially make rapid gains. They are attuned to the complexities of a set of tasks they've never engaged in before, realize they need to practice the basics, and begin to establish a set of skills that initially allow them to overcome their mistakes and muddle through. Over time, if they continue to engage in the task, they refine their skills until they build a level of proficiency that allows them to perform core tasks efficiently and effectively. At this point, their skills are good enough to do well and they stop exerting effort to obtain new skills. Ironically, their learning stops because of their initial success.

At first, experts are no different from novices in their trajectory of learning. They also make mistakes, muddle through, and establish a core set of skills that allow them to be efficient and effective under most circumstances. From here, however, experts take a distinctly different path. Whereas proficient performers settle into the comfort of automaticity, experts intentionally seek out the most challenging conditions that will force them to stay in a steep learning curve until those new, more specialized behaviors become automatic as well. In fact, experts seek out situations that will force them to make new mistakes because they know they continue to learn from them. Research on expertise repeatedly demonstrates this pattern of behavior. Elite figure skaters are more willing to fall on their butts, literally, than their less expert counterparts (Ericsson et al., 2006). They fail at the difficult jumps more often because they continue to practice them anyway. And then, one day, they land the jump. They pushed through the struggle long enough to find success.

Consider your pathway to becoming a proficient driver. Initially, you were bewildered by the components of a car: *Which is the gas pedal and which is the brake? How hard do I push them? Where is the turn signal? How hard do I need to turn the wheel?* In time you develop a set of skills that allow you to drive safely in most conditions. In fact, these skills become so ingrained that they become automatic.

Just as you think you've learned all you need to know about driving, Mother Nature throws some severe weather in your direction. The first time you drive in a snowstorm, you realize you need a different set of strategies. Once again, driving becomes very demanding of your effort and attention. You are a novice again and need to learn new skills. You feel dissonance: *I thought I was a really good driver, but I don't know how to drive in snow.* Here is where the path for the stagnant novice and the budding expert diverge.

The driver on a path toward expertise confronts the dissonance as an opportunity to learn new skills and strategies. She asks experienced drivers for advice. She seeks out some online resources. She goes to an empty parking lot and focuses on learning how her car handles in the snow. She seeks challenge in order to intentionally add new strategies to her repertoire.

The stagnant performer goes out of his way to avoid these conditions. His strategy is one of coping rather than building expertise: *I just don't drive in the snow.* Back to the irony of initial success, he avoids the opportunity to learn new strategies for driving in the snow because he *lacks the necessary strategies to drive in the snow.* He never builds a new skill set. He never improves.

Throughout this chapter we link the concept of expertise to key components of a system of meaningful and purposeful reflection. Experts have an internal locus of control; they believe external conditions inform strategy rather than determine results. They have a growth mindset and believe they can make continuous improvement in any area they choose. Experts engage in deliberate practice, choosing very specific skills to ensure their efforts are focused at a level of practice nuanced enough to improve.

When discussing her comprehensive teaching framework, Charlotte Danielson (2007) stated, "The most powerful use of the framework—and one that should accompany any other use—is for reflection and self-assessment. Research has clearly demonstrated that reflection on practice improves teaching" (p. 168). We wholeheartedly agree and would add that teachers also need the protocols, practice, and permission to ensure this happens. As Hammersley-Fletcher and Orsmond (2005) state, "Reflection is something more than simply thinking, and, just as we need to be taught how to think effectively, so we need to learn how to be effective reflective practitioners" (p. 222).

Although most systems of evaluation and supervision talk about the importance of reflection, they seldom align processes or protocols to support teachers' efforts, or develop their ability to be reflective. Across various professions such as science, nursing, medicine, law, and teaching, the need for individuals to develop their understanding about how they conduct work and become skilled practitioners is important in informing their professional growth (Loughran, 2002).

These individuals demonstrate the capacity to be self-monitoring, self-regulating, and self-evaluating (Ellison & Hayes, 2003; Flavell, 1977; Wilson & Clarke, 2004). John Hattie (2009) adds that deliberate practice is "focused on improving particular aspects of the target performance, to better understand how to monitor, self-regulate, and evaluate their performance, and reduce errors" (p. 30).

The Payoff: An Expert Teacher in Every Classroom

A system of evaluation and supervision cannot be effective unless it builds teachers' capacity to become experts—gathering information about their own practice; critically discerning what is working, what is not working, and what can be improved; and constantly finding ways to close the gap between current and next practice. Expertise develops when teachers cultivate the habits of mind that support an ongoing cycle of awareness, reflection, and modification of practice (Ericsson et al., 2006). These reflective habits occur while "in the moment" of teaching as well as after a lesson, unit, or course has been completed (Schon, 1987). Figure 4.3 summarizes the key elements of a system of reflection that supports deliberate practice and expertise.

Aligning Protocols, Processes, and Practice to Purpose: Meaningful, Purposeful Reflection

When something is meaningful, it is both relevant *and* understandable. If you've ever had the unfortunate experience of finding out someone you love was diagnosed with a serious illness, you understand *meaningful*. Information that meant nothing to you only a few minutes earlier is suddenly relevant. You may read about the illness or talk to a friend who survived the illness. You value the information because it is of personal importance to you. But the information also needs to be something that you understand. If you try to read a medical journal to learn more about the disease, you may not be able to make meaning of the information. Conversely, if you'd come across a reader-friendly article on the disease a day earlier, it would not have been relevant, and you likely would have ignored the information entirely. So meaningfulness implies both relevance and understanding.

FIGURE 4.3

Key Elements of Reflection to Support Deliberate Practice and Expertise

Purpose	For teachers to engage in *meaningful* thought processes that result in *purposeful* action that results in growth toward expertise.
Premise	Reflection is the foundation for the purposeful, aware, responsive decisions and actions made by experts.
Owned by . . .	Teacher
Payoff	Expert performance
Primary Effort	Teachers engage in meaningful, reflective, purposeful, and deliberate practice to support intentional change.
Processes	Metacognition and deliberate practice
Informed by . . .	Student data, teacher data, collegial dialogue, modification, and intentionality
Purpose of Instructional Framework	To inform shared language of reflection and deliberate practice
Type of Feedback	Formative, developmental, self-generated
Frequency of Feedback	Continuous
Disposition	Growth mindset + internal locus of control + learning orientation
Active Participants	Teachers, colleagues, students
Primary Users	Teacher, colleagues
Leadership Role	Supporting
Focus	Metacognition and modification of specific teaching behaviors based on student response to teaching
Controlled by . . .	Teacher
Key Process Question	How will teachers use continuous feedback in meaningful ways to ensure the autonomy support, ownership, and purposeful, deliberate practice associated with developing expertise?
Key Outcome Question	How will I develop expertise in the complex craft of teaching?

Meaningful reflection on one's professional practice implies a belief that our practice matters. We believe the information we can gather about teaching, about our students—and the interrelationship between the two—is relevant to our ability to succeed. We believe there is no such thing as an unteachable student; only students who have yet to be sufficiently motivated or challenged. We reflect in meaningful ways because we see any information about our practice as a pathway to deeper understanding about our students. As reflective practitioners, we are always trying to make sense of our craft. We have a voracious appetite for feedback.

When something is purposeful, it is relevant *and* strategically actionable. Consider the earlier example of meaningfulness. Distraught about your friend or family member's illness, you gather meaningful medical information to learn more. Once you access that information, purposefulness is concerned with how you use that information. You could gather medical information for the purpose of trying to cure the disease, but it is doubtful that you could devise an actionable strategy to make that happen. Or your purpose could be to learn more about the disease so you can be more empathetic to your loved one. This purpose is actionable. It may help you discern which questions to ask to ensure the highest-quality treatment or allow you to demonstrate patience and provide an appropriate level of emotional support.

When reflecting on professional practice, it is critically important that the reflection be both meaningful and purposeful. Meaningful reflection implies that we can discern the relevant components of our practice with greater clarity by understanding the feedback we have received. Deriving meaning, however, is irrelevant unless that information results in a change in practice. If our reflection doesn't result in purposeful action, it was merely a cognitive exercise or just enough reflection to complete a transactional form to gain compliance.

Figure 4.4 summarizes the areas of focus for a system of reflection that is both meaningful and purposeful. We discuss these attributes in detail in the sections that follow.

FIGURE 4.4		
Areas of Focus for a Quality System of Reflection		
Criteria for Quality	**Key Question**	**Action Steps**
Meaningful	*Is reflection meaningful?*	• Teachers operate from an internal locus of control; they believe their classroom practices matter profoundly to influence student learning. • Teachers have a growth mindset; they believe they can make dramatic improvements in any area they choose. • Teachers are metacognitive in their effort to clarify the gap between current and ideal performance.
Purposeful	*Are reflection and action purposeful?*	• Teachers are increasingly purposeful about, aware of, and responsive to the relationship between student learning and effective teaching. • Teachers embrace dissonance; they develop a nuanced view of the gap between current and expert practice. • Teachers use the comprehensive teaching framework and a variety of structured processes to engage in continuous reflection, deliberate practice, and modification as they progress toward expert performance.

A Meaningful Approach to Reflection

In a system that balances evaluation, supervision, and reflection, teachers reflect on meaningful components of their practice. Meaningful reflection is exemplified in systems that emphasize the following beliefs and practices.

1. Teachers operate from an internal locus of control; they believe their classroom practices matter profoundly to influence student learning. High-quality reflection is rooted in the belief that we can exercise control over the connections among our thoughts, our effort, and intended outcomes. Individuals with an internal locus of control believe that they are the active agent in their experiences. Reflection allows them to be more efficient in linking their efforts to intended results. Conversely, individuals with an external locus of control believe that what *they do* doesn't matter as much as what *others do to them.* They tend to engage in a continuous process of justification to explain the external forces they believe they are powerless to control.

2. Teachers have a growth mindset; they believe they can make dramatic improvements in any area they choose. High-quality reflection is rooted in the belief that effective teaching is a set of skills and understandings to be developed, not something you either "have" or "don't have." Individuals with a growth mindset believe that they get better with effort. Conversely, individuals with a fixed mindset don't see any relationship between their effort and results. Therefore, they can be exposed to the same opportunities, challenges, and feedback as an individual with a growth mindset, yet how they choose to engage in, or disengage from, those opportunities will result in dramatically different learning experiences.

3. Teachers are metacognitive in their effort to clarify the gap between current and ideal performance. High-quality reflection is rooted in a habit of being metacognitive. Teachers who strategically think about their own thinking are continuously more self-aware, better able to accurately self-evaluate, and better able to regulate their own behavior—which leads to more effective efforts to improve.

In the sections that follow, we describe these beliefs and practices in more detail. We refer to them as "action steps" and include specific information about how to develop a system that incorporates all the elements necessary to ensure that reflection is meaningful.

Meaningful Reflection Action Step 1

Teachers operate from an internal locus of control; they believe their classroom practices matter profoundly to influence student learning. How do we explain our successes and failures? This question was addressed as a key component of Julian Rotter's (1954) "attribution theory." Rotter theorized that people tended to explain their success or failure as a function of either *external* or *internal* attributes. Consider the following anecdote.

Two students have just had tests returned to them. Both earned a 70 percent—a lower score than either had expected. The first student thinks the test was unfair, the teacher didn't teach the material well, and he was unable to study because of too many assignments in his other classes. The second student thinks the test was fair, given what was taught in the unit, but acknowledges that he didn't ask clarifying questions throughout the unit when he was confused and that he waited until the last minute to study. The factors to which each student attributes his score hold significant implications for how each may perform on the next test.

People who explain outcomes as being largely beyond their control exhibit what Rotter would call an *external locus of control*. They often describe luck, fate, or unpredictable behaviors of others to explain away the challenges or struggles they experience. Rather than accept negative feedback as evidence of their skill or effort, they ascribe blame to the fact that the task was unreasonable or the situation was unfair. Over time, these individuals may cope with repeated failures by avoiding the task or discrediting the individuals who hold them accountable. We call this "the *ABC* approach" to dealing with challenge: *avoiding, blaming, and complaining*. Eventually, people who attribute challenges primarily to external forces may exhibit learned helplessness—the belief that there is nothing they can do to yield satisfactory results. In truth, the external attribution may simply be compensation for their failure to develop and implement an action plan, and a lack of self-efficacy (Bandura, 1991).

At the other end of the spectrum are people who explain outcomes as largely being within their control. Rotter calls this an *internal locus of control*. To explain challenges and struggles, these individuals often describe their preparation, effort, and strategy. Rather than casting blame on others or avoiding challenge when confronted with disappointing results, they use results as feedback about the need to try a different strategy. In fact, they may welcome failure because it clarifies where they need to invest future efforts in order to improve (Zimmerman & Kitsantas, 2005).

Given these differences, let's return to the two students who received a score of 70 on the test. The first student clearly demonstrates an external locus of control. He attributes his score to factors beyond his control. As the next unit approaches, he may think, "It doesn't really matter what I do; the test will be unfair, and the teacher is out to get me." Not surprisingly, he does even more poorly on the next test. If he truly has an external locus of control, he will accept the results as further evidence of the fact that the test is unfair and the teacher did a poor job. The voice in the student's head says, "I was right. I did just as poorly as I thought I would, given how unfair this is!"

The second student clearly demonstrates an internal locus of control. He attributes his score to factors within his control. As the next unit approaches, he thinks, "I didn't ask questions throughout the unit when I was confused, and I didn't start studying early enough. I need to do both of those things this time around." Not surprisingly, the student does better on the next test. The voice in his head says, "I was right. I knew if I asked questions and started preparing earlier, I would understand the content better. I need to continue to do that."

Both students were given the same learning opportunities. The student with the external locus of control missed out on a valuable opportunity to improve his skills because of his external locus of control. The student with the internal locus of control, on the other hand, turned his initial struggle into an important learning opportunity.

Like students, teachers can exhibit an internal or external locus of control. A teacher with an external locus of control related to her professional practice would be likely to explain how her year was going in terms of what others were doing: *Kids these days don't . . . , My principal doesn't let me . . . , The new evaluation system is unfair.* Although any of these statements may be true, what matters most is what the teacher does about them. If the teacher simply avoids, blames, or complains, it is unlikely she will change her practice, and the points of contention that she has identified will remain exactly the same for the remainder of the year.

A teacher with an internal locus of control would be more likely to explain how his year was going in terms of what he was doing: *Because kids these days are less likely to ask questions, I need to learn some new strategies to increase response rates. My principal's feedback on my classroom management was hard for me to hear; I need to use a different approach to ensure students are ready to learn when class begins. The new evaluation system really emphasizes student engagement; I wonder what strategies other teachers are using.* Rather than expecting others to change their behavior, the teacher with an internal locus of control identifies strategies to improve areas that are of concern.

The greatest inhibitor to growth that we've seen throughout our careers is actually a close cousin to reflection. Like reflection, it requires individuals to think critically about their practice and to connect effort to outcomes. It also can occur in collaborative teams, in the staff room, and in clinical post-conferences. The similarities end there. This inhibitor occurs when we are reflective but do not have an internal locus of control. This inhibitor is justification.

Justification uses *if, then, therefore* logic to explain an outcome in terms of forces that are completely beyond one's control. Imagine a child dribbling a basketball through your living room. The child fakes left, cuts to the imaginary hoop, and . . . breaks an antique lamp. The child understands that what she did was not acceptable. She knows she is in trouble. What might she do?

First, she might leave the scene to *avoid a* scenario in which her parents connect her actions to the broken lamp. Furthermore, she may *avoid* her parents as much as possible for as long as possible. Unfortunately, because she is an only child, her parents know that she must have broken the lamp. When they ask her what happened, she acknowledges that the lamp is broken but tries to place *blame* elsewhere. She runs through a string of scenarios: *Maybe the cat did it? A gust of wind?* or simply *I don't know; maybe it fell because it was so old.* Finally, in desperation, she acknowledges the relationship between her actions and the outcome but *complains* that what occurred could not have been avoided: *It's not my fault that our living room is so small!*

This anecdote demonstrates the *ABC*s of justification (see Figure 4.5). Rather than reflecting on the link between our strategies and results, justification appeals to the desire to *avoid* difficult situations, *blame* others for outcomes, or *complain* about forces that are beyond our control.

FIGURE 4.5

ABCs of Justification That Prevents Reflection

Characteristic	Defined	Sounds Like
Avoiding	Intentionally staying away from an individual, a task, or a situation because of anxiety, apathy, or a lack of efficacy	• I don't like teaching that class/that group of students . . . • I tried that once and it didn't work . . . • If I have time to get back to [person, strategy, task] someday, I might . . .
Blaming	Attributing outcomes to the actions of others rather than accepting responsibility	• These students don't care about . . . • The buses don't always arrive on time so I can't . . . • No one told us we could . . . or I would have . . . • The students aren't able to . . . so I can't . . .
Complaining	Bringing attention to concerns that cannot be addressed by those who are present or articulating concerns that one has no intent of addressing	• It is ridiculous to expect us to . . . • These kids are just too . . . [negative attribute] • If only the parents would . . . • How can he/she expect me to . . .

Once locus of control becomes a component of shared vocabulary in a school culture, it can create a shorthand for diagnosing the extent to which children—and adults—feel as though they can control outcomes for which they are accountable. When working with children or adults with an external locus of control, it is imperative that teachers or principals reframe the learner's thinking to an internal locus of control. As we've heard Jeff Howard, founder of the Efficacy Institute, say numerous times, "Attribute your success to your ability and your failures to a lack of effective effort." Or as Jon Saphier and Robert Gower (1997) say, the most important message we can communicate to learners is "This is important. You can do this. I won't give up on you" (p. 335).

Meaningful Reflection Action Step 2

Teachers have a growth mindset; they believe they can make dramatic improvements in any area they choose. Are good teachers developed or born? An integral part of adopting a system that balances evaluation, supervision, and reflection is the belief among teachers and administrators that they can continuously improve and reach higher levels of expertise. We believe teaching is a skill that can be developed (Marzano et al., 2011). Unfortunately, as we discussed earlier in this book, systems of evaluation often provide early-career or preservice teachers with ratings that imply they have mastered the complex craft of teaching with only a few years, or months, of experience. The consequences of this practice may inadvertently result in teachers attributing their capacity to innate skills rather than to the use of strategies and protocols that will help them improve.

Stanford University professor Carol Dweck (2000, 2008) has spent much of her career looking at how people's beliefs about intelligence affect the effort they put forth to improve. According to Dweck, people tend to approach certain tasks in one of two ways: either they believe they have a fixed ability to be effective based on genetic capacity, or they believe they have the unlimited capacity to improve based on the use of effective strategy, perseverance, and dedication. Dweck calls these two ways of viewing one's capacity a *fixed mindset* or a *growth mindset*.

Consider two teachers given the same set of experiences to improve their instructional skills. One teacher has a fixed mindset, and the other has a growth mindset.

Teacher 1: In her preservice teaching, perhaps the fixed-mindset teacher received copious amounts of feedback as affirmation (*You do such a great job with the kids! Wow! Great lesson! You are a natural!*), but little constructive developmental feedback in the form of coaching in her preservice teaching. She is energetic and engaging and does a great job establishing effective relationships with students. She received the highest evaluative ratings through each of her preservice clinical placements and in her student teaching. In her first two years of teaching, she received nothing but positive feedback on her evaluations. She saw herself as what she had been repeatedly told that she was: a "naturally gifted teacher" who had "a way with kids."

A few years into her teaching, she was asked to teach in a different grade level. The students were older, and the academic content was unfamiliar to her. She protested the move for a variety of reasons, but deep down, she didn't see herself as having the capacity to handle the new assignment because she had never taught that grade before. She asked few questions because she didn't want to be perceived as ignorant. In her first few weeks in the new assignment, she struggled but didn't tell anyone for fear that she would be exposed as not being a gifted, great teacher. By March, she'd lost confidence: *I knew I couldn't teach this grade.* When her evaluator told her that she would need to receive help from a veteran teacher, she was offended and disheartened. A few years later, she left the profession.

Teacher 2: Early in the career of the growth-mindset teacher, she received specific praise that helped her link her use of strategies to student outcomes. She also received copious amounts of judgmental feedback. At first the feedback would sting a little, but she knew that if she were going to become a great teacher, she had a lot to learn. In her first few years of teaching, she was constantly asking veteran colleagues for tips and pointers and told her supervisor she welcomed any feedback. She was energized by continuously finding new ways to improve.

A few years into her teaching career, she was asked to teach at a different grade level. Although the students were older and the academic content was unfamiliar to her, she told her principal she hadn't taught that grade yet and asked if she could visit some of her soon-to-be colleagues' classrooms before the school year ended so she could start to develop an understanding of some of the nuances of her new assignment. She asked for sets of instructional resources to familiarize herself with the new content over the summer months. At the start of the school year, she had a plan in place to visit the classroom of a veteran teacher throughout the year and engage in a reflective dialogue with her colleague after each visit. She dove into the learning curve with a full head of steam and within a few years was doing innovative things in her new grade level. She was thriving and continued to do so.

Given the same set of opportunities, teachers with a fixed mindset can find themselves on dramatically different trajectories for improvement when compared with teachers with a growth mindset. The fixed-mindset teacher adopts what Dweck (2008) calls a *coping response*, whereas the growth-mindset teacher adopts a *thriving response*. Figure 4.6 illustrates the differences.

FIGURE 4.6
Fixed Mindset Versus Growth Mindset

Fixed Mindset "Teaching is an innate skill set. Good teachers are born, not made."	Situation	Growth Mindset "Teaching is a set of skills that can be developed through practice."
Coping Response		**Thriving Response**
"This is difficult. I will be better off avoiding the situation entirely."	**Facing a Challenge**	"This is difficult. I am going to have the opportunity to learn something new."
"If it looks like I have to try hard, people might think I am not a good teacher."	**Need for Effort**	"I will have to try hard to accomplish this. Teaching is tough, and I will need to invest time to get this right."
"I've never seen a problem like this before; I can't do this."	**Being Confronted with the Unknown**	"This is new to me. I am going to need to be strategic and learn some new skills."
"I already am a good teacher. Why do I have to do this?"	**Opportunity to Engage in Professional Development**	"This will be a learning opportunity that will affirm me, challenge me, or help me improve."
"Who are you to tell me I need to improve?"	**Receiving Feedback (Developmental or Judgmental)**	"Feedback focuses my efforts to get better. Give me more."
limited capacity to improve and stagnation.	***Results in . . .***	*unlimited capacity to improve and continuous growth.*

To help teachers move from a *fixed* to a *growth* mindset in teaching, do the following:

- Establish a shared language related to fixed mindset and growth mindset to create a clearer link among strategy, effort, and improvement.
- Acknowledge the premise that teaching is a complex, challenging profession.
- Help teachers reflect on the range of more and less effective teaching practices they've experienced as students.
- Have leaders share stories of challenges they've faced in the classroom. Doing so creates a culture where it is OK to acknowledge that teaching can be difficult, doesn't always go as planned, and we can all learn from mistakes as feedback that guides our efforts to improve.
- Celebrate the effort put forth to acquire new skills or roll out new initiatives. The need for significant effort indicates breakthrough learning, not a deficiency in the learner.
- Use protocols that help teachers articulate questions about the unknown, a particularly challenging student, implementation of new curricula, the use of a new strategy, or other matters in a manner that honors putting questions "on the table" as an asset rather than as a liability.
- Articulate high expectations for everyone with the understanding that teaching is a complex craft that requires ongoing professional development, meaningful reflection, and purposeful effort and is worthy of a career's worth of growth.
- Have leaders ask for feedback from teachers in the same manner that teachers ask for feedback among students. Principals can model how to respond to feedback by articulating their summary of the feedback and how that feedback will help them focus efforts for growth.
- Reframe learning for adults using what Dweck (2008) calls the most powerful word in a teacher's vocabulary: *yet*. It is not true that a teacher "can't find a way to meet a student's learning needs"; the teacher just hasn't found the best way to do so *yet*.

If principals or teachers believe great teachers are born and not made, there is little reason to invest in efforts to improve. Fortunately, teaching is a complex set of skills that can be developed by anyone willing to invest time and effort to engage in the deliberate practice that helps individuals improve. These opportunities are most likely to be seized by individuals with a growth mindset.

Meaningful Reflection Action Step 3

Teachers are metacognitive in their effort to clarify the gap between current and ideal performance. If you've ever put a puzzle together, you've probably listened to a voice in your head that guided you to successfully complete it. *"OK, I am going to look at the picture on the box so I am clear about what this will look like when I am done. I need to lay out all of the border pieces first. Does this one have a straight edge? No. But this one does. Now I'm going to start to lay these out here. The colors on these two are nearly identical; I bet they fit together. . . ."* The name for this strategic internal dialogue is *metacognition.*

At its most basic level, metacognition can be described as *thinking about one's own thinking.* Although that explanation articulates the gist, it misses many key components. According to John Flavell (1977), the father of research on this topic, metacognitive thinking

- Is intentional in its focus; it deliberately moves an individual's thoughts and actions toward a goal.
- Allows one to monitor and adjust one's own learning.
- Brings to mind and selects from a variety of problem-solving strategies.
- Is directed toward thinking about one's awareness of one's own learning processes.

So metacognition is not a string of random thoughts; it is an intentional and purposeful process in moving from thought to action to achieve a goal. Metacognition is the "awareness individuals have of their own thinking, their evaluation of that thinking, and their regulation of that thinking" (Wilson, 2001). Awareness makes individuals attuned to what needs to be done, what has been done, and what might be done in specific situations to optimize the use of their own cognitive resources. Given this efficiency, it is not surprising that those with better metacognitive abilities tend to be more successful in cognitive tasks (Livingston, 2003).

The payoffs of metacognition don't occur by awareness alone; they occur by linking thought to action. Specifically, metacognition links self-awareness to self-evaluation and self-regulation.

To be *aware*, individuals need to be able to "step outside" of themselves and understand that their perceptions are guided by thoughts. Whatever they are perceiving and explaining is a *choice*. They could pay attention to something else, but they are aware of what matters. This is captured by Robert Tremmel's (1993) explanation of awareness as teachers and students "working together in a dance-like pattern, simultaneously involved in design and in playing various roles in virtual and real worlds, while at the same time remaining detached enough to observe and feel the action that is occurring, and to respond" (p. 436).

To *evaluate*, individuals think about their thinking and ask themselves questions about the extent that their current thoughts and actions are productive. *Am I perceiving this accurately? What might I be missing? Why are the students still confused?* This is not evaluation to render a judgment ("I am good" or "I am bad"); it is about connecting intent to action. Consider the anecdote from earlier in this chapter about driving in the snow. When a driver says to herself, *I wonder if I am going too fast for these conditions*, she is evaluating her actions.

To *regulate*, individuals actively modify their thoughts and actions in a manner that links strategies to results. Here, they are acting in a purposeful manner based on their *awareness* and *evaluation*. Practitioners who are more expert engage in a series of adjustments, in real time, to fine-tune their efforts as related to their intended outcomes (Zimmerman, 2006). Individuals whose performance stagnates over time tend to get overwhelmed as they think about all of the components involved in a performance, which simply leads to "inconsistent or superficial tracking" (p. 711).

Practitioners with greater expertise not only regulate while engaged in the midst of a task but also are more likely to be metacognitive about their needs between tasks. Therefore, they are more likely to seek help from books, coaches, or models that can clarify specific areas where they believe they can improve their technique. An individual who is metacognitive is aware of the internal dialogue that is required to create and close the gap among awareness, evaluation, and regulation.

In their research on metacognition and expertise, Gyhoo Hatano and Kayoko Inagaki (1986) coined the phrase *adaptive expertise* to distinguish it from *routine expertise*. Routine expertise can be applied to a highly complex yet repetitive task like playing a piano concerto. Adaptive expertise, on the other hand, requires fluid understanding of a constantly changing set of variables. The National Research Council describes the essence of adaptive expertise as follows:

> In research with experts who were asked to verbalize their thinking as they worked, it was revealed that they monitored their own understanding carefully, making note of when additional information was required for understanding, whether new information was consistent with what they already knew, and what analogies could be drawn that would advance their understanding. These meta-cognitive monitoring activities are an important component of what is called adaptive expertise. (Bransford et al., 2000, p. 18)

When the following questions become habits of mind for teachers to guide their path toward adaptive expertise, they cannot help but engage in a purposeful, metacognitive dialogue that informs meaningful reflection:

- What evidence do I have right now that my students are learning?
- How are my actions challenging and supporting their efforts to learn?
- What should I continue to do or what should I do differently to improve results?

A Purposeful Approach to Reflection

In a system that balances evaluation, supervision, and reflection, teachers reflect in a purposeful way; they connect reflection to deliberate actions to improve their instructional practice. Purposeful reflection is exemplified in systems that emphasize the following beliefs and practices.

1. Teachers are increasingly purposeful about, aware of, and responsive to the relationship between student learning and effective teaching. A system of purposeful reflection links strategic questions to the frameworks for effective practice in order to guide teachers' pathway toward expertise. There is never enough time for learning; therefore, teachers need to be purposeful in our intentions to guide student learning. Learning experiences rarely go as planned; thus, we need to be aware of whether or not our teaching is actually supporting learning as intended. As teachers become aware of the gap between their intent and the actual effects, they need to be responsive by modifying their practice to ensure they are providing necessary levels of challenge and support.

2. Teachers embrace dissonance; they develop a nuanced view of the gap between current and expert practice. Purposeful reflection honors the fact that structured approaches to reflection can guide teachers' efforts and purposeful action to make specific changes in behavior, rather than merely thinking about how things went. Reflection is often viewed as being personal and private. This typically leads to individuals reflecting in many different ways (journaling, note taking, making mental notes, and so on), which may or may not be conducive to making changes in behaviors that result in improvement. Teachers are more likely to close the gap between current performance and expertise when they use a systematic approach that helps them see their classroom through the eyes of their students and their own performance through new eyes.

3. Teachers use the comprehensive teaching framework and a variety of structured processes to engage in continuous reflection, deliberate practice, and modification as they progress toward expert performance. Purposeful reflection honors the fact that teaching is complex and requires attention to practicing the nuances of instructional strategies so they are used in a way that best supports student learning. Experts seek to improve by breaking complex tasks into small, actionable components that can be improved through *deliberate practice*. Deliberate practice involves refining a complex process by applying a strategy, responding to feedback, and modifying the strategy until it can be used in the right way, at the right time, to obtain the desired results.

In the sections that follow we describe these beliefs and practices in more detail. Again, we refer to them as "action steps," and we include specific information about how to develop a system that incorporates all the elements necessary to ensure that reflection is purposeful.

Purposeful Reflection Action Step 1

Teachers are increasingly purposeful about, aware of, and responsive to the relationship between student learning and effective teaching. Comprehensive teaching frameworks for instruction can be used for more than just evaluation. Teachers can use them as a shared language of effective practice that clarifies expectations for, and a pathway toward, expertise. However, merely looking at the frameworks to justify a rating or establish a goal when an evaluator is present will not result in improved practice. Teachers must internalize questions that guide purposeful reflection as a daily habit of mind.

We advocate the use of specific questions to help teachers build the habits of mind that ensure they are purposeful, aware, and responsive (PAR) about the connection between their teaching and students' learning. This approach facilitates structured analysis of, and reflection upon, their professional practice. When used effectively, the PAR questions can become the foundation for a culture of meaningful reflection that results in purposeful, accelerated growth.

The PAR framework separates reflection about teaching into three components:

- Purposeful—Reflective teachers are purposeful in their efforts to plan meaningful, engaging learning experiences that support and develop each student's understanding.
  Key question: How should I best invest limited instructional time around prioritized learning goals and aligned strategies to maximize engagement and learning?
- Aware—Reflective teachers are aware of students' learning needs and assess the effectiveness of their lessons in real time. They are open to understanding the perceptions, needs, and actions of students without judgment as a pathway to understanding how the classroom looks through students' eyes.
  Key question: How are the instructional strategies I am using right now supporting each student's active engagement in the learning process?
- Responsive—Reflective teachers are responsive as they make intentional adjustments to their teaching based on students' learning needs in real time, as determined by observations of students' response to the lesson.

They are open to adjusting their own perceptions, strategies, and efforts to more effectively confront, motivate, or support the needs of another. *Key question: What is working and what might I do differently to even more effectively maximize each student's learning?*

These key questions lay the foundation for additional, specific questions that can be used to focus teachers' efforts to engage in meaningful, purposeful reflection. Every question is not intended to be addressed every time a teacher teaches a lesson. Instead, the questions represent the broad range of the terrain that teachers need to be reflective about to best support student learning.

Figure 4.7 lists reflective questions for the three PAR components. The questions aligned to *purpose* are arranged on a continuum from outcomes to instruction; those aligned to *awareness* are arranged on a continuum from classroom management to student engagement; and those aligned to *responsiveness* are arranged on a continuum from modifying classroom management strategies during the lesson to the identification and implementation of new instructional strategies that support deep understanding.

Using a framework to help narrow teachers' focus greatly enhances the depth of teachers' analysis and the potential for more effective professional practice. The PAR framework creates a foundation for powerful reflection and respectful collaboration. The purpose of these questions is to guide inquiry rather than to provoke interrogation. Inquiry is the use of open-ended questions that invite an exploration of possible answers. Interrogation is an ineffective evaluative approach that uses questions to get someone to acknowledge they know nothing, or to admit guilt.

Figure 4.8 (page 146) provides examples of the deep, sophisticated level of reflection that can be elicited through the inquiry-driven PAR approach. Each example illustrates components of meaningful reflection, growth mindset, internal locus of control, and metacognition. By contrast, the nonexamples are either superficial or fall into the traps that are pervasive in the "avoiding, blaming, and complaining" behaviors associated with justification. Notice the difference in the additional examples in Figure 4.9 (page 146), which demonstrate purposeful, aware, responsive reflection as compared to the counterexamples in the *ABCs* of justification listed in Figure 4.5 on page 133.

FIGURE 4.7

Questions That Invite Purposeful, Aware, Responsive (PAR) Reflection

Purposeful Reflective teachers are purposeful in their efforts to plan meaningful, engaging learning experiences that support and develop each student's understanding.	• What learning goals will guide my teaching and students' efforts for learning? • What do students already understand? • What are students already able to do? • What are students likely to be confused about? • What assessment items/tasks will reveal understanding? • What criteria will be used to measure success? • What might students find engaging about this topic? • What formative assessment strategies will be used? • What instructional strategies will be used to support student learning? • What activities will students engage in to build understanding/skill?
Aware Reflective teachers are aware of students' learning needs and assess the effectiveness of their lessons in real time.	• Are students paying attention? • Are students aware of, and do they understand, the learning goal? • Are students engaged? • Are students making connections to existing knowledge/skills? • Are students responding to my directions? • Are students responding to my questions? • Are students transitioning effectively from one task to the next? • Are students confused? • Are students asking questions to clarify assignments/tasks? • Are students asking questions to clarify learning? • Are students asking questions that delve into the unknown and unknowable? • Are students on track to successfully achieve the learning goal? • Are students ready to successfully engage in tasks and activities with guidance? Independently? • Which students are engaged/learning? • Which students are disengaged/not learning? • What teaching strategies are working successfully? • What teaching strategies need to be modified? • What was the high point of the lesson? • What was the low point of the lesson?

Responsive Reflective teachers are responsive as they make intentional adjustments to their teaching based on students' learning needs in real time. Changes are made based on teachers' observations of their students' response to the lesson.	• What management strategies did I use to affirm, or redirect, student behavior? • What instructional strategies did I enact "on the spot" to engage students? • What instructional strategies did I use as a result of feedback from formative assessments? • What clarifying questions did I ask when misunderstanding was evident? • What reteaching occurred when misunderstanding was evident? • What affirmation did I give to students when they made progress or attained the goal? • What instructional strategies did I use to provide additional challenge? • What instructional strategies did I use to provide additional support? • What changes to the original lesson plan did I make, and why? • What other changes might I have made, and why? • What modifications did I make based on individual students' needs? • Were changes made based on "data" or on "feel"? • What opportunities to be responsive were missed and should be addressed next time the situation occurs? • What are next steps in student learning, and how I will support their learning needs?

The reflective questions in the PAR framework can be used in all three components of a balanced system of evaluation, supervision, and reflection. What matters most is who is asking the questions and for what purposes.

For evaluation

• Use the categories Purposeful, Aware, and Responsive to determine areas of focus for evaluative visits.
• Use the questions to delve deeper into conversations about expectations for quality teaching and opportunities for growth.
• Use the questions to focus data collection to an aligned portion of the comprehensive framework for effective instruction.

For supervision

• Use the questions to determine specific goals for growth.
• Use the questions to determine how specific types of data can be collected by teachers to establish and monitor progress toward goals for growth.

FIGURE 4.8
Examples and Nonexamples of PAR-Inspired Reflections

Purposeful
Reflective teachers are purposeful in their efforts to plan meaningful, engaging learning experiences that support and develop each student's understanding.

> **Example:** *"Many of my students this year are struggling with using reliable resources and using multiple sources. They will have a difficult time with the research project I have done in the past. I will need to make some modifications for the students who are struggling by incorporating some more skill-building lessons. The students who aren't struggling can complete the project, and I will add some enrichment activities for them as well."*

> **Nonexample:** *"I will use the same research project we did the last few years because it has been very successful in the past."*

Aware
Reflective teachers are aware of students' learning needs and assess the effectiveness of their lessons in real time.

> **Example:** *"Students are having a hard time with this activity. I need to find out why. I need to determine if they don't understand the content, the learning goal, or if I gave unclear directions."*

> **Nonexample:** *"Students are really having a hard time with this activity. This group is not nearly as bright as last year's class."*

Responsive
Reflective teachers are responsive as they make intentional adjustments to their teaching based on students' learning needs in real time. Changes are made based on teachers' observations of their students' response to the lesson.

> **Example:** *"That didn't work out as I planned. I observed some of my students doing the activity correctly, but the exit ticket I gave revealed that 21 out of 26 students couldn't correctly restate the learning goal and only 3 out of 26 could make a real-world connection. Based on this information, tomorrow I am going to . . . ."*

> **Nonexample:** *"I'm not sure if the kids got that, but we need to move on to the next lesson tomorrow."*

FIGURE 4.9
Examples of Reflection, Rather Than Justification, Through the PAR Framework

Component	Sounds Like
Purposeful	• I get nervous when I talk to _____, so I wrote a list of questions ahead of time . . . • My students always get confused when dividing fractions, so I made a graphic organizer for them to . . . • The buses come late as soon as winter hits, so this year I've set up a process so if students come in a little late, they know they need to . . .
Aware	• I noticed my students were not paying attention, so I . . . • I wanted the students to _____, but instead they _____, so I . . . • I wonder why every time I _____, my students . . . • I am not asking enough higher-order thinking questions. I wonder how I might . . . • Today I tried _____ a bit differently, and my students did great on their group work!

Component	Sounds Like
Responsive	• I noticed my students were _____, so I . . . • Kendrick stopped doing his homework; I need to . . . • This unit is really challenging my students this year. My review of exit slips shows nearly half the class is unsure of some of the key concepts. I need to slow down and reteach those concepts.

Note how the "Sounds Like" column stands in stark contrast to the ABCs of justification in Figure 4.5.

- Use the questions to guide supervisor/coach and teacher discussions. Alternatively, use them in collaborative group discussions to guide dialogue.
- Use the questions to focus instructional rounds and other protocols designed to allow teachers to reflect on their own practice by observing others.

For reflection

- When completing written reflections, use selected PAR questions to guide inquiry and reflection around specific areas of focus.
- Use PAR as a way of being metacognitive and reflective about intentions, actions, and results when teaching.
- When participating in a variety of protocols, use selected PAR questions to guide analysis and discussion of the gap between current performance and expertise.
- Embrace the questions in the PAR framework as a habit of mind to guide reflection in every class, every day.

When used mindfully across evaluation, supervision, and reflection, the PAR framework can be a powerful tool that builds teacher ownership for being a reflective practitioner.

Purposeful Reflection Action Step 2

Teachers embrace dissonance; they develop a nuanced view of the gap between current and expert practice. As we discussed in Chapter 3 on supervision, cognitive dissonance occurs when we are aware that our actions are not aligned to our beliefs. A textbook example is when people know that smoking is bad for them (belief) but do it anyway because of habit (action). The most powerful cognitive dissonance occurs when it is *discovered* in a meaningful context rather than merely *delivered* as a point of information. Consider a father who is a smoker. The father's children share articles with him about the dangers of smoking and encourage him to quit. Delivering the information, however, typically doesn't create dissonance. The information is easier to dismiss than the complexities associated with adopting new behaviors. However, suppose a friend of the father's dies of lung cancer, or the father has a health scare that forces him to recognize his own mortality. This startling news creates dissonance that cannot be dismissed. The father's observations cause him to discover a new set of understandings and beliefs that, ultimately, cause him to adopt new behaviors.

When engaged in the complex process of trying to improve performance, cognitive dissonance is also a good thing. Someone who thinks his existing practice is the ideal of human performance will never make progress toward expertise. He may increase his fluency in certain skills through repetition, but the belief that *there must be a better way* comes from an external spark to move from improvement as simply doing more of the same, to transformational growth based on new beliefs and behaviors that result in expertise.

Unfortunately, in systems that primarily emphasize evaluation, the only opportunity to experience dissonance often comes in the form of judgmental external feedback that is delivered rather than developmental feedback that is discovered. Garmston (2000) argues that "external feedback reduces the capacity for accurate self-reflection . . . [; therefore,] staff developers must eliminate systems and processes that foster dependency on external sources of correction and judgment in order to increase each person's capacity to be self-reflective" (p. 64). We agree. Teachers' own use of various protocols to gather information that results in meaningful reflection creates powerful insights into improved performance.

Charlotte Danielson (2011) emphasizes that effective teacher evaluations that lead to teacher growth will come from processes that engage teachers in self-assessment and reflection. Although external feedback effectively documents strengths and needs, it also invites defensiveness. Even a teacher who is completely open to feedback will not benefit from judgmental evaluation that occurs only a few times a year. Teachers who engage in structured processes that allow them to continuously reflect on their own performance with greater accuracy and articulate components of expert performance more clearly are more likely to embrace dissonance. This dissonance invites reflection about what the next level of high-quality performance will look like on the path toward expertise.

Given what we described in the chapter on supervision, it is important to honor teachers as adult learners and support each teacher's autonomy. Choice is a good thing. However, as Jim Knight (2011) explains, choice without structure is chaos. Unlimited, unstructured opportunities to find pathways to improvement are likely to result in goals without focus and reflection without purpose. As Graham Nuthall (2007) states, "There are distinct limits on the extent to which teachers can learn effective teaching methods from their own experience" (p. 275). Although reflection can lead us through stages of being unaware of what we don't know, conscious awareness of what we know, action toward new practice, and refinement of new skills (Hall & Simerall, 2015), the process can be calibrated and accelerated in a number of ways. These include using a shared language of effective practice, the critical component of observing others' teaching, collecting data, and engaging in written reflection and dialogue with others to clarify ways to close the gap between current practice and what is possible.

Current Performance: Reflecting on "Where Am I Now?"

"Where am I now?" is the first question that must be addressed in a system of reflection. *Reflecting on one's own performance without an accurate awareness of the quality of that performance results in reflection that is not valid.* If I cannot accurately assess the strengths and weaknesses of my current performance, I don't know where I'm starting from. This flaw is pervasive in systems where individuals are isolated, and teaching is among the most isolated professions in the world. When thinking about their answer to the critical question "Where am I now?" their response is a version of Descartes' *"I think, therefore I am,"* in the form of *"I think I am good, therefore I am good."*

Reflection should begin by gathering information about current performance from a variety of sources. A clearer understanding of current performance creates dissonance because teachers can see their position on a continuum toward expertise. In a learning orientation, self-assessment is not an attempt to justify a component of evaluation; it is an opportunity for teachers to affirm their own strengths and willingly identify areas to improve their teaching.

Actions teachers can take to reflect on the question "Where am I now?" include the following:

- Use a survey tool to obtain feedback from students that focuses on the presence or absence of specific teaching behaviors. This process views teaching through students' eyes.
- Collect and analyze data of evidence of student learning through the use of exit slips and other formative assessments.
- Record a video of the classroom from a variety of perspectives (place the recording device in the back of the classroom to capture teaching behaviors or in the front to see students' response to teaching) and analyze the teaching using select questions from the PAR framework or from another protocol.

Expert Performance: Reflecting on "What Could Be?"

"What could be?" is the second question that must be addressed in a system of reflection. *Reflecting on our own performance without understanding alternatives results in complacency.* If we never see alternative methods or approaches, it can be easy to strive for incremental improvement but fail to see what could be. Seeing what is possible in other classrooms creates the dissonance that fuels future-focused reflection.

This kind of purposeful reflection can be facilitated by observing other practitioners as much as possible. *Again, the purpose of observing others is not to evaluate another's performance, but to reflect on how that person's skills and strategies can inform our own performance.* The shared language of a comprehensive framework of instruction can create a powerful language of reflection and dialogue. Observing expert teaching creates dissonance because it expands our understanding of what is possible in the classroom. Things that teachers can do to reflect on "What could be?" include the following:

- Use protocols to guide inquiry into the analysis of video clips of expert practitioners. Observe through a lens of "What can I learn about my own practice?" rather than a lens of "What I am doing is wrong."
- Use protocols to guide analysis of their own performance after visiting classrooms of teachers who have been identified as having expertise using

specific strategies, and focus on the connection between teacher behaviors and student responses.

- Engage in focused, collegial dialogue to discuss how specific strategies were used in the expert classroom and how those strategies challenge or affirm their existing practice.

By observing someone who is expert, teachers can place themselves in a healthy state of cognitive dissonance: *I thought I had figured out the best way to do this [old action and belief], but now I see there are skills and nuances that I can't do yet [new belief].* This dissonance can serve as a catalyst for envisioning, and attempting, new skills and strategies.

Next Performance: Reflecting on "What Does the Next Level of Quality Look Like?"

"What does the next level of quality look like?" is the question that serves as a catalyst to closing the gap between current performance and expert performance. *If teachers can accurately assess their current performance and articulate a vision of expert performance, they can be reflective about the next level of skills and strategies that will move them along the path toward expertise.* The goal is not to instantly move from novice to expert, but to discern what new strategies can be adopted or what existing strategies can be augmented to improve. Things teachers can do to consider the next level of performance include the following:

- Operate from a premise of meaningful reflection; an internal locus of control and a growth mindset ensure that teachers are metacognitive about their performance in a manner that embraces possibility. It is about growth, not judgment.
- Engage in focused, collegial dialogue to discuss the relationship among current, expert, and next performance.
- Use the comprehensive teaching framework to clarify and discern specific strategies that might be selected or improved upon to add to, or improve, current performance.
- Use protocols to visit classrooms, engage in video analysis, and read articles about the use of those identified instructional strategies.

Once teachers have identified what specific instructional strategies can be used to move toward expertise, they can engage in deliberate practice like that used by experts to make dramatic improvements in any area they choose.

Purposeful Reflection Action Step 3

Teachers use the comprehensive teaching framework and a variety of structured processes to engage in continuous reflection, deliberate practice, and modification as they progress toward expert performance. Although cognitive dissonance makes a learner aware of the gap between beliefs and behaviors, it can support change only if those new beliefs are a catalyst for developing new skills. Such development requires practice. Using those skills with the nuance of an expert requires the specific approach to improvement called *deliberate practice,* which we have mentioned previously in this chapter. Quite simply, deliberate practice is how experts become expert. It is not simply trying something a few times, nor is it engaging in the same day-to-day performance for years and years. It is an intentional process focused on improving the ability to more effectively use specific aspects of a complex skill with the goal of improved performance (Ericsson et al., 1993).

Earlier in this chapter we described how experts differ from novices. According to Ericsson and his colleagues (1993), those differences are not due to innate abilities, but to intentionality, focus, and strategy. They make the following points about expert performance:

- Individuals usually improve their skills for a limited time until they reach a level of competence and then plateau.
- Increased time in a profession does *not* necessarily translate into improved performance.
- The pathway to expert performance requires deliberate practice, which Ericsson describes as repeated practice focused on specific aspects of performance, feedback on that performance, and modification.
- Whether focusing on a new skill or augmenting an area that is already perceived to be a strength, deliberate practice requires participants to break strategies into small, actionable opportunities for growth.
- Experts are not afraid to take calculated risks and make repeated mistakes as they move from novice to expert levels of performance.

- Expertise can be developed by concentrating on carefully selected aspects that need improvement and refinement through repetition and feedback.

Throughout this process, specificity is critical. Consider working toward a goal of "becoming a more engaging teacher." It's a noble outcome, but it's not a strategy that can be practiced. As a teacher we worked with noted after participating in a series of instructional rounds:

> [I saw] the ways different teachers responded to students who were not engaged, or the way they managed and responded to different students had a direct effect on the class spirit, individual engagement, and the quality of the lesson. Pacing, enthusiasm, and physical movement were critical pieces of the classroom.

Using deliberate practice to "be more engaging" is not possible. However, using deliberate practice to improve pacing and demonstrate appropriate levels of enthusiasm, and using instructional strategies that give students the opportunity to move around the room during well-managed learning activities are specific behaviors that can be practiced in a manner that builds expertise in the specific skills required to improve student engagement.

Deliberate practice includes the following components (Ericsson, 1996; Ericsson et al., 1993):

- The goal is improved performance, not merely transactional compliance.
- Skills to be developed should be based on specific identified needs.
- Sustained effort of repetitive, specific tasks are designed to improve areas of need.
- Activities provide opportunity for learning and skill acquisition.
- Practice should be outside one's comfort zone.
- Performance is carefully monitored.
- Access to feedback is critical.
- The ability to self-monitor is critical.
- The process may not be enjoyable, but pleasure comes from the development of enhanced performance.
- Expert performance is acquired gradually and incrementally.

Figure 4.10 presents examples for each of these components and lists relevant protocols. (See Appendixes A through D for the actual protocols.)

Emphasizing the importance of feedback, Ericsson and his colleagues (2006) state that "to assure effective learning, subjects ideally should be given explicit instructions about the best method and be supervised by a teacher to allow individualized diagnosis of errors, informative feedback, and remedial part training" (p. 367). Teachers need other teachers to provide feedback and resources that can help them attain their goal. "Research on what enabled some individuals to reach expert rather than mediocre achievement, revealed that expert and elite performers seek out teachers and engage in specially designed training activities" (Ericsson et al., 2006, p. 61).

Educational researcher David Boud and his colleagues write that what is important is not experience itself but "the intellectual growth that follows the process of reflecting on experience . . . effective learning does not follow from a positive experience but from effective reflection" (Boud, Cohen, & Walker, 1993, p. 162). Creating opportunities for meaningful, purposeful reflection increases the likelihood of improvement.

Protocols to Align the Purpose of Reflection to the Payoff

As we have stated before, the purpose of reflection is to develop each teacher's capacity to engage in an ongoing internal dialogue that results in purposeful action to improve professional practice and move toward expertise.

Meaningful reflection occurs in systems that emphasize the following beliefs and practices:

- Developing teachers' internal locus of control
- Nurturing a growth mindset within all staff members of the school
- Clarifying the gap between current and ideal performance to increase teacher metacognition

Purposeful reflection occurs in systems that emphasize the following beliefs and practices:

- Using a structured, systematic approach to reflection
- Engaging teachers in deliberate practice guided by a teaching framework and supported by a systematic process

FIGURE 4.10

Deliberate Practice Applied to Teaching

Key Components of Deliberate Practice	Example Applied to Teaching	Protocols to Use
Goal is improved performance, not merely transactional compliance.	Teachers establish a goal to improve in a specific instructional strategy: *I will use scaffolding techniques to ask students appropriate higher-level questions on a daily basis.*	• Teaching Inventory • The Ideal Classroom • Meaningful Goal Setting • Determining Focus
Skills to be developed should be based on specific identified needs.	Teachers identify the need for improvement of specific skills, with emphasis on improving skills that will have the greatest impact on achievement: *Internal and external feedback helped to determine that transition time between activities should be improved to recapture instructional time.*	• Teaching Inventory • Determining Focus: The Ideal Classroom • Clinical Observation • Formative Classroom Walkthrough • Evaluative Classroom Walkthrough
Sustained effort on specific tasks are designed to improve weakness.	Teachers focus on improving very specific instructional strategies, such as *previewing questions before reading, having students summarize what they have learned, communicating the purpose of homework, chunking content, etc.*	• Teaching Inventory • Determining Focus: The Ideal Classroom
Activities provide opportunity for learning and skill acquisition.	Teachers visit other classrooms, observe video, or engage in professional development around acquisition of specific instructional strategies.	• Reflective Peer Visit • Video Analysis of Others' Teaching • Peer Sharing • Collegial Fishbowl
Practice should be outside one's comfort zone.	Teachers should work to improve specific skills that are beyond their current level of performance. For example, teachers who excel at using graphic organizers should select a different focus area.	• Teaching Inventory • Meaningful Goal Setting • Peer Sharing
Performance is carefully monitored.	Teachers monitor the goal/skills identified for improvement on a regular basis (every 2–3 weeks), using internal or external means.	• Motivational Interviewing • Structured Reflective Writing • Formative Classroom Walkthrough • Evaluative Classroom Walkthrough • Clinical Observation

continued

FIGURE 4.10

Deliberate Practice Applied to Teaching (*continued*)

Key Components of Deliberate Practice	Example Applied to Teaching	Protocols to Use
Access to feedback is critical.	Teachers use feedback generated internally and externally from multiple perspectives. Feedback can come from students informally and through structured surveys; feedback from others' observations or experiences can be used, along with self-generated feedback.	• Student Surveys • Structured Reflective Writing • Peer Sharing • Timely, Specific Developmental Feedback • Timely, Specific Judgmental Feedback • Receiving Feedback
The ability to self-monitor is critical.	Teachers develop their self-monitoring skills and become more self-aware of their performance, as well as how their situation relates to the expectations of the teaching framework.	• Determining Focus: The Ideal Classroom • Video Analysis of Own Teaching • Reflective Peer Visit • Defining the Issue Using the "On PAR Framework" • Structured Reflective Writing
The process may not be enjoyable, but the pleasure comes from the development of enhanced performance.	Teachers struggle through failed attempts but by the end of the year have improved in the identified focus areas. The true enjoyment comes from realizing that they can increase their impact on student achievement and create more opportunities for students.	• Celebrating Success
Expert performance is acquired gradually and incrementally.	Teachers improve dramatically over time. When improvement efforts are focused on 2–3 instructional strategies, teachers can realize significant gains, making the improvement process less overwhelming and motivating teachers to engage in the process. When improvement cycles are repeated, expert performance is a reachable goal.	• Focused Goal Setting

- Developing teachers' reflective and metacognitive skills by using the PAR framework

The protocols listed in the Reflection section of Appendix E can be used to help ensure that the reflection process is both meaningful and purposeful. Each protocol is categorized by main user, purpose, and outcome. See Appendixes

C and D for more detailed explanations of the specific purpose and process for each protocol, as well as the actual protocols.

A Case in Balance: When Reflection Works Effectively

At the start of the school year, Mrs. Jones was ready to make the move from teaching 3rd grade to 5th grade. When goal-setting forms were due, she had gathered enough data to realize that she needed to make some significant changes in practice. The 3rd grade routines that had worked well for her in the past would not work for this group of students. Her goals were to (1) increase students' cognitive engagement by turning attention into higher-order thinking and (2) increase students' behavioral engagement in meaningful tasks aligned to standards.

Mrs. Jones had learned she'd be moving grade levels near the end of the previous year. She soon asked for release time to visit the 5th grade classrooms. Through her observations, she realized two important things. First, the academic content of the work the students were doing was much more focused and rigorous than what she was doing with her 3rd graders; and second, the students seemed to be drawn into activities built around meaningful, authentic problem solving and were very resistant to busywork. She discussed these observations with the 5th grade teacher who would be retiring and listened intently to her advice about what does, and does not, work with 5th graders.

When she greeted her 5th graders for the first time, Mrs. Jones acknowledged that she knew many of them from 3rd grade and asked them to respond to the following prompts:

- The best thing about 3rd grade was:
- What I liked least about 3rd grade was:
- The best thing about 4th grade was:
- What I liked least about 4th grade was:
- This year I am excited to:
- This year I am nervous about:

She identified a number of clear patterns in student responses that helped her gain a better understanding of how the students had changed and how they had stayed the same. Near the end of the third week of class, she placed her phone in front of the room and told students she'd be capturing video of the day's language arts lesson so she could become an even better teacher. The students asked her many questions about how she would use the video, and she explained that after a football team plays a game or actors give a performance, they "study the tape" to think about how they can get even better the next time; she was doing the same thing.

That evening when she watched the video, she noticed several things she had done that caused the kids to be confused by the directions for the day's activity. She made a mental note to be sure to write down the steps on the whiteboard next time so that students could refer to them while she had other content projected on the interactive whiteboard. She also realized that all of the questions the kids asked were about the activity, but no one asked any clarifying questions about the content. She wrote a note to herself: "There were seven questions about how to do the activity 'right' but not a single question about the content. Do they really understand why they are doing this?"

Finally, three days before the goal-setting forms were due to her principal, she gave students a 15-question survey. She noted that although 96 percent of her students agreed or strongly agreed with the statement "My teacher cares about me as a student and a person," only 63 percent agreed or strongly agreed with the statements "If there is something I don't understand, I ask my teacher," and "The projects we do in this class help me understand important ideas and concepts."

After she set her goals, she was placed on a collaborative team of teachers who were working on improving students' cognitive and behavioral engagement. The team met four times throughout the year and discussed strategies they were using; and based on their self-assessment of their video clips and student surveys, they talked about things that were going well and areas where they needed to improve. Additionally, Mrs. Jones found out that one of the 5th grade teachers in a different elementary school in the district had established a goal the previous year of using academic games to improve student engagement. Mrs. Jones's principal arranged for her to visit his classroom and see what he was doing. She had so many lightbulb moments while watching him (inconsequential competition, the difference between attention and engagement, using games as a quick hook activity to grab kids' attention) that the very next day she started implementing some new strategies that had an immediate, positive impact on her students' engagement.

When she administered the student survey again in early December, she saw an increase in the percentage of students agreeing or strongly agreeing with the statements about asking questions and connecting projects to concepts. She was pleased to see the data moving in a positive direction. Additionally, she added four open-ended questions to the survey to gain even better insight into her students and their needs:

- One thing Mrs. Jones does that helps my learning:
- One thing Mrs. Jones could do to help me learn even more:
- One thing that I've done as a 5th grader that has helped my learning:
- One thing I could do as a 5th grader to help me learn even more:

When she started her midyear reflection to share with her principal, the words came easily: "Moving from 3rd grade to 5th grade has been among the most humbling and rewarding things that has happened to me in my 15 years of teaching . . . ."

5

Guidelines for Navigating Change That Results in Balancing Evaluation, Supervision, and Reflection

In the opening chapter of this book, we shared an anecdote of three nomads convening to trade with one another. They were unable to work together because they got in an argument about the color of a great pyramid. Each thought that his view of one side of the pyramid had to describe all of the sides of the pyramid. This anecdote speaks to the importance of acknowledging the form and function of different components of a system. Rather than arguing about evaluation, supervision, and reflection, we believe that our time would be better spent clarifying the purpose of these three components and then aligning protocols and processes associated with each component to ensure desired results.

Mindful implementation of these protocols requires all stakeholders to be attuned to three components: establish and understand a shared purpose, develop an awareness and shared language of ways to understand growth toward expertise, and implement protocols in a manner that is responsive to the strategy and patience required to implement transformational change.

Establish and Understand a Shared Purpose

If members of the school community are to utilize comprehensive teaching frameworks in a manner that improves—rather than merely measures—teacher expertise, they will be most likely to do so in a context where a shared purpose for a balanced system of evaluation, supervision, and reflection has been established. Stakeholders will

- *Understand organizational mission and purpose.* There is clarity as to why we exist, who we serve, and to whom we are accountable as individuals and as an organization.
- *Honestly address challenges and opportunities of relational trust.* Keep in mind the importance of transparency, honesty, and clarity as related to organizational history, adoption, and implementation of the balanced components.
- *Understand the importance of credibility.* Consistent, ongoing professional development that ensures valid and reliable utilization of comprehensive frameworks for effective teaching ensures that the system is seen as fair and criterion referenced.
- *Understand the form and function of evaluation, supervision, and reflection.* These are three different systems that serve three different purposes. The existence of one of these systems neither supersedes nor replaces another.

Develop an Awareness of the Language of Growth and Expertise

If members of the school community are to move beyond transactional implementation of new systems of evaluation—in other words, keep the same assumptions of the old system but with some new forms to fill out and some new deadlines to meet—then new beliefs about learning and expertise need to be developed and understood. Stakeholders will require time to develop a shared understanding of the following:

- The nature of expertise: Teaching is an extremely complex and challenging profession. Experts can utilize the right strategy, in the right way, and at the right time to obtain desired results. Expertise only develops through years of deliberate practice, which consists of focused goals, continuous feedback related to those goals, and thoughtful reflection that results in meaningful action.
- The distinction between growth and fixed mindsets: Effective teachers are made, not born. With effective effort, anyone can dramatically improve his or her capacity to engage in even the most complex tasks. Teachers who

consistently improve are those who seek out challenges, embrace obstacles as learning opportunities, and have a voracious appetite for feedback.

- The distinction between a performance environment and a learning environment: Beliefs and actions associated with organizations focused exclusively on summative outcome measures are very different from organizations focused on getting consistently better. In a learning environment, mistakes are processed as an essential component of the learning process. In a learning environment, questions are viewed as a sign of strength rather than weakness.

- The potential of collegiality and collaboration: Experts spend a significant amount of time watching others engage in their craft, talking with others about the strategies they use, and seeking out individuals who can challenge and support them to improve their practice.

- The distinction between internal and external locus of control: Individuals with an internal locus of control understand that all change starts from within. If you expect different results, then you need to engage in different behaviors. External attribution that results in avoiding, blaming, or complaining about colleagues or students will not change results. Individuals with an internal locus of control are purposeful, aware, and responsive to the need to change their own strategies in order to be more effective.

Responsive Implementation of Transformational Change

If members of the school community are to implement a balanced system of evaluation, supervision, and reflection, it will require patience. The old ways of thinking about what evaluation is, how comprehensive teaching frameworks are used, and improvement as a liability cannot be addressed through a memo of understanding. Recalibration of such a deeply entrenched system requires focused effort and patience. Leadership will need to intentionally and strategically balance evaluation, supervision, and reflection by

- Emphasizing growth as a vital process and not evaluation as an event. Everyone is on a path toward expertise.

- Building awareness and understanding of the components of the comprehensive framework for effective teaching. The framework must be used formatively by teachers and not just summatively by evaluators.
- Using a concept-attainment teaching model when implementing a balanced system. Collaboratively read and synthesize articles that define key concepts, and articulate examples and nonexamples of the shared beliefs described in this book.
- Starting small with relatively low stakes to build shared understandings of key concepts and shared skill sets in implementing new protocols.
- Ensuring that everyone who uses the comprehensive framework for effective teaching understands the distinction between formative and summative feedback. This includes both how to deliver and receive that feedback.
- Considering the augmentation of an evaluation framework with a list of specific, discrete instructional skills and strategies that can be used for formative—rather than summative—feedback.
- Working to create positive norms around the use of protocols that may have been seen as punitive in the past. Even the strongest teachers derive tremendous benefits from collaborative and reflective protocols. In the past, many of the practices described in this framework were solely used to support struggling teachers. If these practices are perceived as a liability rather than an opportunity for teachers, then they need to be renormed.
- Piloting these protocols with the strongest teachers, which communicates a clear message that the protocols described in this balanced framework are strength based, not liability based.
- Using a gradual release of responsibility when implementing a balanced system. Collaboratively learn and practice protocols described in this book. Engage each protocol using low-stakes examples with groups of learners. For example, rather than jumping into instructional rounds, collaboratively watch short video clips of teachers who are not part of your own school community. This allows for the development of skills in using protocols without alienating colleagues—or the processes—while engaged in the learning curve of new protocols.

Through our framework for reflective teaching (described in Chapter 4), we've articulated a process to support teachers' efforts to be more purposeful, aware, and responsive to learners' needs. We've intentionally echoed these three components in these guidelines for implementing transformational change. Teachers need to be purposeful, aware, and responsive to create classrooms that best support each child's growth. Leaders need to be purposeful, aware, and responsive to mindfully implement protocols that best support each teacher's growth. The protocols on the pages that follow can be used to support a balanced approach to evaluation, supervision, and reflection that makes teachers better.

Appendix A

Protocols to Support Systems of Valid, Reliable Evaluation

The purpose of evaluation is to ensure competent teaching in every classroom through a valid, reliable ratings process. Successful evaluation systems can be developed when administrators are consistent in their expectations and processes, communicate clearly with teachers and fellow administrators, and use collaborative problem solving with other administrators when issues arise.

Balancing the needs of reflective practice, supervision, and evaluation can be a delicate process. Too much of one and not the others leads to a system that either lacks accountability or can be overbearing and limit teachers' growth potential. The tools and protocols in this appendix give evaluators the structure that can produce dramatic results within their school. Although each has a slightly different purpose, these "evaluation protocols" share one commonality: they are designed to help administrators improve the validity and reliability of their evaluations. We advise exploring two or three very specific teaching strategies for each teacher, focusing on those that will be most beneficial. Concentrating on a small number of specific skills makes the evaluation process more manageable, which in turn can be motivating, energizing, and ultimately more effective.

The protocols presented here are ideal for generating high-quality feedback and ensuring the evaluation system is fair, valid, and reliable. These tools help to (1) improve the consistency of the process, (2) improve the quality of feedback, (3) allow for multiple perspectives, and (4) improve communication across multiple levels of the organization. In the next paragraphs we briefly describe each protocol and its purpose.

Culture Check Survey

All components of a balanced evaluation system rely on having a high level of relational trust and credibility. Ensuring that leaders are nurturing this type of environment is essential for success. The Culture Check Survey enables school leaders to gather data about the current level of trust and credibility. It can be used to identify areas that should be addressed to improve those foundational components. (See p. 170.)

Establishing and Maintaining Interrater Reliability Among Evaluators

Having a common districtwide vision for high-quality teaching and learning is essential when creating a reliable and consistent supervision and evaluation process. Ensuring that evaluators are consistent in their expectations and feedback is vital to success. Watching videos of teaching and having group discussions about observations, expectations, and generating potential feedback can establish and maintain a common vision of teaching and learning. (See p. 172.)

Clinical Observation

Clinical observations allow teachers and evaluators to engage in focused conversations about teaching and learning both before and after an evaluator has observed an entire lesson. Pre-conferencing helps to provide evaluators an opportunity to fully understand what has occurred, is occurring, and will occur during the classroom visit. The classroom observation allows evaluators an extended opportunity to see the teachers in action. The post-conference allows teachers and evaluators an opportunity to engage in collaborative (or directive, if necessary) dialogue to help teachers understand their status across various criteria. (See p. 174.)

Evaluators' Collegial Fishbowl

The Collegial Fishbowl gives supervisors an opportunity to gain a deeper understanding of a specific challenge related to supporting a teacher's professional growth by listening and responding to questions from colleagues. Evaluators are able to pool their collective knowledge to create better solutions. This protocol also ensures that instructional practices are aligned across the district and promotes interrater consistency through conversations that build a common language and vision. (See p. 176.)

Establishing and Maintaining Interrater Reliability Across Faculty

Having a common vision for teaching and learning within the teaching staff is important to unite staff toward the same goal. Teachers need opportunities to view and discuss what good teaching looks like as related to evaluation criteria. Watching videos of teaching and having group discussions about observations, expectations, and identifying potential resources and in-house experts can help to establish and maintain a common vision. (See p. 178.)

Written Reflection and Face-to-Face Dialogue Between Teacher and Evaluator

Written reflections allow participants to synthesize and create meaning from their experience. This protocol allows teachers to focus on selected aspects of their teaching and to improve their teaching through increased awareness and implementation of new or previously abandoned strategies. Written reflections enhance learning, clarify meanings, and lead to ownership and commitment to change. Combining written reflections with face-to-face dialogue creates a powerful experience that can lead to focused discussions about specific needs and next steps for improvement. (See p. 180.)

Timely, Specific Judgmental Feedback

Giving teachers timely, specific judgmental feedback gives them a clear understanding of their current performance. All feedback should be developed using the district's comprehensive teaching framework as a guide for the specific language and criteria. This approach helps to promote regular use of the framework for both teachers and evaluators and affirms common language and expectations. (See p. 182.)

Multiple Perspectives

Multiple perspectives should be considered to ensure teachers are being given unbiased performance feedback and are being evaluated reliably. This protocol ensures accurate feedback and ratings are being generated across the building or district. Also, this protocol can improve alignment of expectations across the district for both administrators and teachers. (See p. 184.)

Evaluative Classroom Walkthrough

Classroom walkthroughs can be used to gather information about the culture, climate, and instructional practices of teachers within the building or district. Making brief (3- to 10-minute) visits to classrooms can help observers gain a great deal of information about the current status of building priorities and initiatives. Walkthroughs are really a two-part process: Part 1 is the actual classroom visit, and Part 2 is the communication that takes place afterward. Evaluative walkthroughs allow administrators to be more visible and accessible for both staff and students. Although the primary motivation for walkthroughs is to gain information to make better decisions regarding professional development and instructional focus, the ancillary effect of visibility and the potential for relationship building can be just as profound. Ideally the classroom walkthrough is followed by either a face-to-face meeting or an e-mail that poses a question to help teachers reflect on the purposefulness, awareness, and responsiveness of their teaching. Walkthroughs should not be viewed as a simple checklist of present or absent teacher behaviors or teaching strategies. (See p. 185.)

Data Collection for Teacher Evaluation

Validity and reliability of teacher evaluation should be a primary concern of every teacher evaluator. This protocol provides a tool for evaluators to determine how they will collect data for each of the evaluation criteria that have been established by the school district and its teaching framework. It ensures that evaluators are using consistent data-collection processes and that multiple pieces of data are being considered when making evaluative judgments. It can be customized to include points of emphasis within schools, such as engagement, differentiation, or personalized learning. Sharing the information with teachers helps to build transparency in the evaluation process. (See p. 187.)

Celebrating Success and Effort

It is important to celebrate the wins we encounter on our journey toward expertise. Celebrating can help to sustain success, boost morale, motivate staff, and build a positive work atmosphere. It is important not only to celebrate the successes for reaching a certain test score or achievement level but also to recognize others for sustained efforts that showcased their perseverance or their willingness to attempt something new. This balance of rewarding achievement and effort helps create a growth mindset within the organization. (See p. 189.)

Culture Check Survey

PURPOSE: Enables school leaders to gather data about the current level of trust and credibility within their school. This survey can be used to identify areas that should be addressed to improve relational trust and credibility.

PROCESS/PRACTICE:

1. Issue a survey to staff asking them to respond to specific statements about their experience with the school's system of teacher supervision and evaluation. Allow staff to complete the survey anonymously. Some sample survey statements have been provided.
2. Analyze the results and identify one or two specific areas to target for improvement.
3. Create an action plan to improve the target areas.

Potential sample survey statements:

This survey is being given to gauge the amount of trust and credibility within the school regarding the teacher evaluation system. Please respond to the following statements as they relate to your experience at this school.

1. The district uses a comprehensive teaching framework to determine teacher ratings.

   a. Strongly disagree   b. Disagree   c. Agree   d. Strongly agree

2. Administrators focus on gathering quality data, not just a quantity of data.

   a. Strongly disagree   b. Disagree   c. Agree   d. Strongly agree

3. Administrators provide timely and accurate judgmental feedback about my performance.

   a. Strongly disagree   b. Disagree   c. Agree   d. Strongly agree

4. Teachers are actively involved in the data collection for the evaluation process.

   a. Strongly disagree   b. Disagree   c. Agree   d. Strongly agree

5. Different administrators produce accurate, consistent ratings for all evaluations.

   a. Strongly disagree   b. Disagree   c. Agree   d. Strongly agree

6. I feel that my perspectives are valued by the administration regarding the evaluation process.

   a. Strongly disagree   b. Disagree   c. Agree   d. Strongly agree

7. Administrators ask "what is possible" versus merely pointing out what is wrong.

   a. Strongly disagree   b. Disagree   c. Agree   d. Strongly agree

8. I feel that my administrator cares about me as a person.

   a. Strongly disagree   b. Disagree   c. Agree   d. Strongly agree

9. I trust the judgment of my administrator regarding the evaluation process.

   a. Strongly disagree   b. Disagree   c. Agree   d. Strongly agree

10. Teachers use the teaching framework for more than just an end-of-the-year evaluation.

    a. Strongly disagree   b. Disagree   c. Agree   d. Strongly agree

11. Teachers are involved in continuous data collection for the purpose of improving their daily instruction.

    a. Strongly disagree   b. Disagree   c. Agree   d. Strongly agree

12. Teachers are allowed to make mistakes, and questions are encouraged.

    a. Strongly disagree   b. Disagree   c. Agree   d. Strongly agree

13. Teachers receive frequent, high-quality, developmental feedback from a variety of sources that support teacher growth.

    a. Strongly disagree   b. Disagree   c. Agree   d. Strongly agree

PAYOFF: Leaders have a more accurate assessment of how teachers perceive the current teacher evaluation and supervision system.

Establishing and Maintaining Interrater Reliability Among Evaluators

PURPOSE: To ensure that more reliable and accurate feedback and ratings are being generated across the district. Also, this protocol helps to align expectations among all evaluators.

PROCESS/PRACTICE:

1. Evaluators/instructional coaches review the district's teaching framework.
2. A facilitator shows a short video (5–15 minutes) of a classroom teacher teaching.
   a. If possible, obtain videos of teachers within the district, which helps to add credibility to the conversations. Initially it may be difficult to do so because people may feel uncomfortable discussing people they know in a group setting. Videos that are available online are good starting points.
   b. Facilitators may also give a focal point for the viewing, such as transitions, pace, student management, effective questioning, etc.
3. Participants take notes on what they observe during the video. Observers should approach this the same way they would approach a normal walkthrough.
4. Participants are given three to five minutes to organize and analyze their notes.
5. A facilitator then leads a discussion about the video and participants' observations.
   a. If the group consists of more than eight people, having initial small-group discussions ensures that all participants can share their experience and ask questions.

   b. Recommendation: A whole-group share-out to summarize
      the observations will ensure that all participants have the
      same expectations.
6. Discussion questions include the following:
   a. What portions of the video were most relevant?
   b. What rubric descriptors were aligned to specific teacher and
      student behaviors?
   c. How would you rate this teaching in _____? (Select the
      appropriate domains and indicators from the comprehensive
      framework.)
   d. The facilitator asks each participant to report his or her score.
   e. Discrepancies in scores are discussed until consensus as to the accu-
      rate score is reached.
   f. The accurate score is shared

PAYOFF: Evaluators/create/maintain a common vision of expectations for quality within the district. Teachers receive more valid ratings from evaluators, and
evaluators increase their level of interrater reliability.

Clinical Observation

PURPOSE: Clinical observations give teachers and evaluators an opportunity to engage in focused conversations about teaching and learning.

PROCESS/PRACTICE:

Robert Goldhammer (1969) developed a five-phase process of clinical supervision that was designed to involve teachers and evaluators in a reflective dialogue. The process includes a pre-observation conference, a classroom observation, analysis of the data collected, a conference, and a post-conference analysis.

1. **Pre-observation Conference:** Teacher and evaluator meet to clarify the following (ideally, the teacher brings written responses to the pre-observation):

    a. What is being taught during the lesson? What was taught before this point? Is this new material, or are students deepening their knowledge?

    b. How is it being taught? What instructional strategies are being used?

    c. What is the intended outcome?

    d. How will students be assessed?

    e. Are there special circumstances for the lesson or students that I should be aware of?

    f. What strategies would you like me to focus my efforts on? What do you want your feedback to be focused on?

2. **Classroom Observation:** The evaluator observes the teacher and records information and evidence, including the following:

    a. Teacher and student interaction during the lesson

    b. Condition and status of the classroom environment

    c. Student behavior and engagement

    d. Sample work

3. **Analysis:** The evaluator analyzes the data collected and determines two or three specific points to discuss with the teacher. Guiding questions for the analysis include the following:
   a. Are there any patterns evident in the data?
   b. Were there any turning points doing the lesson?
   c. What should be the focus of the dialogue during the conference with the teacher?
   d. What discussion point can have the biggest impact on improving teacher practice?

4. **Conference:** The teacher and the evaluator meet to engage in a reflective dialogue about the lesson. Potential questions* to consider include the following:
   a. What was the purpose of the lesson? (purpose)
   b. What was the high point of the lesson? (awareness)
   c. What was the low point of the lesson? (awareness)
   d. What would you do differently next time? (responsiveness)

5. **Post-Conference Analysis:** The supervisor evaluates the actions taken in the previous steps to determine if the teacher is making appropriate growth.

PAYOFF: Evaluators can engage in a structured process to gather data about each teachers classroom performance. This ensures focused data collection that supports a valid rating through a reliable process. Teachers can engage in a structured process to receive judgmental and developmental feedback about their performance. This supports teachers' efforts to set goals in, and be reflective upon, the most valid areas of need.

* For additional reflective prompts, see the PAR framework on pages 234–235.

Evaluators' Collegial Fishbowl

PURPOSE: The Collegial Fishbowl gives evaluators an opportunity to gain a deeper understanding of a specific challenge they are facing by listening and responding to questions from colleagues.

PROCESS/PRACTICE:

1. In preparation, evaluators should bring a short, written reflection about a challenge they are facing as related to supervision or evaluation. (See prompt 4a below.)

2. Place supervisors in groups of four or five. Arrange three or four chairs in a semicircle and put another chair in front of the semicircle (this chair represents the "fishbowl").

3. Invite one evaluator who is interested in addressing an evaluation-related challenge to sit in the fishbowl. This person will do most of the talking. People sitting outside the fishbowl should focus on listening intently and asking thoughtful questions, but they should not dominate any aspect of the conversation.

4. Describing the Case

   a. The person in the fishbowl has three to five minutes to respond to the following prompt with as much detail as possible:

      • *Tell us about a specific teacher or a specific component of our system of supervision and evaluation that is presenting a challenge for you. As specifically as possible, what is the challenge, what have you done to address the challenge, and what next steps are you considering?*

5. Questions and Dialogue

   a. Clarification: Colleagues sitting in the semicircle have 5 minutes to ask *clarifying questions*. The purpose of clarifying questions is to clarify the relevant details for all participants, but especially for the individual in the fishbowl.

   b. Probing: Colleagues have 10 minutes to ask *probing questions*. The purpose of probing questions *is not to give advice* but to push the individual in the fishbowl to new levels of reflection about the situation.

c. Suggestions: Finally, the person in the fishbowl may ask others if they are aware of or have had a related experience and ask them to give suggestions about strategies or resources.

6. Summarizing the Case and Next Steps

a. The person in the fishbowl responds to this prompt: *Based on your questions and my reflection,*

- *The challenge I'm facing is . . . .*
- *Specific steps I will take to address this challenge include . . . .*

b. The individuals outside the fishbowl respond to this prompt: *This discussion has given me the opportunity to think more clearly or critically about how I . . . .*

c. After one round, participants take one to three minutes to write notes about their next steps, affirmations, or concerns.

7. The process continues with a new person in the fishbowl.

Stems for Questions

a. Clarification:

- *Could you share an example of . . . ?*
- *Could you say a little more about . . . ?*
- *Are you saying . . . ?*
- *Does that mean . . . ?*

b. Probing:

- *Why did you . . . ?*
- *How do you know . . . ?*
- *What might happen if . . . ?*
- *What other strategies/approaches might . . . ?*

c. Suggestions to the person in the fishbowl (if requested):

- *Something you might consider trying is . . . .*
- *Sometimes it's helpful to . . . .*
- *A couple of things to keep in mind are . . . .*

PAYOFF: Evaluators have an opportunity to share their concerns, suggestions, and experiences with peers, which leads to group learning and collaboration and helps to develop the culture of the district as a learning organization. This process also aligns instructional practices and resources across the district, improving the validity and reliability of the process.

Establishing and Maintaining
Interrater Reliability Across Faculty

PURPOSE: To create a common vision for teaching and learning, define expectations for quality. and calibrate teachers' perceptions of various levels of quality. (Note. This supports teachers efforts to reflect on their rating more accurately. It is not to prepare teachers to evaluate other teachers.)

PROCESS/PRACTICE:

1. Teachers review the district's comprehensive teaching framework.
2. A facilitator shows a short video (5–15 minutes) of a classroom teacher teaching.
   a. The video should be of high-quality teaching of a teacher from outside the district.
   b. Teachers are given a focal point for the viewing, such as transitions, pace, student management, effective questioning, etc.
3. Participants take notes on what they observe during the video.
4. Participants are given three to five minutes to organize and analyze their notes.
5. A facilitator then leads a discussion about the video and participants' observations.
   a. If the group consists of more than eight people, having initial small-group discussions ensures that all participants will have an opportunity to share their experience and ask questions.
   b. Recommendation: A whole-group share-out to summarize the observations will ensure that all participants have the same expectations.

6. Discussion questions include the following:
    a. What portions of the video were more relevant?
    b. What rubric descriptors were aligned to specific teacher and student behaviors?
    c. How would you rate this teaching in _____? (Select the appropriate domains and indicators from the comprehensive framework.)
7. The facilitator asks each participant to report his or her score.
8. The accurate score is shared.
9. Discrepancies in scores are discussed through the facilitator to ensure consensus as to why that is the valid score.

PAYOFF: Teachers and coaches create/maintain a common vision of expectations for quality within the district. Teachers are better able to reliably calibrate their perceptions of their own teaching relative to expectations for quality within the district.

Written Reflection and Face-to-Face Dialogue Between Teacher and Evaluator

PURPOSE: Written reflections allow participants to synthesize and create meaning from their experience while enhancing learning. This process also facilitates ownership and commitment to change.

PROCESS/PRACTICE:

1. Teachers should review the district's selected teaching framework to help guide their thought process.
2. This protocol should be used in conjunction with the Clinical Observation protocol.
3. The teacher prepares written answers to questions regarding a recent lesson that was taught. (See below for suggested questions.)
4. The teacher and the evaluator meet to discuss the written reflection.
5. The evaluator reviews the written responses and engages in a conversation about the reflection with the intent of specifying one or two specific areas of improvement and a plan for follow-up.

Guiding Questions for Post-Lesson Reflection

1. What was the purpose of the lesson? (purpose)
2. What was the high point of the lesson? (awareness)
3. What was the low point of the lesson? (awareness)
4. What new or different strategies will you implement based on your reflection? (responsiveness)
5. What new questions about your teaching have emerged after reflecting on this lesson? (responsiveness)
6. What would you do differently next time you teach this lesson? (responsiveness)

Face-to-Face Meeting

1. Refer to the Guiding Questions to start the dialogue.
2. The evaluator engages the teacher in a dialogue to offer support and to facilitate the learning process for *both* individuals.
3. Use the following question stems for clarification, paraphrasing, and suggestions.
   a. Clarification:
      - *Could you share an example of . . . ?*
      - *Could you say a little more about . . . ?*
      - *Are you saying . . . ?*
      - *Does that mean . . . ?*
   b. Paraphrasing:
      - *In other words, ...*
      - *You are saying . . . .*
      - *You are feeling . . . .*
      - *Your opinion is . . . .*
   c. Suggestions to the teacher:
      - *Something you might consider trying . . . .*
      - *Sometimes it's helpful if . . . .*
      - *A couple of things to keep in mind . . . .*

PAYOFF: Teachers have a systematic, reliable way to reflect on their improvement efforts. Teachers take the time to reflect about specific teaching strategies and develop new questions about their teaching. This process also aids goal setting and provides accountability for both teachers and evaluators.

Timely, Specific Judgmental Feedback

PURPOSE: To help teachers and supervisors clarify an individual's standing relative to specific criteria for quality.

PROCESS/PRACTICE:

1. Observation/data collection: The evaluator observes the teacher and records information and evidence, including the following:
   a. Teacher and student comments and interaction during the lesson.
   b. Condition and status of room.
   c. Student behavior and engagement.
   d. Sample work.
2. Analysis: The evaluator analyzes the data collected and determines one or two specific points to focus on, using the following questions to guide the analysis:
   a. Are there any patterns evident in the data?
   b. Were there any turning points in the lesson?
   c. What should be the focus of the dialogue during the conference with the teacher?
   d. What discussion point can have the biggest impact on improving teacher practice?
3. Use the district's comprehensive teaching framework to generate feedback.
   a. Rubric descriptors in comprehensive frameworks for effective practice (see examples in chart) provide the criteria upon which all judgmental feedback should be based.
   b. Communicate the feedback to the teacher within 48 hours of the data collection.

Example Rubric Descriptors for Judgmental Feedback			
	Danielson	**Stronge**	**Marzano**
Learning Target	Ms. Smith clearly stated what the students will be learning at the beginning of the lesson.	Ms. Smith reinforced the learning goal consistently throughout the lesson, referencing it at least 3 times.	Ms. Smith referred 3 times during the lesson to the learning goal that was posted on the whiteboard.
Questioning	Ms. Smith used a variety of questions to challenge students and promoted higher-level thinking during the discussion.	Ms. Smith only used higher levels of questioning when leading the discussion. At least 5 students were unable to participate in the discussion because they did not understand the questions.	Ms. Smith asked students to explain how the activity helped them to understand the content better by using an analogy to examine similarities and differences.
Assessment	Ms. Smith did no monitoring of student learning. She gave no feedback to students.	Ms. Smith used pre-assessment data to guide instructional planning and to differentiate her instruction.	Ms. Smith used formative data to chart the progress of individual students toward the learning objective.
Responsiveness	Ms. Smith attempted to modify the lesson when trying to respond to student questions but was unsuccessful in her attempts.	Ms. Smith did not differentiate her instruction for students who needed remediation.	Ms. Smith did not allow enough time to adequately respond to students' questions about the upcoming assignment.

PAYOFF: Evaluators clearly communicate how teachers are currently performing in relation to the district's teaching framework. Expectations are explicitly linked to the teaching framework, thus improving the validity and reliability of the evaluation process.

Multiple Perspectives

PURPOSE: To ensure teachers are being given unbiased performance feedback and evaluations.

PROCESS/PRACTICE:

1. The primary evaluator contacts a secondary evaluator and asks that individual to observe the teacher.
2. The primary evaluator does not share his or her current perceptions or ratings.
3. The primary evaluator may give the new evaluator two to three focal points for the observation.
4. The secondary evaluator conducts one or more observations (either formal or informal) independent of the original evaluator.
5. The secondary evaluator discusses the observations with the teacher.
6. Evaluators discuss their findings after the secondary evaluator has completed observations.
   a. Evaluators should discuss the following:
      • Observed strengths
      • Specific observed areas for growth
   b. Evaluators should identify two to three focal points for the teacher's targeted growth.
7. The original evaluator meets with the teacher to do the following:
   a. Discuss the outcome of multiple observations.
   b. Review the district's teaching framework to discuss areas of need.
   c. Agree on two to three focal points for targeted growth.
   d. Develop an action plan to address targeted growth areas.
   e. Set the time for the next follow-up conversation.

PAYOFF: Teachers receive feedback from multiple evaluators, thus helping to ensure that the ratings are valid and reliable. The feedback is used in conjunction with the district's preferred teaching framework to set specific improvement goals.

Evaluative Classroom Walkthrough

PURPOSE: To help evaluators learn about current strengths and weaknesses of individual staff members and of the collective school staff.

PROCESS/PRACTICE:

1. Enter the classroom to observe a teacher while teaching, for the purpose of gathering information in the following areas:

   a. What is being taught? (curriculum)

   b. How is it being taught? (instructional strategies)

   c. How are students responding? (student engagement)

   d. How are students behaving? (student behavior)

   e. What is the classroom environment? (appearance of classroom, items posted within classroom, use of resources)

2. When possible, and if it isn't a distraction—

   a. Ask students questions:

   - Why are you learning this?

   - What are you learning today?

   - How does this connect to what you learned yesterday?

   - What will you do with this? What is the next step?

   - How will you be assessed on this information?

   b. Review questions from exams or handouts.

3. Keep track of observations either in writing or an electronic format.

4. Develop a reflective question or coaching point to discuss with the teacher either face-to-face or via e-mail. Limit the focus to the one question or coaching point that will have the most impact.

5. Have either a brief discussion or pose the reflective question in an e-mail to the teacher, being sure to identify the time, class, and context of the question.

   a. Today in your classroom, I saw _____. (see protocol on timely, specific, judgmental feedback)

        b. How did this strategy support the purpose of the lesson?

        c. Did students respond as you expected they would? Explain.

        d. What are the next steps in student learning, and how will you support their learning needs?

6. Establish clear expectations for staff as to whether they are to respond to e-mails or whether responses are optional.

7. Track data throughout the building to help inform decisions on building priorities, initiatives, and professional development.

PAYOFF: Evaluators are able to collect valid data across the entire school year and provide timely, accurate, judgmental feedback. Dialogue with teachers can be used as a reflective and collaborative process.

Data Collection for Teacher Evaluation

PURPOSE: To ensure that multiple data points and perspectives are considered when generating judgmental feedback and decisions about teacher performance.

PROCESS/PRACTICE:

1. Evaluators should determine what data-collection techniques will be used to develop a teacher rating. The team should consult the district's comprehensive teaching framework to determine the main components that will be used for teacher evaluation.
2. Once the main components of the evaluation criteria have been reviewed, the team should then discuss how data will be gathered to create a rating for each main component. This can be done using a chart similar to the one included in this protocol.
3. Evaluators should list all of the evaluation criteria that will be considered during the evaluation process. Most frameworks will include variations of the following: (1) instructional planning, (2) classroom environment, (3) instructional delivery, (4) assessment, and (5) professional responsibilities. A generic sample is included here.
    a. Each main component is listed in the first column. Other components that are being emphasized within schools may be included, such as engagement, differentiation, or personalized learning. This allows evaluators to create common expectations for all teachers and helps to highlight points of emphasis for teachers.
    b. The column headings in the table show potential data-collection sources that could be used for each main component. Teams should list all of the data-collection techniques that are used within their organizations.
4. Evaluators should place a checkmark in each box that will be used by the team to gather data about teacher performance. This process should include discussion that ensures that all evaluators are following the same processes and data-collection techniques. Evaluators should come to a consensus on how data will be collected and on the evaluation criteria.

Evaluation Criteria	Classroom Observation	Teacher Goal Setting	Documents/Artifacts	Survey Data	Portfolio	Self-Evaluation	Student Achievement Data	Student Work Samples
Instructional Planning								
Classroom Environment								
Instructional Delivery								
Assessment								
Professional Responsibilities								
Engagement								
Differentiation								
Personalizing Learning								

5. It is recommended that multiple administrators evaluate each teacher to generate reliable ratings.
6. Also recommended is sharing the final consensus as to how artifacts align to specific criteria with teachers to build transparency into the evaluation process.

PAYOFF: Administrators develop a consistent data-collection process that ensures that multiple pieces of data are being considered when making evaluative judgments. This protocol helps to improve reliability of the evaluation process.

Celebrating Success and Effort

PURPOSE: To recognize the achievements of individuals and of the organization. Celebrating success motivates employees, relieves stress, and helps to sustain individual and organizational improvement efforts.

PROCESS/PRACTICE:

1. Leaders should create various recognition opportunities for individuals that connect individual efforts to the purpose, vision, and initiatives of the school.
2. Be sensitive to individual needs. Some staff seek public recognition; others abhor it. Determine what is right for each individual on the staff.
3. When recognizing individuals or groups, don't just reward those that get great results. Also reward those who either persevered through a difficult task or tried something new. Doing so will help to foster a growth mindset within the organization and put the focus on the process instead of just the result.
4. Here are some potential ways to celebrate success:
   a. Send staff handwritten thank-you notes.
   b. Give staff a few minutes at the start of a meeting to write thank-you notes to each other. Provide a blank thank-you card for the staff to complete.
   c. Recognize efforts in your weekly staff letter.
   d. Start a Teacher of the Month award. Ask for nominations from the staff and let the staff vote anonymously. The winner gets preferred parking for the month.
   e. At the start of a meeting, in small groups, have staff share individual stories of their recent personal successes within their classroom. This activity helps teachers to remember why they are teachers, and it serves as a way to share successful strategies with their colleagues.
   f. Plan a surprise achievement celebration for an employee or group of employees.
   g. Invite and recognize the efforts of support staff during teacher meetings.

h. Pass along positive comments or e-mails from parents to staff during meetings.

i. Send an e-mail to staff thanking them for their efforts on a recent accomplishment.

j. Start a "purposeful theme" or award for staff. For example, in his book *The Last Lecture*, Randy Pausch (2008) describes how he started a "First Penguin Award" that was given to students who dared to do something great. The award is aptly named, as it takes a brave penguin to be the first to jump into the water because of unseen dangers that may be lurking below the surface. The award focuses on efforts and process rather than just the end result (process over product). Staff could be given small penguin pins to attach to their staff ID, as a constant reminder to dare to be great. This is a great way to foster the growth mindset within your staff. Be creative and find a theme that fits the organization.

PAYOFF: Staff enjoy coming to work and become more dedicated and committed to the organization. Positive reinforcement can create a more persistent, resilient, and successful staff.

Appendix B

Protocols to Support Systems of Empowering, Focused Supervision

Supervision plays a critical role in empowering teachers to attain focused goals. Some of this work is done by helping teachers gain a better understanding of what is occurring in the classroom by giving them unbiased feedback, asking reflective questions, and giving them another perspective to consider. In these protocols, the term *observer* includes supervisors, administrators, instructional coaches, or peers. When observers can effectively play the role of "critical friend," they can accelerate teachers' improvement. The goal should be to help teachers become as purposeful, aware, and responsive as possible by developing their reflective skills and by providing the resources, structure, and support necessary.

The tools and protocols in this appendix give observers a structure that can produce dramatic results in the classroom. Although each has a slightly different purpose, each of these "supervisory protocols" share one commonality: they are designed to give participants a better understanding of the current condition and context of a teacher's performance. Each protocol also creates opportunities for dialogue that can improve performance. The key to improvement is focusing on two or three very specific teaching strategies. Concentrating on a small number of specific strategies makes the supervision process more manageable, which in turn is more motivating, energizing, and ultimately more effective for teachers and observers.

The protocols presented here can help observers facilitate teacher improvement by enhancing their ability to be reflective and by promoting deliberate practice. These protocols are ideal for helping teachers achieve goals for professional growth by generating formative feedback. These tools provide observers the structure to (1) better understand the teacher's current needs, (2) construct formative feedback, and (3) more effectively deliver feedback. In the next paragraphs we briefly describe each protocol and its purpose.

Meaningful Goal Setting

By ensuring that goals are based on data related to student learning and teacher practice, teachers can identify areas of need most likely to improve their professional practice. Individuals on a path toward expertise establish "stretch goals" in areas outside their comfort zone. Those who plateau tend to set goals that are easily obtained in an area where they already are confident in their skills and abilities.

Sharing learnings and questions with peers leads to collaboration and development of a culture that identifies the school as a learning organization. This process also aligns instructional practices and resources across the school. (See p. 195.)

Plan-Do-Study-Act Instructional Coaching Process

Plan-Do-Study-Act (PDSA) is a continuous improvement method that was made popular by Dr. W. Edwards Demming, an American engineer, professor, and management consultant who has been given credit for helping Japan's economic success following World War II. In this adaptation of PDSA, teachers and observers collaborate to select an instructional strategy to target for improvement. This protocol helps to align protocols from this book that are helpful in each stage of PDSA. (See p. 197.)

The Seven Coaching Hats

Observers can use the Seven Coaching Hats protocol to help define their current role when talking with teachers. This protocol gives observers some guidance
on the different roles they play and some potential questions or next steps. (See p. 199.)

Formative Classroom Walkthrough

Formative classroom walkthroughs can be used to give developmental feedback to teachers on a limited number of specific teaching practices. They differ from evaluative classroom walkthroughs because they emphasize delivering formative feedback to the teacher about a specific instructional strategy. After the walkthrough, the observer and the teacher should discuss what was observed and collaborate on next steps. Using classroom walkthroughs in a formative manner can stimulate teacher growth by offering timely feedback that is directly related to the teacher's current improvement efforts. (See p. 200.)

There are numerous protocols available that detail processes for completing classroom walkthroughs. Carolyn Downey's *The Three-Minute Classroom Walk-Through* (Downey, Steffy, English, Frase, & Poston, 2004) and Kim Marshall's *Rethinking Teacher Supervision and Evaluation* (2009) offer two different perspectives.

Active Listening

Active listening can be used to help observers become better listeners and to improve communication. Active listening is about the willingness and ability to understand another person's point of view. Empathy is a key component of active listening. When active listening is done well, individuals can communicate at a deeper level, which helps to correctly identify core issues as well as potential solutions. Active listening also builds the learning culture of the school and improves trust by allowing people the opportunity to be truly heard. (See p. 202.)

Motivational Interviewing

Motivational interviewing can help teachers and observers have a collaborative conversation that increases a teacher's motivation and commitment to change. This protocol also helps observers understand where teachers are on the change continuum. The protocol is adapted from the work of Linda Sobell, Mark Sobell, and Jim Braastad. (See p. 204.)

Timely, Specific Developmental Feedback

Timely, specific developmental feedback supports teachers in their efforts to improve their daily professional practice and solve issues and to help align expectations across the school. When developmental feedback is tied directly to specific improvement goals and to the district's comprehensive teaching framework, growth opportunities are maximized because teachers have the opportunity to continuously improve their craft and meet their full potential. Observers open up lines of communication, develop a common language, standardize expectations, and develop relationships that improve overall school performance and culture. (See p. 207.)

Receiving Feedback

Feedback involves two groups: feedback givers and feedback receivers. Typically, a great deal of emphasis is placed on developing the skills of individuals giving feedback. This protocol focuses on improving the skills of the receiver. If individuals are better able to receive, process, and implement feedback, they can increase their chance of improving. (See p. 209.)

Meaningful Goal Setting

PURPOSE: By ensuring that goals are based on data related to student learning and teacher practice, teachers can identify the areas of need most likely to improve their professional practice. Individuals on a path toward expertise establish goals in areas outside their comfort zone. Individuals who plateau tend to set goals that are easily obtained in an area where they are already confident in their skills and abilities. This protocol is based conceptually on work developed by Edwin Locke and Gary Latham (Locke, 1996; Locke & Latham, 1990).

PROCESS/PRACTICE:

1. Data should be used to identify a student learning goal. Then teachers should create a goal that links improvement in their professional practice to the student learning goal. Here is an example:

    a. Student Learning Goal: By the end of the 2016–2017 school year, 80 percent or more of my students will demonstrate proficiency in all writing standards as assessed through the departmental rubrics for narrative, informative, and argumentative writing.

    b. Professional Practice Goal: To increase the effectiveness of my writing instruction, I will implement the ongoing use of graphic organizers for prewriting activities and create opportunities for students to receive more formative feedback.

2. The teacher uses the prompts in the following table to develop a goal that connects student learning with professional practice.

Establishing Focused Improvement Goals	
Locke's Components of Effective Goal Setting	**Prompts**
Specificity of the goal—Specific goals focus efforts on the actionable components of a complex process.	*The goal is to:*
Challenge—The more difficult the goal, the more likely it will be obtained, given commitment to the goal and access to the knowledge, practice time, and resources necessary to achieve it.	*This goal will challenge me to strive toward my ideal classroom because:*
Commitment—A goal that is specific and challenging will require effort to be attained, making commitment to the goal crucial for success.	*I will demonstrate my commitment to develop the strategies required to obtain this goal by:*
Feedback—Feedback allows people to check and track their progress toward the goal. Feedback allows the learner to modify strategies in a manner that actually yields different results.	*I will obtain feedback on my progress toward this goal by:*
Task complexity—The more complex the goal, the more it will require (1) sufficient time to meet and (2) opportunities and resources to visualize, practice, and learn specific components of the strategies that are involved.	*Because of the complexity of the skills and strategies required to attain this goal I will need:*

3. Write the goal in the SMART format. SMART goals are specific, measurable, attainable, results oriented, and time bound.
   a. Example: By May 1, I will have incorporated the use of graphic organizers for prewriting activities for 90 percent of common assessments given to my students and will have given students opportunities to receive formative feedback on each of these assignments.
4. The observer should use the prompts and goals to facilitate discussion, feedback, and action plans for teacher support.

PAYOFF: Teachers create a specific goal linked to instructional practices and establish a plan that empowers them to achieve focused goals.

Plan-Do-Study-Act Instructional Coaching Process

PURPOSE: To give teachers and observers a process to plan and engage in focused efforts for growth.

PROCESS/PRACTICE: See chart.

	Teacher	Observer	Supporting Protocols
Plan	• Gather data on student achievement/perceptions. • Analyze data. • Consult comprehensive teaching framework. • Research strategies as needed. • Select strategy to focus on.	• Help analyze data. • Connect to teaching framework. • Create dissonance. • Support research efforts. • Narrow focus of potential strategies; suggest options.	• Teaching Inventory • Student Surveys • Motivational Interviewing • Self-analysis Framework Dig • Determining Focus: The Ideal Classroom • Active Listening • Meaningful Goal Setting • Defining the Issue Using the "On PAR Framework"

Do	• Attempt strategy.
	• Gather data.
	• Track outcomes.
	• Record what has been learned (positive and negative).
	• View others teaching.
	• Video-record own teaching for self-review.
	• Share information, resources with peers.
		• Support teacher as needed by
		  – Supplying resources/examples.
		  – Modeling.
		  – Coteaching.
		  – Observing to give formative feedback.
		  – Substituting for teachers so they can observe peers.
		• Create/facilitate peer sharing groups.
		• Discuss videos.
		• Connect to teaching framework.
		• Provide specific developmental feedback.
			• Instructional Rounds
			• Peer Sharing
			• Collegial Fishbowl
			• Defining the Issue Using the "On PAR Framework"
			• Reflective Peer Visit
			• Active Listening
			• Receiving Feedback
			• Timely, Specific Developmental Feedback
			• Formative Classroom Walkthrough
			• Video Analysis of Others' Teaching
			• Video Analysis of Own Teaching

continued

	Teacher	Observer	Supporting Protocols
Study	• Analyze data gathered in previous step. • Compare results to teaching framework. • Summarize learning in written reflection.	• Follow up with resources as needed. • Help analyze data. • Connect to teaching framework. • Review/discuss written reflection. • Provide specific developmental feedback.	• Structured Reflective Writing • Defining the Issue Using the "On PAR Framework" • Self-analysis Framework Dig

Act	• Record
	  – Key learnings.
	  – New questions.
	  – Next steps.
	• Commit to incorporating into daily practice.
	• Repeat process.
		• Confer/collaborate on new learnings/questions/next steps.
		• Monitor key learnings and new questions to locate trends for whole staff.
			• Structured Reflective Writing
			• Active Listening
			• Receiving Feedback
			• Timely, Specific Developmental Feedback
			• Defining the Issue Using the "On PAR Framework"

PAYOFF: Teachers and observers are empowered to utilize specific protocols that they believe will best focus their efforts to achieve improvement goals.

The Seven Coaching Hats

PURPOSE: To help observers identify which coaching role they are playing and how to become more effective within that role.

This protocol is based on the concepts presented by Robert Hargrove's *Masterful Coaching* (2008).

PROCESS/PRACTICE:

Observers take on many roles when coaching teachers. The following chart helps to distinguish seven different "hats" that coaches wear and some potential questions that can be used to guide dialogue between teachers and observers.

Coaching "Hat"	Potential Questions or Next Steps
1. Declaring new responsibilities	"What would you do differently if you had to hold all kids to high standards, you couldn't give grades, and kids could come and go as they pleased?"
2. Serving as thinking partner	"What do you think?" "I know you don't know the answer now, but if you did, what advice would you give yourself?"
3. Drawing others out	"I am curious to hear what you are thinking." "I think you are on to something; tell me more about that."
4. Reframing thinking and attitudes	"It sounds like you feel that the new reading program is limiting how you can teach. What are some things you still have control over in your classroom, and how might you focus on those practices?" "It sounds like you have an energetic group of students in that class. What are some ways you could harness that energy into some active learning?"
5. Teaching and advising	If someone wearing the teaching and advising hat has advice to share, it can be offered when relational trust and credibility have been established. The advice, however, must be thoughtful. Draw from a common value base, but give advice with quiet confidence that honors the intelligence and strengths of the people to whom it is offered.
6. Forwarding action	Coaching can create the conditions that lead an individual to say, "I can see the possibility, but what do I do next?" Here it is important to help the teacher focus on a new (or refine) an instructional strategy or a new approach to curriculum or assessment. Focus is essential to engage in the deliberate practice that results in growth.
7. Giving honest feedback	It is essential that the feedback be objective and based on a shared set of criteria for quality. Objective feedback that holds up a mirror to one's own practice can harness the capacity of a shared framework by creating parameters around what "better" looks like.

PAYOFF: Observers are given a tool to help define their "hat" and be more effective in their efforts to empower teachers to achieve improvement goals.

Formative Classroom Walkthrough

PURPOSE: To help provide teachers with timely feedback on a limited number of specific instructional strategies.

PROCESS/PRACTICE:

1. Enter the classroom to observe a teacher while teaching, for the purpose of gathering information on specific instructional strategies that have been previously identified. Ideally, the focus should be limited to one to three specific strategies.
2. (Complete this step only if it will yield relevant information.) When possible and if it isn't a distraction,
   a. Ask students questions:
      - Why are you learning this?
      - What are you learning today?
      - How does this connect to what you learned yesterday?
      - What will you do with this? What is the next step?
      - How will you be assessed on this information?
   b. Review questions from exams or handouts.
3. Keep track of your observations either in writing or an electronic format.
4. Connect the observations that have been made to the district's comprehensive teaching framework to create context.
5. Develop a reflective question or coaching point to discuss with the teacher either face-to-face or via e-mail. Limit the focus to one question or coaching point that will have the most impact. The question should be related to the instructional strategies that have been targeted for improvement. (See the PAR framework on pp. 234–235 for suggestions.)

6. Discuss the current progress with the teacher and offer the appropriate support needed, such as
   a. Supplying resources/examples to help clarify expectations and provide context.
   b. Modeling how the instructional strategies could be implemented.
   c. Coteaching with the teacher, using the targeted strategies.
   d. Observing again to provide formative feedback.
   e. Giving context of performance as it relates to the teaching framework.
   f. Creating opportunities for the teacher to
      • Discuss the specific instructional strategies with peers.
      • Observe peers using the specific teaching strategies.
      • View videos of the specific teaching strategies.
7. Establish clear expectations about next steps and potential follow-up that may be required.
8. Track data throughout the building to help inform decisions on building priorities, initiatives, and professional development.

PAYOFF: Teachers are given timely and specific developmental feedback on the specific instructional practices that have been targeted for improvement. This empowers teachers to focus their efforts to achieve improvement goals.

Active Listening

PURPOSE: To help teachers and obsevers become better listeners and to improve communication. Active listening is about the willingness and ability to understand the other person's point of view.

PROCESS/PRACTICE:

1. During the dialogue, pay close attention.
    a. Pay attention to both verbal and nonverbal communication. People communicate a great deal of information through their tone of voice, pace, facial expressions, and gestures.
2. Approach the dialogue with an open mind.
    a. It is important to withhold any type of judgments or criticisms until there is a complete understanding of the situation.
3. Paraphrase during the dialogue.
    a. Restate the message briefly to ensure that the receiver has correctly interpreted what has been said.
4. Clarify when necessary.
    a. Ask questions to get more information, clear up misunderstandings, and delve deeper into the dialogue. This encourages others to expand on their ideas and be more thoughtful and reflective in their responses. Use question stems such as these:
       *   *"Could you share an example of . . . ?"*
       *   *"I don't quite understand what you are saying. Could you repeat that?"*
5. Summarize key points.
    a. Restate key points during the dialogue. Briefly summarize your current understanding and ask your counterpart to do the same. Summarizing helps to clarify next steps and responsibilities for follow-up steps if necessary. Use prompts such as the following:
       *   *"Let me see if I understand this so far. . . ."*
       *   *"Here's what I have heard. . . . Have I missed anything?"*
       *   *"What you've said is important. . . ."*

6. Respond appropriately.

   a. Active listening is first about understanding the other person, then about being understood. When you have an understanding of the other's point of view, you can then share ideas, feelings, and suggestions. Prompts for responses include the following:

- *"Sometimes it's helpful if . . . ."*
- *"A couple of things to keep in mind . . . ."*

7. Clarify next steps.

   a. The power of active listening is in clarifying the issue and attempting to find support, resources, and potential solutions. Clarifying the next steps with specific goals, timelines, and expectations is essential to being an active listener. Here are some prompts for clarifying:

- *"So we agreed that our goal is . . . ."*
- *"I will see you on [date] to check in/support your efforts in . . . ."*

PAYOFF: Individuals are able to communicate at a deeper level, which helps to correctly identify core issues as well as potential solutions. Active listening also builds the culture of the school, empowers teachers, and improves trust by allowing everyone the opportunity to be truly heard.

Motivational Interviewing

PURPOSE: To help teachers and observers have a collaborative conversation that increases a teacher's motivation and commitment to change. This protocol also helps observers understand where teachers are on the change continuum.

PROCESS/PRACTICE:

1. Interviewers use four basic skills to engage in a dialogue that can help teachers address issues within their classroom. The four skills are open-ended questions, affirmations, reflective listening, and summary statements, or "OARS."

   a. **Open-ended questions** are used to help teachers explore their own thinking, and they deter supervisors from "giving the correct answer." The goal is to have teachers do most of the talking, which leads to reflective statements. Examples:
      - *"How can I help you with . . . ?"*
      - *"How would you like things to be different?"*

   b. **Affirmations** are used to acknowledge positive behaviors and strengths, building the teacher's confidence. Affirmations should convey empathy, respect, and support for teachers. Examples:
      - *"That's a good suggestion."*
      - *"That shows great [perseverance/patience/skill/understanding]."*

   c. **Reflective listening** is used to paraphrase teachers' comments by repeating back what they have said. This is done to ensure that both parties have a clear understanding of what has been said. Examples:
      - *"It sounds like . . . ."*
      - *"So, what I hear you saying is . . . ."*
      - *"So, you feel/think . . . ."*

   d. **Summary statements** can be used for transitioning to the next topic. The interviewer can ask what the teacher has gained from the experience in attempts to use it as a learning opportunity. Examples:
      - *"Let me see if I understand this so far. . . ."*
      - *"Here's what I have heard. . . . Have I missed anything?"*
      - *"What you've said is important. . . ."*

2. Using OARS, the interviewer strives to implement the "DEARS"—the 5 Principles of Motivational Interviewing:

a. **Develop discrepancy**—Point out discrepancies to show the gap between the current performance and the preferred performance. The goal is to motivate individuals by making them aware of the need for change. Examples:

- *"What do you feel you need to change to reach your goals?"*
- *"If you continue to do things the same way, what will be the consequences?"*

b. **Express empathy**—This is the key to motivational interviewing. It is important to see things from the other person's perspective. When people feel understood, they are willing to share more information, which allows us to better understand how to support them. Examples:

- *"I understand how difficult this is."*
- *"Making changes is very hard work."*
- *"That must have been difficult for you."*

c. **Amplify ambivalence**—Being ambivalent to change is normal. Talking through both sides of the issue with people helps them work through the process, which can promote long-lasting change. Examples:

- *"If you keep doing what you are doing, what do you see happening?"*
- *"How has this been a problem for you? How has it been a problem for others?"*

d. **Roll with resistance**—Resistance to change is normal, and creating a power struggle with individuals often is counterproductive. Encourage teachers to come up with their own solutions. If you meet resistance, it may be a sign to respond differently. Examples:

- *"That is OK. It is your choice."*
- *"Where do you want to go from here?"*
- *"What do you want to do? How do you want to proceed?"*

     e. **Support self-efficacy**—A teacher's belief that change is possible can be very motivating. In motivational interviewing, there is no right way to change. Create an environment that allows the person to explore difficult issues, and convey the idea that change is both possible and attainable.

3. The interviewer and teacher attempt to create a plan that will support the teacher's attempts to change.

PAYOFF: Observers have a deeper understanding of what is preventing teachers from improving their practice. This gives observers an opportunity to better support teachers through the change process. Teachers are empowered to engage in reflective dialogue to stimulate change and improve their craft.

Timely, Specific Developmental Feedback

PURPOSE: To help support teachers in their efforts to improve their daily professional practice and solve issues, and to help align expectations across the school. When feedback is tied directly to specific improvement goals and to the district's comprehensive teaching framework, it maximizes growth opportunities.

PROCESS/PRACTICE:

1. Recognize and state the desired goal, using the district's comprehensive teaching framework. Example:
    - *"You are working on stating clear learning goals in order to empower students to establish action plans to demonstrate proficiency in identified goals."*

2. Discuss evidence of present position in relation to the goal. Example:
    - *"You clearly stated the learning goals. This was evidenced by the goal being articulated, appropriately, on top of the assignment sheet. Student evidence of use of the goal was clear when students restated the goal in their own language, discussed two ways they would accept evidence from a learner who successfully obtained the goal, and wrote one goal-related thing they already do well and one goal-related thing they are still learning."*

3. Develop a shared understanding of how to close the gap between the current situation and the desired goal. Examples:
    - *"Some of the students didn't articulate the goal correctly; they stated an activity. You might consider starting by telling them the difference between a goal and an activity and then giving them a T-chart with examples."*
    - *"What do students find most challenging when using learning goals to establish action plans?"*
    - *"How might _____ be made even clearer to students?" (Teacher discusses strategy.)*
    - *"How might you incorporate [strategy] into the goal-setting process?"*

4. The teacher needs to understand the pathway between the current position and the desired position. This is accomplished through a continuous process that guides and modifies the teacher's efforts in a way that will most efficiently build skills and understandings associated with the goal.

5. The feedback needs to be timely and should be developmental, not judgmental. Feedback should be targeted toward the specific performance and strategies that may improve the understanding or skills of the teacher. Statements of judgment about an individual's worth, intentions, or innate ability are rarely effective. Example:

   - *"It was clear that students could articulate the goal in their own words. This clarifies the fact that the learning goals are for the students, and not just the teacher, to use to guide their efforts."*

PAYOFF: Teachers have the opportunity to continuously improve their craft and meet their full potential. Observers open up lines of communication and develop relationships that can improve overall school performance and culture by empowering teachers to focus their efforts toward professional growth.

Receiving Feedback

PURPOSE: To improve the skills of the person receiving the feedback. If individuals are better able to receive, process, and implement feedback, their chance of improving is increased.

PROCESS/PRACTICE:

1. Receive the feedback with an open mind.
   a. Focus on the concepts of a growth mindset and treat feedback as an opportunity for learning and improvement.
   b. Do not make snap judgments about the feedback.
   c. Do not reject the feedback; try to understand why someone would say it.
   d. Attempt to understand the other person's point of view.
2. Focus on *what* is being said, not *who* is saying it.
3. Assume all feedback is being delivered with the intention of improving your performance. This helps to eliminate an emotional reaction to the feedback.
4. Analyze the feedback to see how you could apply it to your situation.
5. Identify a focal point for improvement.
   a. Find a specific process or product to focus efforts for growth.
   b. Ask for specific examples from the person giving the feedback.
6. Try acting on the feedback and making changes in a limited fashion, in a safe setting. For example, if the concern was lack of student engagement, then employ a new instructional strategy for student engagement with students who are most likely to show positive results. This allows an opportunity to implement and refine the strategy successfully.
7. Each of these criteria can be addressed by responding to the following prompts.
   a. What specific feedback affirms your own perceptions of your teaching?
   b. What feedback is most difficult for you to see/hear and why?

c. How might the more difficult feedback focus your efforts to be more purposeful, aware, and responsive in your efforts to improve?

d. What clarifying questions do you have about the feedback?

e. How might you break this feedback into smaller, actionable efforts to improve?

f. What support might you access to interpret the feedback in a manner that productively focuses your efforts to improve?

g. What personal incentives might you use to focus your improvement efforts?

PAYOFF: Individuals improve their ability to process and use feedback, in a manner that empowers them to focus their efforts to attain goals for professional growth.

Appendix C

Protocols to Support Individuals' Meaningful, Purposeful Reflection

Throughout this book we've argued that evaluation, supervision, and teacher reflection are out of balance. Too often, comprehensive frameworks for effective instruction are used solely by evaluators and solely for summative evaluation. Too often, supervision is about the analysis and synthesis of the supervisor, while the teacher is relegated to a role of relying on the supervisor for the "right answer" or articulating an occasional transactional reflection. Too often, focused reflection is something that occurs primarily during post-conference summary meetings—if it happens at all. To fulfill the potential of systems of supervision and evaluation to improve—rather than merely measure—professional practice, teachers need to be the central users of these comprehensive frameworks for professional practice.

If we believe that teachers should play the central role in their continual improvement process, then we should provide them with the resources to develop proficiency in a set of strategies that support their efforts to become expert teachers. When given the opportunity, almost all teachers are interested in improving their daily practice. They often have the will to improve but lack the opportunities and processes to do so. Protocols structured around the tenets of reflective and deliberate practice can vastly enhance teachers' abilities to self-monitor and improve their practice.

The tools in this appendix provide teachers a structure that can produce dramatic results in the classroom. Although each has a slightly different purpose, these "teacher protocols" share one commonality: they are designed to give teachers formative feedback about their current practice and, when paired with a teaching framework, give meaning to their performance.

The protocols presented here can help teachers to understand their current status in the classroom and to identify specific components or instructional strategies of their teaching to improve. They provide teachers with a way to (1) clarify self-perceptions of their current performance, (2) better understand student perceptions of their performance, and (3) collaborate and learn from peers about specific learning strategies. We advise focusing on two or three specific teaching strategies. Doing so makes the process more manageable, which in turn can be motivating, energizing, and ultimately more effective. In the next paragraphs we briefly describe each protocol and its purpose.

Teaching Inventory

The Teaching Inventory protocol builds teachers' awareness of instructional strategies that are new to teachers or are familiar to them but have not been fully integrated into their practice. Completing a teaching inventory affirms the range of strategies in each teacher's instructional repertoire and raises awareness of strategies that might be added to that repertoire to meet student needs even more effectively. (See p. 215.)

Determining Focus: The Ideal Classroom

When teachers accept the challenge of continuous improvement and of becoming an expert teacher, it is essential that they identify specific skills to improve and develop those skills. This protocol is adapted from the Intentional Change Model developed by Richard E. Boyatzis (Boyatzis & McKee, 2005), which asks teachers to identify areas of strength and improvement through a set of reflective questions. Once specific skills for improvement are identified, they become the primary focus of improvement efforts. The partner sharing helps teachers process information as well as generate new or alternative solutions. (See p. 217.)

Self-analysis Framework Dig

Seeing how current instructional practices align with a teaching framework can help to build context for the link between the framework and the use of specific instructional strategies. This protocol breaks down the teaching framework and allows teachers to make connections between specific instructional strategies and the framework itself. The interaction between peers can also stimulate collaboration and new learning for each teacher. The teacher is given an opportunity to identify strengths and areas for growth based on the teaching framework. (See p. 219.)

Student Surveys

Gathering information from students can uncover strengths and areas of improvement for teachers. It also allows teachers to see themselves from their students' perspective. Students are often very honest when asked to give feedback about their classroom experience. This strategy targets areas for improvement from the "customer" perspective. The real power of student surveys is when the results lead to further discussions with students about current learning activities and policies. These discussions have the potential to lead to effective changes within the classroom. (See p. 221.)

Video Analysis of Own Teaching

Analyzing video of a teacher's own teaching uncovers strengths and areas for improvement. It also allows teachers to see themselves from their students' perspective. Because the video is viewed by the teacher only, the anxiety of recording a lesson is reduced. This strategy targets areas for improvement. When used in conjunction with the district's comprehensive teaching framework, it contributes to a more accurate assessment of current performance as related to ideal performance. (See p. 223.)

Reflective Peer Visit

Observing other teachers during their daily practice is extremely beneficial for teachers. This protocol targets areas for improvement and identifies areas of strength. When used in conjunction with the Teaching Inventory protocol, it provides a more accurate assessment of current practice. The Reflective Peer Visit protocol also provides a context for the teaching inventory or the district's selected teaching framework. Seeing strategies in action helps to significantly deepen professional learning. The key to having a successful experience is to focus directly on two or three specific teaching strategies during the visit.

Note that reflective peer visits differ from conventional peer observations in a significant way. *Whereas peer observations are typically used to provide feedback for the teacher being observed, reflective peer visits are focused on what the observer can gain from the visit.* Cosh (1999) states that in the reflective model, the emphasis is on what the observer has learned. Reflective peer visits are not performed to judge others but to "encourage self-reflection and self-awareness about our own teaching. The focus is on the teacher's own development, rather than the presumed ability to develop the teaching of one's peers or colleagues" (p. 25). (See p. 225.)

Structured Reflective Writing

The structured reflection process allows participants to synthesize and create meaning from their experiences. Written reflections lead to ownership and commitment for teachers to modify and improve their practice. This process allows teachers to focus on selected aspects of their teaching and increase their awareness and implementation of new or previously abandoned strategies. The real power of structured reflective writing comes from answering common questions with the intent of sharing learning with others by using other protocols, such as the Peer Sharing protocol. Written responses enhance understanding, making the experience more memorable, and participants make connections to previous learning and identify areas of strength or weakness. The protocol provides a common structure, and questions that prompt reflective, open-ended responses create an opportunity for significant peer learning and increase awareness of strengths and needs for both teachers and supervisors. (See p. 227.)

Teaching Inventory

PURPOSE: To build teachers' awareness of their current strengths and weaknesses in relation to the district's selected teaching framework.

PROCESS/PRACTICE:

1. The teacher reviews the Teaching Inventory Template (below) and completes the level-of-use scale for each strategy. (Note: The template could cover the full instructional framework, or it could be for a specific portion of the framework. It is important that the inventory focus on specific strategies and not general outcomes.)

2. After completing the inventory, the teacher identifies a focus strategy to learn, try, use, or integrate.

3. The teacher uses the Instructional Strategy Reflection Template (next page) to guide reflection and deliberate practice.

4. After a predetermined period of time (weeks or months), the teacher completes the bottom portion of the Strategy Reflection Template, "What I've Learned," to articulate new understandings.

5. The teacher returns to the Teaching Inventory Template, noting areas of growth by placing a plus sign (+) and the date at the new level of use.

Teaching Inventory Template				
Instructional Strategy (Examples)	**I am not yet aware of this strategy.** **(New to me)**	**I have tried or I use occasionally.** **(Tried it)**	**I use frequently and/or refined.** **(Used)**	**I've adapted and modified to apply in an innovative way.** **(Integrated)**
Advanced organizers to guide student thinking around key concepts and skills				
Think-pair-share				
Graphic representations				

continued

Instructional Strategy Reflection Template		
Instructional strategy: Benefit to students: Key steps in this strategy include:		
Date: Lesson:	How I used the strategy: How students responded:	Next time I will:
Date: Lesson:	How I used the strategy: How students responded:	Next time I will:
Date: Lesson:	How I used the strategy: How students responded:	Next time I will:
What I've Learned (Synthesis)		
The purpose of [name of strategy] is to help students _____. To use this strategy effectively, I've learned that it is important to _____. Additional lessons where I might use this strategy, or innovative ways this strategy could be adapted or integrated into my repertoire, include_____ _____.		

PAYOFF: Teachers have selected a specific instructional strategy to focus their improvement efforts on. Sharing this information with an observer leads to targeted and specific feedback. The teachers' interaction with the district's comprehensive teaching framework can clarify expectations and ensure meaningful reflection that results in purposeful action to support professional growth.

Determining Focus: The Ideal Classroom

PURPOSE: To have teachers identify areas they perceive as strength or growth areas and develop goals through a reflective process.

This protocol is conceptually based on the Intentional Change Model developed by Richard E. Boyatzis (Boyatzis & McKee, 2005). It can be completed individually or, ideally, in small groups.

PROCESS/PRACTICE:

1. Teachers are asked a series of questions to reflect on; the questions help to identify important qualities of teachers, what is within their control, and specific skills to focus on.

2. Working in small groups, ask teachers to respond to Guiding Questions 1 and 2 (see below) in writing. Question 1 is designed to help teachers focus on effective teaching practices; Question 2 is designed to focus on what they can control within their classroom.

3. Have teachers share brief responses to the following questions with two to four others in their group. Teacher sharing can lead to deeper questioning, innovation, or confirmation of current beliefs.
   - What would your ideal classroom look/sound like?
   - What strategies would you use?
   - How would you assess students?

4. Ask teachers to respond to Guiding Questions 3 through 6 in writing.

5. Have teachers share brief responses to the following questions with two to four others in their group:
   - What skills are you focusing on, and what are the barriers to achieving your ideal classroom?

6. Teachers then focus their improvement efforts on the specific strategies that were identified in Guiding Question 6. A good first step is to locate these strategies within the district's selected teaching framework and reference how the teaching strategies can be applied proficiently according to the framework.

GUIDING QUESTIONS:

1. Who was the best teacher you ever had? What made that teacher great?
2. Generate a list of things you can control in your classroom.
3. Focusing on what you can control, what would your ideal classroom look/sound like?
   a. What instructional strategies would you use?
   b. How would you assess students in your ideal classroom?
4. What are your current strengths as a teacher?
5. What areas in your current teaching represent the biggest gaps from your ideal classroom to your current classroom?
6. Identify two to three strategies to focus on that will help close the gaps between your current classroom and your ideal classroom.

PAYOFF: Teachers compare their vision of the ideal classroom and their current perception of their own teaching performance. Understanding this gap allows teachers to engage in meaningful reflection that results in purposeful action to support professional growth.

Self-analysis Framework Dig

PURPOSE: To provide teachers with an opportunity to interact with the district's preferred teaching framework and to develop a focus for improvement efforts.

PROCESS/PRACTICE:

1. Provide teachers with a copy of the district's comprehensive teaching framework.
2. Provide teachers with a document that is aligned to the teaching framework to record which specific instructional strategies are used for each indicator of the framework, as well as what questions or insights have been generated. *Assure teachers that this document will not be collected and that it is for their own professional learning.*

    The following is an example of a document that could be used for the Stronge teaching framework.

Performance Standard 4: Assessment for and of Learning

Stronge Performance Indicator	What instructional strategies do you use that support this indicator? (How do you _____?) List 3–5 for each.	Affirmations/needs
4.1 Uses pre-assessment data to develop expectations for students, to differentiate instruction, and to document learning.		
4.2 Involves students in setting learning goals and monitoring their own progress.		
4.3 Uses a variety of informal and formal assessment strategies and instruments that are valid and appropriate for the content and for the student population.		

3. Provide teachers an opportunity to complete the document by brain-storming specific instructional strategies used, along with any questions or insights that arise during the process.
4. Teachers identify an area of strength and an opportunity for growth.
5. Create an opportunity for peer sharing in small groups, which allows teachers to share the instructional strategies they use in the areas of their strength. Teachers sharing their expertise with one another can help to stimulate further insights and questions from the group.
6. After the small-group sharing, have teachers identify one or two areas that they will focus their improvement efforts on and specific potential instructional strategies that could be incorporated to help them improve.

PAYOFF: Teachers have the opportunity to align their current instructional practices with the comprehensive framework, collaborate with peers, affirm current practice, and identify needs for growth toward expertise.

Student Surveys

PURPOSE: To have teachers gather perception data from students about their teaching. The data can also be used to facilitate discussions with students about specific strategies, activities, and policies that are being used.

PROCESS/PRACTICE:

1. The teacher develops a survey to give to students (see an example on the next page) to gather feedback about student perceptions. These surveys will vary in length and type of questions based on grade level.
2. The teacher develops a second survey asking the same questions from the teacher's perspective (see the next page).
3. The teacher completes the teacher survey.
4. The teacher has students complete the student survey. Teachers who teach multiple sections of students may elect to survey one or two of their classes instead of all students.
5. The teacher tallies the results of the student survey.
6. The teacher compares the results of the student and teacher surveys.
7. The teacher analyzes the results and creates a specific focus for improvement efforts. (See Guiding Questions for some questions that can facilitate the process.)
8. After gathering the results, the teacher has conversations with classes about why they answered certain questions the way they did. The intent is to help teachers target specifically what students either like or find challenging about the class, with the goal of faster improvement and results. Often when teachers have deeper conversations with students, they are able to make minor adjustments that have a significant impact on their effectiveness.

Sample STUDENT survey questions for grades 6–12:

1. The learning goals for this class are clear to me.

○ Strongly disagree	○ Disagree	○ Agree	○ Strongly agree

2. When I don't understand something the first time, my teacher can teach it in a different way.

○ Strongly disagree	○ Disagree	○ Agree	○ Strongly agree

3. I think my teacher believes I can do well in this class.

○ Strongly disagree	○ Disagree	○ Agree	○ Strongly agree

Sample TEACHER survey questions for grades 6–12:

1. Learning goals for this course have been clearly communicated to students.

○ Strongly disagree	○ Disagree	○ Agree	○ Strongly agree

2. When students don't understand something, I can teach it in a different way.

○ Strongly disagree	○ Disagree	○ Agree	○ Strongly agree

3. I believe all students can do well in this class.

○ Strongly disagree	○ Disagree	○ Agree	○ Strongly agree

GUIDING QUESTIONS:

1. On what areas and specific questions were you rated highest by your students?
2. On what areas and specific questions were you rated lowest by your students?
3. Were you surprised by any of the results or comments?
4. What did you learn from the survey?
5. Based on the survey results, what have you identified as your area of focus?
6. How will you improve in this area? (Be as specific as possible when targeting an area of improvement, ideally identifying a specific skill or strategy.)

PAYOFF: Teachers have a better awareness of how students respond to their classroom experience. Teachers can use these results to engage in purposeful improvement efforts.

Video Analysis of Own Teaching

PURPOSE: To have teachers affirm or uncover both strengths and areas for improvement by analyzing video of their own teaching. Teachers can become more aware of how students perceive them in the classroom.

PROCESS/PRACTICE:

1. The teacher reviews the results of the Teaching Inventory protocol or the district's selected teaching framework and selects two or three strategies to focus on.

2. The teacher selects a 15-to 20-minute section of a lesson to record and prepares the recording device (e.g., camera, iPad).

   a. Suggestions: Having another person operating the camera is not necessary. However, the placement of the recording device can greatly affect the type of information that is collected. Keep the following points in mind:

   - A recording device positioned in the front of the room captures a great deal of visual information about the students but less about the teacher.

   - A recording device positioned in the back of the room captures most of the teacher action but may make it more difficult to determine student engagement and reaction, depending on where the students are seated.

   - A recording device positioned in the middle of the room pointed toward the teacher is a good way to gather a balance of information about students and teacher.

   b. Also consider the following points when deciding where to place the recording device:

   - What do you want to gather information on?

   - Which students will be recorded, given the placement of the recording device?

   - Where is most of the "action" taking place?

- Where can you position the recording device so it won't be a distraction or interfered with?
- How will you notify students of the recording?

3. Before reviewing the recording, the teacher reviews the Teaching Inventory protocol or the rubric for the district's comprehensive teaching framework to reinforce understanding of proficient and exemplary characteristics of the selected strategies.

4. The teacher reviews the recording and writes down observations, concentrating on the two or three aspects that are relevant to the focus identified earlier (see Step 1). However, the teacher should take notes on any items of interest. Noting exact times from the video is helpful if there is something that the teacher would like to revisit later. (Teachers tend to be their own worst critics. The teacher should note at least two things that were done well during the lesson.) After viewing the recording, use the comprehensive teaching framework to help organize, critique, and align the observations made.

5. Answer the Guiding Questions (see below) *in writing*. Doing so improves the teacher's ability to clarify and precisely articulate the experience and discoveries or affirmations.

GUIDING QUESTIONS:*

1. What was the particular behavior, strategy, or skill you focused on?
2. As a result of viewing the video of your own teaching, what have you learned about teaching?
3. What new or different strategies will you implement as a result of analyzing the video?
4. What new questions about your teaching have emerged after analyzing the video?
   (*See the PAR framework on p. 234 for additional questions.)

PAYOFF: Teachers are able to be metacognitive in their efforts to clarify the gap between current and ideal performance. Additionally, teachers became more objectively aware of, and responsive to, the relationship between student learning and their teaching.

Reflective Peer Visit

PURPOSE: To have teachers learn about their own teaching by observing their peers teach. This protocol is conceptually based on the work of Jill Cosh (1999).

PROCESS/PRACTICE:

1. The teacher reviews the Teaching Inventory protocol or the district's comprehensive teaching framework and selects two or three strategies to focus on. (Limiting the focus to only one strategy would likely minimize the chances of collecting relevant information.)
2. The teacher sets up a classroom visit with another teacher.
3. Immediately before the visit, the teacher reviews the Teaching Inventory or the district's comprehensive teaching framework to reinforce understanding of proficient and exemplary characteristics of the selected strategies.
4. The teacher visits a peer and observes for 15–20 minutes. During the visit, the teacher records observations. Later the teacher consults the teaching framework to organize, critique, and align the observations with the framework.
   a. *Remember:* The focus of the visit is to learn more about *the observer's* teaching. The goal is not to critique the teacher being observed but to find ways to improve the observer's teaching. The visit should bring to light some new questions or insights for the observer's own teaching.
5. The teacher answers the Guiding Questions (see below) *in writing.* Writing the answers improves the teacher's ability to clarify and precisely articulate discoveries or affirmations.

GUIDING QUESTIONS:

1. What was the particular behavior, strategy, or skill you focused on?
2. As a result of the visit to another teacher's classroom, what have you learned about your own teaching?
3. What new or different strategies will you implement as a result of completing the visit?

4. What new questions about your teaching have emerged after completing the visit?

PAYOFF: Teachers will have had the opportunity to realize one of the following:

- Their peers are struggling with the same issues—a realization that can lead to collaboration to solve those issues.
- Their peers are excelling in specific teaching strategies or processes— a realization that helps to motivate teachers to try these practices within their own classroom.
- They are performing better than their peers in specific areas— a realization that can be motivating and energizing.

Thus, depending on the outcome, the visit supports purposeful reflection that results in affirmation of current practice or dissonance as a catalyst to focus efforts that support progress toward expert performance.

Structured Reflective Writing

PURPOSE: The structured reflection process allows participants to be meta-cognitive and create meaning from their experiences. Written reflections support meaningful reflection that leads to ownership and commitment for teachers to modify and improve their practice.

PROCESS/PRACTICE:

1. The teacher reviews the questions to be answered before participating in a data-collection or feedback-gathering activity such as Student Surveys, Video Analysis of Own Teaching, Reflective Peer Visit, Video Analysis of Others' Teaching, or Instructional Rounds. For example, here are questions that might be asked for Video Analysis of Own Teaching:

   Video Self-Evaluation Reflection Questions

   a. Briefly give some background on the lesson (subject, topic, objective).
   b. What was the particular behavior, strategy, or skill you focused on?
   c. As a result of viewing the video of your own teaching, what have you learned about teaching?
   d. What new or different strategies will you implement as a result of analyzing the video?
   e. What new questions about your teaching have emerged after analyzing the video?

2. The teacher participates in the data-collection/feedback-gathering activity.
3. The teacher takes notes during the activity to help answer the questions.
4. Before answering the questions, the teacher reviews the results of the Teaching Inventory protocol or the district's comprehensive teaching framework to reinforce understanding of proficient and exemplary characteristics of the selected strategies.
5. The teacher answers the reflection questions *in writing*. Writing the answers improves the teacher's ability to clarify and precisely articulate discoveries and affirmations.

6. Responses are typically two to four sentences or bullet points for each question. However, there should be no limits on the number of responses allowed. The focus is on the quality of the response, not the quantity.

7. Ideally, groups use their answers to share out in a group setting, using the Peer Sharing protocol (see p. 236) to enhance their learning experience and to share expertise and resources with others.

GUIDING QUESTIONS: See Guiding Questions from other protocols, including the following:

- Video Analysis of Own Teaching
- Reflective Peer Visit
- Video Analysis of Others' Teaching

PAYOFF: Teachers engage in meaningful reflection that focuses efforts for purposeful action to support progress toward expert performance.

Appendix D

Collaborative Protocols to Support Individuals' Meaningful, Purposeful Reflection

Given sufficient time and proper structure, teacher teams can help improve instructional practices across the building. A structured process around the tenets of reflective practice and deliberate practice vastly improves teacher teams' abilities to self-monitor and self-improve their daily practices, but it is important to balance structure with flexibility.

The tools in this appendix give teacher teams a structure that can produce dramatic results within their classrooms. Although each has a slightly different purpose, these "teacher team protocols" share one commonality: they are designed to give teachers an opportunity to share their experiences and to learn from one another as a collective whole.

The nonevaluative protocols presented here can help teacher teams improve their teaching by enhancing their ability to be reflective and by promoting deliberate practice. It is important for teacher teams to have common expectations and the opportunity to learn from one another. These protocols are ideal for generating formative feedback that can inform the improvement process by providing teachers with the tools necessary to (1) observe and discuss specific learning strategies and (2) use the collective wisdom, experience, and talent of the entire teaching staff. We advise focusing on two or three specific teaching strategies. Doing so makes the process more manageable, which in turn can be motivating, energizing, and ultimately more effective. In the next paragraphs we briefly describe each protocol and its purpose.

Video Analysis of Others' Teaching

Analyzing videos gives teachers a flexible and efficient way to observe others' teaching and to affirm or uncover strengths and areas of improvement in one's own teaching. When viewed in small-group settings, a video can also provide the starting point for conversations about specific teaching practices. Discussions based on the video can clarify expectations, articulate and give context to the instructional framework, and set the standards and next steps for current practices. (See p. 232.)

Defining the Issue Using the "On PAR Framework"

It is useful to give teachers a framework to help process their observations and perceptions. Teaching is a complex profession with many intricate, often interwoven nuances. Deciphering how to correctly identify an issue should be the first step in finding a solution. Giving teachers a tool to help narrow their focus enhances the depth of their reflection and analysis and increases the potential for a successful solution. (See p. 234.)

Peer Sharing

Peer sharing provides teachers an opportunity to share their findings, pool their resources, and focus discussions on teaching strategies. Peer sharing is extremely effective when paired with structured protocols that are designed to generate feedback, such as Video Analysis of Own Teaching or Reflective Peer Visit. When teachers have the opportunity to review, discuss, and share their findings with peers, all participants have the opportunity to learn from one another and to improve their daily teaching practices. Peer sharing also builds staff cohesiveness and offers instructional leaders an opportunity to identify potential topics for professional development. Instructional leaders can either be participants or silent observers. This structured process also ensures that all teachers have the opportunity to be equal participants; it prevents a situation in which a few teachers dominate the conversation and allows learning to take place among all group members effectively and efficiently. (See p. 236.)

Instructional Rounds

Observing other teachers during their daily practice can be extremely beneficial for teachers. Instructional rounds are designed so that small groups of teachers observe their peers teaching and then debrief afterward to share observations and insights about their own teaching. Instructional rounds also provide a context for the school district's selected teaching framework. Seeing strategies in action significantly deepens professional learning. In a small-group context, it allows teachers to learn from one another, promoting a schoolwide learning culture. The key to a successful experience is to focus directly on two or three specific teaching strategies during the visit. This protocol is similar to the one for Reflective Peer Visit, but it is done in a group format, with discussion immediately after the classroom observations. Instructional rounds are not performed to judge others; rather, they serve as a catalyst to help teachers reflect on their own practice. (See p. 238.)

The Collegial Fishbowl

The Collegial Fishbowl protocol gives teachers an opportunity to gain a deeper understanding of a specific challenge related to improving student skill or understanding by listening and responding to questions from colleagues. Providing teachers with a structure to discuss current instructional-practice issues leads to identification of core issues and promotes the generation of solutions. The Collegial Fishbowl can be used to access the experience of the staff and to expand the use of effective instructional practices. It can also be used to support teachers who are struggling to find solutions for a current issue within their classroom. The Collegial Fishbowl protocol gives a voice to all teachers and promotes collegiality and learning across the school. (See p. 240.)

Video Analysis of Others' Teaching

PURPOSE: To give teachers a flexible and efficient way to observe others' teaching. This process can affirm or uncover strengths and areas of improvement for teachers, which can clarify expectations and build shared understanding and common language.

PROCESS/PRACTICE:

1. The teacher or small group does one of two things:
   a. Reviews the results of the Teaching Inventory protocol or the district's comprehensive teaching framework and selects two or three strategies to focus on.
   b. Focuses on two or three specified strategies related to identified goals.
2. Before viewing the recording, the teacher or group should clarify the purpose or narrow the focus for viewing. The learning opportunity can be enhanced by a quick review, if possible, of the district's comprehensive teaching framework to reinforce understanding of proficient and exemplary characteristics of the selected strategies
3. The teacher or small group watches a 5- to 15-minute video clip of a lesson or portion of a lesson being taught. Videos can be from outside sources or from teacher volunteers within the school or district. The closer the video matches the viewing teachers' current situation, the more useful it will be. For example, having high school teachers view video from a kindergarten classroom may be less useful than viewing a video from a different but similar high school.
4. Teachers should record their observations, writing down the two or three aspects that are relevant to the focus identified earlier (see Step 1) and giving special attention to these areas. However, they should take notes on any items of interest. After viewing the recording, teachers can use the teaching framework to help organize, critique, and align their observations that were made during the viewing of the video.

5. Answer the Guiding Questions (see below).

   a. For individual teachers, it is recommended that answers be in writing. Writing the answers improves the teacher's ability to clarify and precisely articulate the experience and discoveries or affirmations.

   b. For small groups, give teachers a few minutes to record their thoughts and then discuss their observations. If there are multiple small groups, a final sharing-out will allow all individuals to learn from one another, leaving with a clear understanding of expectations and potential look-fors within the classroom.

GUIDING QUESTIONS:

1. What was the particular behavior, strategy, or skill you focused on?
2. As a result of viewing the classroom video, what have you learned about *your* teaching?
3. What new or different strategies will you implement as a result of analyzing the video?
4. What new questions about your teaching have emerged after analyzing the video?

PAYOFF: Teachers are given an opportunity to experience the dissonance that exists between current and next practice. This dissonance is used as a catalyst to engage in meaningful reflection and purposeful action that supports progress toward expert performance.

Defining the Issue: Using the "On PAR Framework"

PURPOSE: To provide teachers with a framework to process their observations and perceptions and to improve reflection by narrowing the focus of their analysis.

PROCESS/PRACTICE:

1. This protocol is most effective when it is combined with *any* of the other protocols. It presents a framework for teachers or observers to process what has been experienced or observed.

2. Refer to the chart below and ask teachers to determine which part of the lesson their reflection or questions focused on: (1) planning, (2) the teaching of the lesson, or (3) how they adjusted the lesson. Planning is associated with the questions related to "purposeful"; real-time teaching is associated with the questions related to "aware"; and adjusting is associated with the questions related to "responsive."

3. Use the chart and questions to help teachers narrow their improvement efforts.

	Definition	**Reflective Prompts**
Purposeful	Reflective teachers are purposeful in their efforts to plan meaningful, engaging learning experiences that support and develop each student's understanding.	• What learning goals will guide my teaching and students' efforts for learning? • What do students already understand? • What are students already able to do? • What are students likely to be confused about? • What assessment items/tasks will reveal understanding? • What criteria will be used to measure success? • What might students find engaging about this topic? • What formative assessment strategies will I use? • What instructional strategies will I use to support student learning? • What activities will students engage in to build understanding/skill?

	Definition	Reflective Prompts
Aware	Reflective teachers are aware of students' learning needs and assess the effectiveness of their lessons in real time.	• Are students paying attention? • Are students aware of, and do they understand, the learning goal? • Are students engaged? • Are students making connections to existing knowledge/skills? • Are students responding to my directions? • Are students responding to my questions? • Are students transitioning effectively from one task to the next? • Are students confused? • Are students asking questions to clarify assignments/tasks? • Are students asking questions to clarify learning? • Are students asking questions that delve into the unknown and unknowable? • Are students on track to successfully achieve the learning goal? • Are students ready to successfully engage in tasks and activities with guidance? Independently? • Which students are engaged/learning? • Which students are disengaged/not learning? • What teaching strategies are working successfully? • What strategies need to be modified? • What was the high point of the lesson? • What was the low point of the lesson?
Responsive	Reflective teachers are responsive as they make intentional adjustments to their teaching based on students' learning needs in real time. Changes are made based on teachers' observations of their students' response to the lesson.	• What management strategies did I use to affirm, or redirect, student behavior? • What instructional strategies did I enact "on the spot" to engage students? • What instructional strategies did I use as a result of feedback from formative assessments? • What clarifying questions did I ask when misunderstanding was evident? • What reteaching occurred when misunderstanding was evident? • What affirmation did I give to students when they made progress or attained the goal? • What instructional strategies did I use to provide additional challenge? • What instructional strategies did I use to provide additional support? • What changes to the original lesson plan did I make, and why? • What other changes might I have made, and why? • What modifications did I make based on individual students' needs? • Were changes made based on "data" or on "feel"? • What opportunities to be responsive were missed and should be addressed next time the situation occurs? • What are next steps in student learning, and how I will support their learning needs?

PAYOFF: Teachers are more metecognitive about the link between purposeful, aware, and responsive teaching and student learning.

Peer Sharing

PURPOSE: Peer sharing provides teachers an opportunity to share their findings and pool their resources, and to focus discussions on teaching strategies.

PROCESS/PRACTICE:

1. In preparation, teachers should bring written reflections for protocols such as Video Analysis of Own Teaching, Reflective Peer Visit, or others.
2. Place teachers in groups of four to six. Teachers can be from different subject areas or grade levels.
3. Identify one teacher to serve as the leader. This responsibility will rotate during the protocol.
4. The teacher to the right of the leader is the first teacher to be interviewed. This teacher should refer to his or her written reflection while being interviewed by the leader about the experience.
5. The leader asks the interviewee what type of experience he or she will be sharing, such as Video Analysis of Own Teaching, Reflective Peer Visit, etc. The leader then begins by asking the questions from the appropriate protocol.
6. The leader asks clarifying questions and paraphrases what is being said about the teacher's experience so the group has a complete understanding of the experience.
7. The other teachers in the group listen to the conversation between the leader and the teacher who is being interviewed, remaining silent and focusing on what is being said, taking notes as needed.
8. At the end of the interview, the leader asks each of the group members if they have any related experiences to share, as well as suggestions, questions, or resources.
9. The process continues with leader and interviewee rotating to the right until the process is complete.

GUIDING QUESTIONS:

1. Refer to the questions of the protocol being shared; for example, if a peer visit is being shared, the following questions should be used:

   a. What was the particular behavior, strategy, or skill you focused on?

   b. As a result of the classroom visit of another teacher, what have you learned about your own teaching?

   c. What new or different strategies will you implement as a result of completing the visit?

   d. What new questions about your teaching have emerged after completing the visit?

2. The group leader can use the following stems for

   a. Clarification:
      - *Could you share an example of . . . ?*
      - *Could you say a little more about . . . ?*
      - *Are you saying . . . ?*
      - *Does that mean . . . ?*

   b. Paraphrasing:
      - *In other words, ...*
      - *You are saying . . . .*
      - *You are feeling . . . .*
      - *Your opinion is . . . .*

3. The group listeners can use the following stems for suggestions to the interviewee:
      - *Something you might consider trying is . . . .*
      - *Sometimes it's helpful if . . . .*
      - *A couple of things to keep in mind are . . . .*

PAYOFF: By collaborating about teaching through a structured process, teachers engage in meaningful reflection and purposeful action that support progress toward expert performance.

Instructional Rounds

PURPOSE: To have small groups of teachers (three to five) learn about their own teaching by observing their peers teach.

This protocol is an adapted version of instructional rounds as described by Elizabeth City and her colleagues (2009).

PROCESS/PRACTICE:

1. Teachers are notified ahead of time if they will be observed by the small group. Typically, teachers volunteer to have their classroom practice observed.

2. The group reviews the Teaching Inventory protocol or the district's selected teaching framework and selects two or three strategies to focus on. To ensure a productive visit, it is important to be flexible and to have multiple areas to gather information on. Limiting the focus to only one strategy minimizes the chances of collecting relevant information.

3. The group observes their peer engaged in teaching, typically for 3 to 10 minutes, and each teacher records observations. The teachers should take notes and then consult the teaching framework to help organize, critique, and align their observations.

   a. *Remember,* the focus of the visit is to inform *the observers'* teaching. The goal is not to critique the teacher being observed but to find ways to improve the observers' own teaching. The visit should generate some new questions or insights for the observers. Unless an observed teacher specifically asks for feedback, it is recommended to avoid sharing personal comments.

4. Ideally, groups will visit multiple classrooms in order to gather information to have informed conversations.

5. Groups meet to debrief on what they observed.

GUIDING QUESTIONS:

1. What was the particular behavior, strategy, or skill you focused on?
2. As a result of the visit to another teacher's classroom, what have you learned about your own teaching?
3. What new or different strategies will you implement as a result of completing the visit?
4. What new questions about your teaching have emerged after completing the visit?

PAYOFF: Teachers have an opportunity to share their observations and questions with peers, which leads to group learning and collaboration and develops a culture of the school as a learning organization. Observing others' practice to gain insights about one's own practice supports meaningful reflection and purposeful action that leads to expert performance.

The Collegial Fishbowl

PURPOSE: The Collegial Fishbowl gives teachers an opportunity to gain a deeper understanding of a specific challenge related to improving student skill or understanding by listening and responding to questions from colleagues.

PROCESS/PRACTICE:

1. In preparation, teachers should bring written reflections from such protocols as Video Analysis of Own Teaching or Reflective Peer Visit.
2. Place teachers in groups of five to seven. Arrange four to six chairs in a circle and put another chair in the middle of the circle (this chair represents the "fishbowl").
3. Invite one teacher who is interested in addressing a teaching-related challenge to sit in the fishbowl. This person will do most of the talking. People sitting outside the fishbowl should focus on listening intently and asking thoughtful questions, but they should not dominate any aspect of the conversation.
4. Describing the Case
   a. The teacher in the fishbowl has three to five minutes to respond to the following prompt in as much detail as possible:
      - *Tell us about a specific student or specific academic content or skills that are presenting unique challenges for you. As specifically as possible, what is the challenge, what have you done to address the challenge, and what next steps are you considering?*
5. Questions and Dialogue
   a. Clarification: Colleagues sitting in the circle have five minutes to ask *clarifying questions*. The purpose is to clarify the relevant details for all participants, but especially for the individual in the fishbowl.
   b. Probing: Colleagues have 10 minutes to ask *probing questions*. The purpose *is not to give advice* but to push the individual in the fishbowl to new levels of reflection about the situation.
   c. Suggestions: Finally, the person in the fishbowl may ask others if they are aware of or have had a related experience and ask them to give suggestions about strategies or resources.

6. Summarizing the Case and Next Steps
   a. The teacher in the fishbowl responds to this prompt: *Based on your questions and my reflection, ...*
      - *The challenge I'm facing is . . . .*
      - *Specific steps I will take in my classroom to address this challenge include . . . .*
   b. The individuals outside the fishbowl respond to this prompt: *This discussion has given me the opportunity to think more clearly or critically about how I . . . .*
   c. After one round, participants take one to three minutes to write notes about their next steps, affirmations, or concerns.
7. The process continues with a new person going into the fishbowl.

Stems for Questions
   a. Clarification:
      - *Could you share an example of . . . ?*
      - *Could you say a little more about . . . ?*
      - *Are you saying . . . ?*
      - *Does that mean . . . ?*
   b. Probing:
      - *Why did you . . . ?*
      - *How do you know . . . ?*
      - *What might happen if . . . ?*
      - *What other strategies/approaches might . . . ?*
   c. Suggestions to the interviewee (if requested):
      - *Something you might consider trying is . . . .*
      - *Sometimes it's helpful if . . . .*
      - *A couple of things to keep in mind are . . . .*

PAYOFF: Teachers have an opportunity to share their concerns, suggestions, and experiences with peers, which leads to group learning and collaboration and develops the culture of the school as a learning organization. This collaborative process empowers teachers to engage in meaningful reflection and purposeful action that leads to expert performance.

Appendix E

Matrix of Protocols for Balancing Evaluation, Supervision, and Reflection

Category	Protocols	Users					Purpose							Payoff					
		Administrators	Instructional Coaches	Teachers	Groups	Individuals	Generating Feedback	Processing Feedback	Calibrating Expectations	Guiding Dialogue	Defining Expectations	Creating Awareness	Goal Setting	Validity	Reliability	Empowering Teachers	Focused Goal Setting	Meaningful Reflection	Purposeful Reflection
Evaluation	Culture Check Survey	X	X				X					X		X					
	Clinical Observation	X				X	X	X	X			X	X	X					
	Establishing and Maintaining Interrater Reliability Among Evaluators	X	X		X				X		X			X	X				
	Evaluators' Collegial Fishbowl	X			X				X		X			X	X				
	Establishing and Maintaining Interrater Reliability Across Faculty	X	X	X	X				X		X				X				
	Written Reflection and Face-to-Face Dialogue Between Teacher and Evaluator	X				X				X				X					
	Timely, Specific Judgmental Feedback	X				X	X							X					
	Multiple Perspectives	X				X	X		X		X			X	X				
	Celebrating Success and Effort	X	X			X									X				
	Evaluative Classroom Walkthrough	X				X	X							X	X				
	Data Collection for Teacher Evaluation	X				X	X	X	X	X				X	X				

continued

	Protocols	Users					Purpose							Payoff					
		Administrators	Instructional Coaches	Teachers	Groups	Individuals	Generating Feedback	Processing Feedback	Calibrating Expectations	Guiding Dialogue	Defining Expectations	Creating Awareness	Goal Setting	Validity	Reliability	Empowering Teachers	Focused Goal Setting	Meaningful Reflection	Purposeful Reflection
Supervision	Meaningful Goal Setting	X	X	X						X	X		X				X	X	
	PDSA Instructional Coaching Process	X	X	X	X	X	X	X		X		X	X			X			
	The Seven Coaching Hats		X			X		X		X		X				X			
	Motivational Interviewing	X		X			X	X		X		X					X		
	Receiving Feedback	X	X	X	X	X		X		X						X			
	Timely, Specific Developmental Feedback	X	X	X	X			X		X		X				X	X		
	Formative Classroom Walkthrough	X	X			X	X		X							X	X		
	Active Listening	X	X	X	X	X		X		X						X			
Reflection	Determining Focus: The Ideal Classroom	X	X	X			X					X	X					X	X
	Defining the Issue Using the "On PAR Framework"	X	X	X	X	X	X	X	X	X	X		X			X	X	X	X
	Instructional Rounds	X	X	X			X		X			X				X			X
	Peer Sharing	X	X	X			X	X	X	X		X				X	X		X
	Collegial Fishbowl	X	X	X			X	X											X
	Self-analysis Framework Dig	X	X	X			X					X						X	X
	Teaching Inventory			X			X		X									X	X
	Student Surveys			X			X		X			X	X					X	
	Video Analysis of Others' Teaching		X	X			X		X			X	X			X		X	
	Video Analysis of Own Teaching		X	X			X					X	X					X	
	Reflective Peer Visit		X	X			X					X	X					X	
	Structured Reflective Writing			X			X	X		X			X					X	X

References

Ariely, D., Gneezy, U., Loewenstein, G., & Mazar, N. (2005). Large stakes and big mistakes. Working paper series, Federal Reserve Bank of Boston, No. 05-11.

Attinello, J., Lare, D., & Waters, F. (2006). The value of teacher portfolios for evaluation and professional growth. *NASSP Bulletin, 90*, 132–152.

Bandura, A. (1986). *Social foundations of thought and action: A social cognitive theory.* Englewood Cliffs, NJ: Prentice Hall.

Bandura, A. (1991). Self-regulation of motivation through anticipatory and self-reactive mechanisms. In R. A. Dienstbier (Ed.), *Perspectives on motivation: Nebraska symposium on motivation* (Vol. 38, pp. 69–164). Lincoln: University of Nebraska Press.

Bandura, A., & Walters, R. (1963). *Social learning theory and personality development.* New York: Holt, Rinehart & Winston.

BBC (n.d.). Pablo Casals. Retrieved April 11, 2015, from https://www.youtube.com/watch?v=Z20GwENK1-w

Berliner, D. C. (1988, February). *The development of expertise in pedagogy.* Charles W. Hunt lecture presented at the annual meeting of the American Association of Colleges for Teacher Education, New Orleans, LA.

Bill and Melinda Gates Foundation. (2013). *Ensuring fair and reliable measures of effective teaching: Culminating findings from the MET Project's three-year study.* Available: http://files.eric.ed.gov/fulltext/ED540958.pdf

Black, P., & Wiliam, D. (1998). Inside the black box: Raising standards through classroom assessment. *Phi Delta Kappan, 80*(2), 139–148.

Bolman, L. G., & Deal, T. E. (2010). *Reframing the path to school leadership: A guide for teachers and principals.* Thousand Oaks, CA: Corwin.

Boud, D., Cohen, R., & Walker D. (1993). *Using experience for learning.* London: Society for Research into Higher Education and Open University Press.

Boyatzis, R. E., & McKee, A. (2005). *Resonant leadership: Renewing yourself and connecting with others through mindfulness, hope, and compassion.* Boston: Harvard Business School Publishing.

Bransford, J. D., Brown, A. L., & Cocking, R. R. (Eds.) (2000). *How people learn: Brain, mind, experience, and school* (expanded ed.). Washington, DC: National Academy Press.

Brophy, J. (1981). Teacher praise: A functional analysis. *Review of Educational Research, 51*(1), 5–32.

Broussard, C. (2013). Interview with LeBron James. Available: http://espn.go.com/nba/story/_/id/9824909/lebron-james-michael-jordan-fear-failure-35-point-games-more-espn-magazine

Brown Center on Education Policy. (2014). Evaluating teachers with classroom observations: Lessons learned in four districts. Retrieved from www.brookings.edu/~/media/research/files/reports/2014/05/13-teacher-evaluation/evaluating-teachers-with-classroom-observations.pdf

Bryk, A. S., & Schneider, B. (2002). *Trust in schools: A core resource for improvement.* New York: Russell Sage Foundation.

Bryk, A. S., & Schneider, B. (2003). Trust in schools: A core resource for school reform. *Educational Leadership, 60*(6), 40–45.

Burgoyne, J. (1988). *Competency based approaches to management development.* Lancaster, UK: Centre for the Study of Management Learning.

Burton, W. H., & Brueckner, L. J. (1955). *Supervision: A social process.* New York: Appleton-Century-Crofts.

Chi, M. T. H., Glaser, R., & Farr, M. J. (1988). *The nature of expertise.* Hillsdale, NJ: Erlbaum.

City, E. A., Elmore, R. F., Fiarman, S. E., & Teitel, L. (2009). *Instructional rounds in education: A network approach to improving teaching and learning.* Cambridge, MA: Harvard University Press.

Cochran-Smith, M., & Lytle, S. L. (2001). Beyond certainty: Taking an inquiry stance on practice. In A. Lieberman & L. Miller (Eds.), *Teachers caught in the action: Professional development in practice* (pp. 45–60). New York: Teachers College Press.

Cosh, J. (1999). Peer observation: A reflective model. *ELT Journal, 53*(1), 22–27.

Costa, A. L., & Garmston, R. J. (2002). *Cognitive coaching: A foundation for renaissance schools* (2nd ed.). Norwood, MA: Christopher Gordan.

Cubberley, E. (1929). *Public school administration (3rd Ed.).* New York: Houghton Mifflin.

Culbert, S. A. (2010). *Get rid of the performance review! How companies can stop intimidating, start managing—and focus on what really matters.* New York: Business Plus.

Danielson, C. (1996). *Enhancing professional practice: A framework for teaching.* Alexandria, VA: ASCD.

Danielson, C. (2007). *Enhancing professional practice: A framework for teaching* (2nd ed.). Alexandria, VA: ASCD.

Danielson, C. (2011). Evaluations that help teachers learn. *Educational Leadership, 68*(5), 35–39.

Danielson, C. (2013). *The framework for teaching: Evaluation instrument.* Retrieved from www.danielsongroup.org.

Deci, E. (2012). *Promoting motivation, health, and excellence: Ed Deci at TEDxFlourCity.* Available: http://tedxtalks.ted.com/video/Promoting-Motivation-Health-and

Deci, E. L., & Ryan, R. M. (1985). *Intrinsic motivation and self-determination in human behavior.* New York: Springer Science & Business Media.

Deci, E. L., & Ryan, R. M. (2000). The "what" and "why" of goal pursuits: Human needs and the self-determination of behavior. *Psychological Inquiry, 11*(4), 227–268.

Deci, E. L., & Ryan, R. M. (2002). *Handbook of self-determination research.* Rochester, NY: University of Rochester Press.

Downey, C. J., Steffy, B. E., English, F. W., Frase, L. E., & Poston, W. K. (2004). *The three-minute classroom walk-through: Changing school supervisory practice one teacher at a time.* Thousand Oaks, CA: Corwin.

Dweck, C. S. (2000). *Self-theories: Their role in motivation, personality, and development.* Philadelphia: Psychology Press.

Dweck, C. S. (2008). *Mindset: The new psychology of success.* New York: Ballantine Books.

Ellison, J., & Hayes, C. (2003). *Cognitive coaching: Weaving threads of learning and change into the culture of an organization.* Norwood, MA: Christopher-Gordon.

Ericsson, K. A. (1996). The acquisition of expert performance: An introduction to some of the issues. In K. A. Ericsson (Ed.), *The road to excellence: The acquisition of expert performance in the arts and sciences, sports, and games* (pp. 1-50). Mahwah, NJ: Lawrence Erlbaum.

Ericsson, K. A., Charness, N., Feltovich, P. J., & Hoffman, R. R. (Eds.). (2006). *The Cambridge handbook of expertise and expert performance.* New York: Cambridge University Press.

Ericsson, K. A., Krampe, R. T., & Tesch-Romer, C. (1993). The role of deliberate practice in the acquisition of expert performance. *Psychological Review, 100*(3), 363–406.

Flavell, J. H. (1977). *Cognitive development.* Englewood Cliffs, NJ: Prentice Hall.

Frontier, T., & Mielke, P. (2014). Beyond educator effectiveness: Balancing evaluation, supervision, and reflection in the use of comprehensive frameworks for teaching. Paper presented at Cardinal Stritch University Southeastern Wisconsin New Teacher Project, Milwaukee.

Frontier, T., & Rickabaugh, J. (2014). *Five levers to improve learning: How to prioritize for powerful results in your school.* Alexandria, VA: ASCD.

Fullan, M. (2011). Choosing the wrong drivers for whole system reform. 2011 Centre for Strategic Education Seminar Series Paper No. 204, May 2011. Available: www.michaelfullan.ca/media/13436787590.html

Garmston, R. (2000). Why cats have clean paws. *National Staff Development Council, 21*(3), 63–64.

Gladwell, M. (2008). *Outliers: The story of success.* New York: Hachette.

Goldhammer, R. (1969). *Clinical supervision.* New York: Holt, Rinehart and Winston.

Hall, P., & Simeral, A. (2015). *Teach, reflect, learn: Building your capacity for success in the classroom.* Alexandria, VA: ASCD.

Hammersley-Fletcher, L., & Orsmond, P. (2005). Reflecting on reflective practices within peer observation. *Studies in Higher Education, 30*(2), 213–224.

Hargrove, R. A. (2008). *Masterful coaching.* San Francisco: Jossey-Bass.

Haslam, M. B., & Seremet, C. P. (2001). *Strategies for improving professional development: A guide for school districts.* Alexandria, VA: New American Schools.

Hatano, G., & Inagaki, K. (1986). Two courses of expertise. In H. Stevenson, H. Azuma, & K. Hakuta (Eds.), *Child development and education in Japan* (pp. 262–272). New York: W. H. Freeman.

Hattie, J. (2009). *Visible learning: A synthesis of over 800 meta-analyses relating to achievement.* New York: Routledge.

Hattie, J., & Yates, G. (2013). *Visible learning and the science of how we learn.* New York: Routledge.

Hunter, M. (1985). What's wrong with Madeline Hunter? *Educational Leadership, 42*(5), 57–60.

Jackman, J. M., & Strober, M. H. (2003). Fear of feedback. *Harvard Business Review, 81*(4), 101–107.

Joe, J. N., McClellan, C. A., & Holtzman, S. L. (2014). Scoring design decisions: Reliability and the length and focus of classroom observations. In T. J. Kane, K. A. Kerr, & R. C. Pianta (Eds.), *Designing teacher evaluation systems* (pp. 415–443). San Francisco: Jossey-Bass.

Knight, J. (2011). *Unmistakable impact: A partnership approach for dramatically improving instruction.* Thousand Oaks, CA: Corwin.

Knowles, M. S. (1980). *The modern practice of adult education: From pedagogy to andragogy* (Rev. ed.). New York: Cambridge.

Knowles, M. S. (1984). *Andragogy in action.* San Francisco: Jossey-Bass.

Lewis, C., & Hurd, J. (2011). *Lesson study step by step: How teacher learning communities improve instruction.* Portsmouth, NH: Heinemann.

Lezotte, L. W., & Snyder, K. M. (2011). *What effective schools do: Re-envisioning the correlates.* Bloomington, IN: Solution Tree.

Livingston, J. (2003). *Metacognition: An overview.* Retrieved from ERIC database. (ED474273).

Locke, E. A. (1996). Motivation through conscious goal setting. *Applied and Preventive Psychology, 5*(2), 117–124.

Locke, E. A., & Latham, G. P. (1990). *A theory of goal setting & task performance.* Englewood Cliffs, NJ: Prentice Hall.

Locke, E. A., & Latham, G. P. (2006). New directions in goal-setting theory. *Current Directions in Psychological Science, 15*(5), 265–268.

Loughran, J. (2002). Effective reflective practice: In search of meaning in learning about teaching. *Journal of Teacher Education, 53*(1), 33–43.

Marshall, K. (2005). It's time to rethink teacher supervision and evaluation. *Phi Delta Kappan, 86*(10), 727–735.

Marshall, K. (2009). *Rethinking teacher supervision and evaluation: How to work smart, build collaboration, and close the achievement gap.* San Francisco: Jossey-Bass.

Marzano, R. J. (2007). *The art and science of teaching: A comprehensive framework for effective instruction.* Alexandria, VA: ASCD.

Marzano, R. J. (2012). The two purposes of teacher evaluation. *Educational Leadership, 70*(3), 14–19.

Marzano, R. J., Frontier, T., & Livingston, D. (2011). *Effective supervision: Supporting the art and science of teaching.* Alexandria, VA: ASCD.

Marzano, R. J., & Toth, M. D. (2013). *Teacher evaluation that makes a difference: A new model for teacher growth and student achievement.* Alexandria, VA: ASCD.

McGregor, D. (1972). An uneasy look at performance appraisal. *Harvard Business Review.* Available: https://hbr.org/1972/09/an-uneasy-look-at-performance-appraisal/ar/1

Mezirow, J. (1990). *Fostering critical reflection in adulthood: A guide to transformative and emancipatory learning.* San Francisco: Jossey-Bass.

Mielke, P. G. (2012). *Investigating a systematic process to develop teacher expertise: A comparative case study.* Milwaukee, WI: Cardinal Stritch University.

Mielke, P. G., & Frontier, T. (2012). Keeping improvement in mind. *Educational Leadership, 70*(3), 10–13.

Nuthall, G. (2004, May 5). *Discovering the hidden realities of teaching and learning in the classroom.* Talk presented at the University of Canterbury, Christchurch, New Zealand. Available: http://www.nuthalltrust.org.nz/docs/GN_Trust_talk.pdf

Nuthall, G. (2007). *The hidden lives of learners.* Wellington, NZ: NZCER Press.

Patterson, K., Grenny, J., Maxfield, D., McMillan, R., & Switzler, A. (2007). *Influencer: The power to change anything.* New York: McGraw-Hill.

Pausch, R. (2008). *The last lecture.* New York: Hyperion Books.

Piaget, J. (1936). *Origins of intelligence in the child.* London: Routledge & Kegan Paul.

Piaget, J., & Cook, M. T. (1952). *The origins of intelligence in children.* New York: International University Press.

Pianta, R. C., LaParo, K. M., & Hamre, B. K. (2008). *Classroom assessment scoring system.* Baltimore, MD: Brookes.

Pink, D. H. (2009a). *Dan Pink on the suprising science of motivation.* [Video file]. Retrieved from http://www.ted.com/talks/dan_pink_on_motivation.html

Pink, D. H. (2009b). *Drive: The surprising truth about what motivates us.* New York: Riverhead Books.

Ramirez, A., Clouse, W., & Davis, K. W. (2014). Teacher evaluation in Colorado: How policy frustrates practice. *Management in Education, 28*(2), 44–51.

Rogers, C. R. (1961). *On becoming a person: A therapist's view of psychotherapy.* Boston: Houghton Mifflin.

Rotter, J. B. (1954). *Social learning and clinical psychology.* Englewood Cliffs, NJ: Prentice Hall.

Ryan, R. M., & Deci, E. L. (2000). Self-determination theory and the facilitation of intrinsic motivation, social development, and well-being. *American Psychologist, 55*(1), 68–78.

Saphier, J., & Gower, R. (1997). *The skillful teacher: Building your teaching skills.* Acton, MA: Research for Better Teaching.

Scharmer, C. O. (2009). *Theory U: Learning from the future as it emerges.* San Francisco: Berrett-Koehler.

Schon, D. A. (1987). *Educating the reflective practitioner: Toward a new design for teaching and learning in the professions.* San Francisco: Jossey-Bass.

Senge, P. M. (1990). *The fifth discipline: The art and practice of the learning organization.* New York: Doubleday/Currency.

Sergiovanni, T. J., & Starratt, R. J. (1979). *Supervision: Human perspectives.* New York: McGraw-Hill.

Sinek, S. (2009). *Start with why: How great leaders inspire everyone to take action.* New York: Penguin.

Skinner, B. F. (1953). *Science and human behavior.* New York: Free Press.

Stiggins, R. J., Arter, J. A., Chappuis, J., & Chappuis, S. (2004). *Classroom assessment for student learning: Doing it right—Using it well.* Portland, OR: Assessment Training Institute.

Stone, D., & Heen, S. (2014). *Thanks for the feedback: The science and art of receiving feedback well.* New York: Penguin.

Stronge, J. H. (2013). *Evaluating what good teachers do: Eight research-based standards for assessing teacher excellence.* New York: Routledge.

Taylor, F. W. (1911). *The principles of scientific management.* New York, Harper & Brothers.

Thorndike, E. L. (1931). *Human learning.* New York: The Century.

Toch, T., & Rothman, R. (2008). *Rush to judgment: Teacher evaluation in public education.* Education Sector Reports. Washington, DC: Education Sector.

Tracy, S. J. (1995). How historical concepts of supervision relate to supervisory practices today. *The Clearing House, 68*(5), 320–325.

Tremmel, R. (1993). Zen and the art of reflection practice in teacher education. *Harvard Educational Review, 63*(1), 434–458.

van Es, E. A. (2010). Viewer discussion advised. *Journal of Staff Development, 31*(1), 54–58.

Weisberg, D., Sexton, S., Mulhern, J., & Keeling, D. (2009). The widget effect: Our national failure to acknowledge and act on differences in teacher effectiveness. *Education Digest: Essential Readings Condensed for Quick Review, 75*(2), 31–35.

Wheatley, M. J. (2002). *Turning to one another: Simple conversations to restore hope to the future.* San Francisco: Berrett-Koehler.

Whitehurst, G. J., Chingos, M. M., & Lindquist, K. M. (2014). *Evaluating teachers with classroom observations: Lessons learned in four districts.* Washington, DC: Brown Center on Education Policy at the Brookings Institution.

Wiggins, G. P. (1998). *Educative assessment: Designing assessments to inform and improve student performance* (Vol. 1). San Francisco: Jossey-Bass.

Wilson, J. (2001). *Assessing metacognition.* Unpublished doctoral thesis, University of Melbourne.

Wilson, J., & Clarke, D. (2004). Towards the modelling of mathematical metacognition. *Mathematics Education Research Journal, 16*(2), 25–48.

Zimmerman, B. J. (2006). Development and adaption of expertise: The role of self-regulatory processes and beliefs. In K. A. Ericsson, N. Charness, P. H. Feltovich, & R. R. Hoffman (Eds.), *The Cambridge handbook of expertise and expert performance* (pp. 705–722). New York: Cambridge University Press.

Zimmerman, B. J., & Kitsantas, A. (2005). Homework practices and academic achievement: The mediating role of self-efficacy and perceived responsibility beliefs. *Contemporary Educational Psychology, 30*(4), 397–417.

Index

The letter *f* following a page number denotes a figure.

accountability, high-stakes, 1–2
active listening protocol, 193, 202–203
adult learning, 77, 121
advising role in effective coaching, 90
affirmation
    collaboration calibrating, 113–114
    feedback for, 98
    growth and, 112–113
Alice in Wonderland (Carroll), 104, 106
andragogy theory, 77
The Art and Science of Teaching (Marzano), 6
artifacts, 65
assessment
    high-stakes, 1–2
    improvement and, 148
    summative, 45
attainability in effective goal setting, 102
attribution theory, 130–131
autonomy-supportive practices, 79, 84–91, 86*f*
awareness, metacognitive, 139

balanced teaching framework. *See also specific components*
    benefits, 33, 34–35*f*
    credibility component, 38–40, 45–46
    guidelines for change resulting in a, 160–164
    key elements, comparison of, 34–35*f*
    matrix of protocols for, 243–244
    premises, 34–35*f*
    processes and protocols, 33, 34–35*f*

balanced teaching framework. *See also specific components (continued)*
    purpose, 34–35*f*
    pyramid analogy, 3–4, 36
    relational trust component, 36–38
    users of, 18–19
behaviorism, 120
Brown Center on Education Policy, 66

challenge
    ABC approach to, 131
    in effective goal setting, 102–103, 105*f*
change
    commitment to, protocol determining, 193, 204–206
    implementing, 23
    managing the status quo, 24, 27, 28*f*
    responsive implementation of, 162–164
    transactional, 24–25, 27, 28*f*
    transformational, 25–26, 28, 162–164
choice, coaching supporting, 88
clarity, credibility and, 40
classroom, the ideal, 212, 217–218
classroom walkthrough protocol
    evaluative, 168, 185–186
    formative, 193, 200–201
clinical observation protocol, 166, 174–175
coaching
    autonomy-supportive, 88
    collective capacity for, 88–89
    feedback as, 97
    Seven Coaching Hats, 89–91, 192, 199

cognitivists, 120–121
collaboration
   calibrating focused supervision, 100–101,
      110–114
   in effective systems of supervision, 72
   performance evaluations effect on, 9
Collegial Fishbowl, 166–167, 176–177, 231,
   240–241
commitment
   to change, 193, 204–206
   in effective goal setting, 103, 105*f*
competence, evaluating for, 12–13, 34–35*f*
consequences, improvement and, 10–11,
   19–20
consistency, credibility and, 39–40
credibility, 38–40, 45–46, 170–171
criticism, constructive, 9
cross transactions, 98–99
culture check survey, 166, 170–171
current-expert practice gap, 141, 147–152
current-ideal performance gap, 72, 130,
   138–140

Danielson Framework for Teaching, 5, 58*f*
data analysis in a performance environment,
   45, 80
data collection
   for evaluation vs. growth, 108–110
   in focused supervision, 100, 104, 106–110
   in reliable evaluation
      artifacts, 65
      high-quality focus, 61–64
      length and frequency of, 63
      strategic, 63
      teachers involvement, 64–66
      teacher voice, 65–66
data collection protocols
   student surveys, 213, 221–222
   for teacher evaluation, 168–169, 187–188
deliberate practice
   example applied to teaching, 155–156*f*
   expertise and, 77–78, 125–126, 141,
      152–154
   key components, 154, 155–156*f*
   protocols, 155–156*f*
   reflection supporting, 34–35*f*
dialogue face-to-face, teacher-evaluator, 167,
   180–181
dissonance
   collaboration calibrating, 113–114

dissonance (*continued*)
   in developing expertise, 124–125,
      148–149
   example of, 147–148
   growth and, 113
   reflection and, 149
drawing others out, coaching for, 90

effectiveness, systems measuring, 16–17
empowering supervision
   action steps, 31*f*, 78*f*
   beliefs and practices emphasized in, 79
   creates a learning orientation, 79, 80–84
   key questions, 31*f*, 78*f*
   quality criteria, 31*f*
   supports growth, 72–73
   uses autonomy-supportive practices, 79,
      84–91, 86*f*
   uses high-quality, developmental feed-
      back, 79, 92–95, 96*f*, 97–99
empowering supervision, protocols to support systems of
   active listening, 193, 202–203
   classroom walkthrough, formative, 193,
      200–201
   developmental feedback, timely and spe-
      cific, 194, 207–208
   feedback, receiving, 194, 209–210
   goal setting, meaningful, 192, 195–196
   interviewing, motivational, 193, 204–206
   Plan-Do-Study-Act (PDSA), 192,
      197–198
   Seven Coaching Hats, 192, 199
empowerment, self-identifying opportunities
   for, 78
evaluation
   in balance, example of, 67–69
   credible, components of, 47, 49–50, 50*f*
   data collection protocol, 168, 187–188
   feedback as, 97–98
   goal of, 45
   improvement and, 63
   metacognitive, 139
   out of balance, example of, 41–42
   purpose of, 29, 165
   supervision vs., 72, 75–77
evaluation frameworks
   qualitative components, 51–52
   quantitative components, 52–54
   rating scales, analyzing, 52–54

evaluation in a balanced system. *See also* reliable evaluation; valid evaluation
  action steps, 31*f*
  data collection for, 108–110
  framework for, 18–19
  judgment rendered through, 45–47
  key elements to ensure competence, 34–35*f*, 48*f*
  key questions, 31*f*
  overview, 44*f*
  PAR reflective questions for, 145
  payoff, 34*f*, 43, 47
  premise, 34*f*, 45–47
  protocols and processes, 32*f*, 34*f*
  purpose of, 32*f*, 34–35*f*, 43–44, 51
  quality criteria, 31*f*, 47, 50*f*
  unbiased, Multiple Perspectives protocol for, 168, 184
evaluation systems
  efficacy of, 8–11, 21–22, 134
  history of, 12
  managing the status quo, 24, 27, 28*f*
  successful, 165
  transactional change in, 24–25, 27, 28, 28*f*
  transformational change in, 25–26
  validity-reliability relation, 49–50
evaluators
  Collegial Fishbowl protocol, 166–167, 176–177
  data gathering, explicit purposefulness in, 64
  external, 66
  face-to-face dialogue, teacher-evaluator, 167, 180–181
  and improvements in expert teaching, 17
  interrater reliability, 66, 166, 172–173
  meaningful feedback from, 20–21
  new, mentoring, 66
  performance orientation, 45
  power to judge, 80
  valid evaluation ensures ratings from credible, 51, 54–55
excellence, pathways toward, 11–12
expertise
  adaptive vs. routine, 140
  components of, 14
  developing
    deliberate practice and, 77–78, 125–126, 141, 152–154
    dissonance in, 148–149

expertise (*continued*)
    evaluation for, 17, 18*f*
    reflection supporting, 34–35*f*, 122–124, 149–152
    skill sets for, 14–15
    supportive systems for, 11
  evaluating, 13–14
  levels of, 15
  meaning of, 122–123
  metacognition and, 140
experts
  in effective goal setting, 102
  growth mindset, 125
  internal locus of control, 125
  learning trajectory, 124

faculty, interrater reliability, 167, 178–179
feedback
  affirmative, 98, 112–113
  appreciative, 97
  coaching and, 90
  coaching as, 97
  criterion-referenced, 57, 58*f*
  cross transactions, 98–99
  in effective goal setting, 103, 105*f*
  as evaluation, 97–98
  formative, 193, 200–201
  improvement and, 20–21, 148–149
  meaningful, evaluators as sole source of, 20–21
  non-supervisory, 21
  objective, 57, 58*f*
  performance evaluations effect on, 9
  specific, 57, 58*f*
  type given, by component, 35*f*
feedback, developmental
  dissonance and, 148
  effective, components of, 93–95, 96d
  empowering supervision and, 79, 92–95, 96*f*, 97–99
  giving and receiving, 95, 97–99
  opportunities for, 71
  purpose of, 92
feedback, judgmental
  credible, 57
  dissonance and, 148
  giving, 56–57
  quality, characteristics of, 57, 58*f*
  receiving, 59–60
  responding to, action steps for

feedback, judgmental (*continued*)
    break into manageable tasks, 60
    get support, 59–60
    recognize emotions and responses, 59
    reframe, 60
    use personal incentives, 60
    timely and accurate, valid evaluation for,
      51, 55–57, 59–60
feedback protocols
    classroom walkthrough, 193, 200–201
    developmental feedback, timely and spe-
      cific, 194, 207–208
    on instructional strategies, 194, 200–201
    judgmental feedback, timely and specific,
      167, 182–183, 183*f*
    receiving feedback, 194, 209–210
    for unbiased feedback, 168, 184
Five Levers to Improve Learning (Frontier &
  Rickabaugh), 23
Five *W*s and How, 23–24
focused supervision
    action steps, 31*f*, 78*f*
    beliefs and practices emphasized in,
      100–101, 114
    establishes and guides efforts toward
      improvement goals, 100, 101–104
    key questions, 31*f*, 78*f*
    quality criteria, 31*f*
    uses collaboration to calibrate, 100–101,
      110–114
    uses data collection as basis and support
      for for, 100, 104, 106–110
    uses modification of practice as basis and
      support for for, 100, 104, 106–110
focused supervision, protocols to support
  systems of
    active listening, 193, 202–203
    classroom walkthrough, formative, 193,
      200–201
    developmental feedback, timely and spe-
      cific, 194, 207–208
    feedback, receiving, 194, 209–210
    goal setting, meaningful, 192, 195–196
    interviewing, motivational, 193, 204–206
    Plan-Do-Study-Act (PDSA), 192,
      197–198
    Seven Coaching Hats, 192, 199
forwarding action in effective coaching, 90

goal setting
    catalysts for, 21–22
    protocols to support meaningful, 192,
      195–196
goal setting, effective
    attainability in, 102
    by experts, 102
    challenge and, 102–103, 105*f*
    commitment in, 103, 105*f*
    exemplars, 106–107*f*
    feedback and, 103, 105*f*
    specificity in, 102, 105*f*, 153
    task complexity and, 103–104, 106*f*
growth. *See* improvement
growth mindset, 125, 130, 134–139, 136*f*

high performers, acknowledging, 10. *See also*
  experts

improvement
    acknowledging a need for, 8, 9, 10–11
    affirmation and, 112–113
    consequences and, 10–11, 19–20
    data collection for, 108–110
    dissonance and, 113
    evaluation and, 63
    evaluators and, 20–21
    experts desire for, 14–15
    failure in, reasons for, 19–20
    feedback and, 20–21
    focus and, 77–78
    incentives and, 19–20
    pathways to, 20
    punishment and, 19–20, 120
    self-assessment and, 148
    self-identifying opportunities for, 20–22,
      78
improvement plans, 10–11
incentives, improvement and, 19–20
Influencer: The Power to Change Anything
  (Patterson & Senge), 77
instructional rounds protocol, 231, 238–239
interviewing, motivational, 193, 204–206
isolation in professional practice, 17, 73, 82,
  111

judgement. *See also* feedback, judgmental
    evaluation and, 45–47
    summative, 80

justifications preventing reflection, 132–133, 133*f*

language
   of effective practice, 88, 111
   of growth and expertise, 161–162
leaders, role of, 35*f*
learners, adult, 85, 121
learning
   cognitivist vs. behaviorist approach to, 120–121
   high-stakes accountability and, 7
   process of, 122*f*
learning environment
   autonomy-supportive, 88
   collaboration in a, 80, 81
   data collected, use of, 80, 81
   empowering supervision and growth in a, 72, 79, 80–84
   mistakes in a, 80
   performance environment vs., 80–84, 80*f*
   purpose of, 80
   questions validating an established, 83–84
lesson quality, 52
locus of control
   external, 131, 132–133
   internal, 125, 129, 130–134

Marzano Observational Protocol, 6, 58*f*
Masterful Coaching (Hargrove), 89
meaningfulness, 126, 128
meaningful reflection
   action steps, 31*f*, 129*f*
   beliefs and practices emphasized in, 129–130, 154
   beliefs supporting, 128
   on current-ideal performance gap, 130, 138–140
   in efforts to learn, 122*f*
   growth mindset for, 130, 134–139, 136*f*
   improved performance and, 148
   internal locus of control and, 129, 130–134
   key questions, 31*f*, 129*f*
   quality criteria, 31*f*, 129*f*
meaningful reflection, collaborative protocols supporting
   Collegial Fishbowl, 231, 240–241

meaningful reflection, collaborative protocols supporting (*continued*)
   defining the issue using the "On PAR Framework," 230, 234–235
   instructional rounds, 231, 238–239
   peer sharing, 230, 236–237
   video analysis of others' teaching, 230, 232–233
meaningful reflection, protocols supporting
   determining focus: the ideal classroom, 212, 217–218
   peer visit, reflective, 213–214, 225–226
   reflective writing, structured, 214, 227–228
   Self-analysis Framework Dig, 212–213, 219–220
   student surveys, 213, 221–222
   Teaching Inventory, 212, 215–216
   video analysis of own teaching, 213, 223–224
measurement, accurate, 47, 49–50
Measures of Effective Teaching Project (Gates Foundation), 66
metacognition
   defined, 138
   expertise and, 140
   meaningful reflection and, 130, 138–140
   payoffs, 139
   process of, 138
mindset, fixed vs. growth, 130, 134–138, 136*f*
motivation
   in adult learners, 85
   autonomous, 84–85
   controlling, 84
   interviewing protocol, 193, 204–206

nomad anecdote, 3–4, 36

Outliers (Gladwell), 122–123

PAR (purposeful, aware, responsive) reflection
   components of, 142
   examples and non-examples, 146–147*f*
   questions inviting, 144–145*f*
PAR (purposeful, aware, responsive) reflective questions
   for evaluation, 145
   for reflection, 147
   for supervision, 145, 147

peer sharing protocol, 230, 236–237
peer visits protocol, 213–214, 225–226
perception, magnitude of change and, 27–30
performance environment
    data collected, use of, 80
    evaluation rendering judgment, 45–47
    evaluator power in a, 80, 82
    learning environment vs., 80–84, 80f
    mistakes in a, 80, 81–82
performance evaluation systems, efficacy of, 8–9
performance gap, current-ideal, 72, 130, 138–140
perspectives protocol to ensure unbiased feedback, 168, 184
Plan-Do-Study-Act (PDSA), 192, 197–198
possibilities, coaching for, 89
practice gap, current-expert, 141, 147–152
praise for teacher development, 120
principals, saints, cynic, and sinners, 62
proficiency, 124–125
punishment
    improvement and, 19–20, 120
    motivation and, 84
purpose, in navigating change, 160–161
purposeful action, 122f, 128
purposefulness, 128
purposeful reflection
    action steps, 31f, 129f
    beliefs and practices emphasized in, 140–141, 154
    current-expert practice gap, closing the, 141, 147–152
    dissonance is embraced, 141, 147–152
    facilitating, 150–151
    key questions, 31f, 129f
    PAR framework, 140–143, 144–147f
    to progress toward expert performance, 141, 152–154
    quality criteria, 31f, 129f
    "What Could Be?" question, 150–151
    "What Does the Next Level of Quality Look Like?" question, 151–152
    "Where am I now?" question, 149–150
purposeful reflection, collaborative protocols supporting
    Collegial Fishbowl, 231, 240–241
    defining the issue using the "On PAR Framework," 230, 234–235
    instructional rounds, 231, 238–239
purposeful reflection, collaborative protocols supporting (continued)
    peer sharing, 230, 236–237
    video analysis of others' teaching, 230, 232–233
purposeful reflection, protocols supporting
    determining focus: the ideal classroom, 212, 217–218
    peer visit, reflective, 213–214, 225–226
    reflective writing, structured, 214, 227–228
    Self-analysis Framework Dig, 212–213, 219–220
    student surveys, 213, 221–222
    Teaching Inventory, 212, 215–216
    video analysis of own teaching, 213, 223–224
pyramid anecdote, 3–4, 36

ratings, valid, 10, 51–54, 54–55
reflection
    in balance, example of, 157–159
    dissonance and, 149
    growth and, 148
    justifications preventing, 132–133, 133f
    meaningful, 129f
    out of balance, example of, 118–119
    purposeful, 129f
    term derivation, 120
reflection in a balanced system. See also meaningful reflection; purposeful reflection
    action steps, 31f
    key elements to support deliberate practice and expertise, 34–35f, 127f
    key questions, 31f, 129f
    overview, 123f
    PAR reflective questions for, 147
    payoff, 34f, 126
    premise, 34f, 122–126
    protocols and processes, 32f
    purpose of, 29–30, 32f, 34–35f, 119–121
    quality criteria, 31f, 129f
reflective writing protocol, 167, 214, 227–228
reframing, effective coaching for, 90
regulation, metacognitive, 139
relational trust, 36–38, 45–46, 88
reliable evaluation
    action steps, 31f, 50f
    beliefs and practices emphasized in, 61, 67

reliable evaluation (*continued*)
  evaluators, 64, 66
  key questions, 31*f*, 50*f*
  quality criteria, 31*f*, 50*f*
  results of, 47
reliable evaluation, protocols to support systems of
  classroom walkthrough, evaluative, 168, 185–186
  clinical observation, 166, 174–175
  culture check survey, 166, 170–171
  evaluation, data collection for, 187–188
  evaluator interrater reliability, establishing and maintaining, 166, 172–173
  evaluators' Collegial Fishbowl, 166–167, 176–177
  face-to-face dialogue, teacher-evaluator, 167, 180–181
  faculty interrater reliability, establishing and maintaining, 167, 178–179
  function of, 165
  judgmental feedback, timely and specific, 167, 182–183, 183*f*
  multiple perspectives to ensure unbiased performance feedback and evaluations, 168, 184
  success and effort, celebrating, 169, 189–190
  written reflection, 167, 180–181
reliable evaluation data collection
  artifacts, 65
  by evaluators, 64
  high-quality focus, 61–64
  length and frequency of, 63
  strategic, 63
  teachers involvement, 64–66
  teacher voice, 65–66
rewards
  improvement and, 19–20, 120
  motivation and, 84
Rush to Judgment (Toch & Rothman), 13

school improvement, 36, 45–46
Self-analysis Framework Dig, 212–213, 219–220
self-assessment
  of current performance, 149–150
  growth and, 148
self-determination theory, 84
Seven Coaching Hats, 89–91, 192, 199

specificity in effective goal setting, 102, 105*f*, 153
stakeholder perception, magnitude of change and, 27–30
standardized tests, 1–2
status quo, managing the, 24, 27, 28*f*
Stronge Teacher Evaluation Protocol, 6
student survey protocol, 213, 221–222
success and effort, protocol for celebrating, 169, 189–190
supervision
  in balance, example of, 115–117
  evaluation vs., 72, 75–77
  out of balance, example of, 70–71
  purpose of, 29–30
  term use, 72
supervision in a balanced system. *See also* empowering supervision; focused supervision
  action steps, 31*f*
  autonomy's relation to, 86*f*
  focused goal setting, 77
  key elements to influence growth, 34–35*f*, 74*f*
  key questions, 31*f*, 78*f*
  overview, 73*f*
  PAR reflective questions for, 145, 147
  payoff, 34*f*, 72
  premise, 34*f*, 72, 74*f*
  protocols and processes, 32*f*, 34*f*
  purpose of, 32*f*, 34–35*f*, 71–72, 114
  quality criteria, 31*f*, 78*f*
supervision systems
  managing the status quo, 24, 27, 28*f*
  transactional change in, 24–25, 27, 28, 28*f*
  transformational change in, 25–26

task complexity in effective goal setting, 103–104, 106*f*
teacher evaluation
  competencies, 13
  high-stakes, 7
  history of/basis for, 12
  Marzano Observational Protocol framework, 6
  pyramid analogy, 4–5
  stakeholder critical perspectives, 7–8
  Stronge Protocol, 6
teacher evaluation rating scales
  Danielson Framework, 5

teacher evaluation rating scales (*continued*)
    Marzano Observational Protocol, 6
    Stronge Teacher Evaluation Protocol, 6
teacher portfolios, 65
teachers
    coaching effectively, 90
    data collection, involvement in, 64–67
    expert
        evaluation in developing, 17, 18*f*
        percent of total teachers, 10
    incompetent, percent of total teachers, 10
    struggling, improvement plans for, 10–11
teaching
    current-expert practice gap, 141, 147–152
    current-ideal performance gap, 72, 130,
        138–140
    Hunterizaton of, 52
    isolation in professional practice, 17, 73,
        82, 111
teaching frameworks
    Danielson Framework, 5
    effective use of, 18–19
    for evaluation, exclusive use of, 18–19
    Marzano Observational Protocol, 6
    Stronge Teacher Evaluation Protocol, 6
Teaching Inventory protocol, 212, 215–216
teaching protocols
    face-to-face dialogue, teacher-evaluator,
        167, 180–181
    instructional rounds, 231, 238–239
    peer sharing, 230, 236–237
    reflective peer visits, 213–214, 225–226
    student surveys for data collection, 213,
        221–222
    Teaching Inventory, 212, 215–216
    video analysis of others' teaching, 230
    video analysis of own teaching, 213,
        223–224
teamwork, evaluation and, 9
thinking partners, 89
transparency, credibility and, 39
trust, 36–38, 45–46, 88, 170–171
Turning to One Another (Wheatley), 38

valid evaluation
    action steps, 31*f*, 50*f*

valid evaluation (*continued*)
    beliefs and practices emphasized in,
        50–51, 67
    ensures ratings from credible evaluators,
        51, 54–55
    key questions, 31*f*, 50*f*
    provides timely, accurate judgmental
        feedback, 51, 55–57, 59–60
    quality criteria, 31*f*, 50*f*
    results of, 47
    uses a valid, research-based framework to
        determine ratings, 50, 51–54
valid evaluation, protocols to support systems
of
    classroom walkthrough, evaluative, 168,
        185–186
    clinical observation, 166, 174–175
    culture check survey, 166, 170–171
    evaluation, data collection for, 187–188
    evaluators' Collegial Fishbowl, 166–167,
        176–177
    face-to-face dialogue, teacher-evaluator,
        167, 180–181
    function of, 165
    interrater reliability, establishing and
        maintaining across faculty, 167,
        178–179
    interrater reliability, establishing and
        maintaining among evaluators, 166,
        172–173
    judgmental feedback, timely and specific,
        167, 182–183, 183*f*
    multiple perspectives to ensure unbiased
        performance feedback and evaluations,
        168, 184
    success and effort, celebrating, 169,
        189–190
    written reflection, 167, 180–181
video analysis
    of one's own teaching, 213, 223–224
    of others' teaching, 230, 232–233

"What Could Be?" question, 150–151
"What Does the Next Level of Quality Look
    Like?" question, 151–152
"Where am I now?" question, 149–150
The Widget Effect (Weisberg et al.), 13

About the Authors

Tony Frontier is a consultant, award-winning educator, and assistant professor of leadership studies at Cardinal Stritch University in Milwaukee, WI. He consults internationally on topics of effective instruction, student engagement, teacher supervision, and school leadership. A frequent contributor to *Educational Leadership*, he is coauthor of ASCD's *Effective Supervision: Supporting the Art and Science of Teaching* and *Five Levers to Improve Learning: How to Prioritize for Powerful Results in Your School*. He can be reached at tonyfrontier@gmail.com.

Paul Mielke is superintendent of the Hamilton School District in Sussex, WI. Paul is an adjunct faculty member at Cardinal Stritch University in Milwaukee, where he teaches courses in teacher evaluation and organizational learning. He began his career in education in 1999 teaching English and coaching football at Wittenberg-Birnamwood High School. He served three years as an assistant principal/athletic director at Waukesha South High, another five years as a principal at West Allis Central High School, and two more years as a principal at Templeton Middle School. He received a bachelor's degree with a major in English and secondary education from the University of Wisconsin, Oshkosh; a master's degree in educational leadership; and a doctorate in leadership for the advancement of learning and service from Cardinal Stritch University. He can be reached at mielpa@hamilton.k12.wi.us.

Related ASCD Resources

At the time of publication, the following ASCD resources were available (ASCD stock numbers appear in parentheses). For up-to-date information about ASCD resources, go to www.ascd.org. You can search the complete archives of *Educational Leadership* at http://www.ascd.org/el.

ASCD Edge®
Exchange ideas and connect with other educators on the social networking site ASCD Edge at http://ascdedge.ascd.org/

Print Products
Building Teachers' Capacity for Success: A Collaborative Approach for Coaches and School Leaders by Pete Hall & Alisa Simeral (#109002)

Effective Supervision: Supporting the Art and Science of Teaching by Robert J. Marzano, Tony Frontier, & David Livingston (#110019)

Enhancing Professional Practice: A Framework for Teaching, 2nd Edition by Charlotte Danielson (#106034)

Insights into Action: Successful School Leaders Share What Works by William Sterrett (#112009)

Intentional and Targeted Teaching: A Framework for Teacher Growth and Leadership by Douglas B. Fisher, Nancy E. Frey, & Stefani Arzonetti Hite (#116008)

Learning from Coaching: How do I work with an instructional coach to grow as a teacher? (ASCD Arias) by Nina Morel (#SF114066)

The Principal Influence: A Framework for Developing Leadership Capacity in Principals by Pete Hall, Deborah Childs-Bowen, Ann Cunningham-Morris, Phyllis Pajardo, & Alisa A. Simeral (#116026)

Qualities of Effective Principals by James H. Stronge, Holly B. Richard, & Nancy Catano (#108003)

Taking Charge of Professional Development: A Practical Model for Your School by Joseph H. Semadeni (#109029)

THE WHOLE CHILD The Whole Child Initiative helps schools and communities create learning environments that allow students to be healthy, safe, engaged, supported, and challenged. To learn more about other books and resources that relate to the whole child, visit www.wholechildeducation.org.

For more information: send e-mail to member@ascd.org; call 1-800-933-2723 or 703-578-9600, press 2; send a fax to 703-575-5400; or write to Information Services, ASCD, 1703 N. Beauregard St., Alexandria, VA 22311-1714 USA.

WHOLE CHILD
TENETS

 HEALTHY
Each student enters school healthy and learns about and practices a healthy lifestyle.

 SAFE
Each student learns in an environment that is physically and emotionally safe for students and adults.

 ENGAGED
Each student is actively engaged in learning and is connected to the school and broader community.

4 **SUPPORTED**
Each student has access to personalized learning and is supported by qualified, caring adults.

5 **CHALLENGED**
Each student is challenged academically and prepared for success in college or further study and for employment and participation in a global environment.

ASCD's Whole Child approach is an effort to transition from a focus on narrowly defined academic achievement to one that promotes the long-term development and success of all children. Through this approach, ASCD supports educators, families, community members, and policymakers as they move from a vision about educating the whole child to sustainable, collaborative actions.

For more about the Whole Child approach, visit www.ascd.org/wholechild.

LEARN. TEACH. LEAD.